PISANELLO

ENIO SINDONA

PISANELLO

HARRY N. ABRAMS, INC. PUBLISHERS

NEW YORK

Translated from the Italian by
JOHN ROSS

Library of Congress Catalog Card No. 63-12780

Copyright in Italy, 1961, by Istituto Editoriale Italiano, Milan

Printed and bound in Italy

CONTENTS

THE LEGEND OF SAINT GEORGE

Around the lofty arch high above the Pellegrini Chapel in the Church of Sant'Anastasia in Verona, a fantastic optical trick seemed to flatten the fresco depicting *The Legend of Saint George* against the wall; in its almost terrifying verticality, the scene seemed suspended in emptiness. Over the centuries, anyone who succeeded in seeing Pisanello's masterpiece must have found the position of the figures most unconvincing: thrust forward and distorted, they appeared to be slipping down the only plane that provided any support, as if they were on the point of falling headlong into the surrounding space.

Even now that one can have a closer view of the fresco,[1] it is impossible to imagine these characters in their fabulous setting other than with this distortion, petrified forever on the brink of the chasm. Time's corrosion has stripped them of their splendid garments, so that in spite of the material life that was theirs in the legend which originally served as a pretext for the work, they have become purely and simply symbols—unadulterated, eternal forms. Furthermore, the fresco is composed in stifling, tightly compressed planes, without space for air to circulate between them, and the understanding of these planes is governed exclusively by the passage from light to shadow and by the over-all flatness which, in accordance with the medieval conception, equates verticality with the abyss.[2]

Thus, at first sight the *Legend* does not seem to depend on any unifying principle; every element exists in isolation, absorbed in its own state of delirious suffering and totally cut off from the feelings of the others. This, however, is a mere appearance: we shall see that Pisanello succeeds nevertheless in welding the scene solidly together.

One naturally wonders why the artist saw fit to give his composition this air of a fleeting apparition, suddenly caught and fixed forever in its very impermanence, why he did not take pains to create a more broadly set out, narrative, unified pictorial composition which could be admired with ease and pleasure. As it was, he paid little attention to the actual wall on which he had to work and preferred to place his characters in an almost absurd position. The fact that they would undergo almost no normal foreshortening did not trouble him, for he was concentrating entirely on situating them in a kind of endless enchantment.

In expressing the fullness of his poetic fancy in the *Legend*, Pisanello's main ambition was to preserve a particular moment in the history of culture, eschewing decorative effects and following only his own very personal reaction to a critical historical reality. In this composition the spirit of the Middle Ages is still present, and in a very positive way, but at the same time it seems on the point of yielding, though not of disappearing completely, to give way to a different reality. Indeed, the one thing lacking in the *Legend* is a proposal for a final solution; the work itself is an affirmative effort by figurative art to leave a well-defined image of this fundamental unique moment of crisis, an image which would be universally valid in its precision and concreteness.

But one may also ask if the stress so desperately laid on the transitional nature of the times, and the melancholy atmosphere that troubles every part of the painting, stem from an exaltation of the period and a love for the Middle Ages, or from the artist's personal hostility toward the forces that resulted in the breakdown of a culture; whether the characters have been exaggerated and inflated to provide the symbols of a time cherished by Pisanello, or represent only the dialectical terms of a world dying of its own contradictions. All this is possible, but in any case it is certain that this masterpiece exhibits a profound nostalgia for some of the more superior medieval traits, such as the aesthetic refinement that sprang from Late Gothic art and was now endangered in its most inherent properties by the inevitable collapse of its world. Pisanello, then, extracted the most fantastic and the truest elements from this polished, aristocratic aestheticism which the late Middle Ages were to pass on to the Renaissance. He could no longer use these elements to narrate and exalt episodes from a disappearing way of life, for these episodes were no longer relevant to the times; yet Pisanello's art seizes the most indestructible characteristics of these situations, and in "saving" them translates them into eternally living poetry.

Thus, poetry rises to celebrate the vision and so the process of palingenesis becomes an accomplished fact. There is no longer the slightest shadow of complaint, of grief or irony; such emotions presuppose hope, an unrealized integration into a rejected reality. All that remains, besides creation, is anguish over the conclusive act.

The Legend of Saint George [Plates 49-54, 59, 60, 65, 66, 74-85], of which only the most essential parts have been saved from the ravages of time, and those only with difficulty, is Pisanello's most outstanding painting and, without doubt, one of the most disconcerting works of art of all time. Before approaching this masterpiece it is essential to comprehend, at least summarily, the vast range of cultural elements and formal and psychological factors that come

1 - THE MADONNA ENTHRONED - *Palazzo Venezia Museum* - ROME

2 - STUDIES OF THE MADONNA, ANIMALS, AND DEMONS - *Louvre* - PARIS

3 - STUDY OF FIGURES AND THE MADONNA SUCKLING THE INFANT JESUS - *Louvre* - PARIS

together in it, and above all it is necessary to consider the moment in which such different elements were united by the artist's exceptional act of expression. Purely on the level of intellectual synthesis, three different aspects of fifteenth-century artistic culture converge suddenly in the Veronese painter: International Gothic, northern art (Bohemian in part, but mainly French), and the earliest forms of Renaissance humanism. A fourth element makes a discreet appearance: the recrudescence of a Hellenistic sentiment, revealed in the poses of painful surrender and in the brooding presence of metaphysical suffering. The poetic drama of Pisanello's work owes its form to the juxtaposition of these different expressive languages. The knights and the savage-looking Kalmucks that crowd the scene almost all originate in the North and bear its imprint in their faces, their costumes, and their ornaments. Primitive down to the last mustache bristle, they typify the far-off lands where, in spite of immeasurable economic changes, the Middle Ages still reigned supreme with its legends, its ritual and its hallucinating fantasy. These figures, lined up in an isolated group, are as different from one another as the pages in an album of human types, yet they have in common an expression of tormented, disheartened expectation. They have come in their finest trappings, as if they had been summoned to the enactment of some tragic ritual that nothing—not even repentance transformed into will power, far less blind force—can now possibly halt.[3] Barbarians beyond any doubt, they stand there, mute and impotent; they are caught up, perhaps for the first time, in a tragedy that cannot be imputed to human responsibility and behave as if struck down by fate, by a cruel supernatural phenomenon. Some lean slightly forward and their barbaric appearance is softened; others stiffen; while others again show signs of sadness. It is indispensable to study them one by one.

From left to right the expressions show a gradual affirmation of consciousness in three stages [Plates 50-52]. The first stage ends with the Kalmuck whose hair hangs lankly down on either side of his fierce muscular face. He is shown with a corpulent expressive power and an exemplary correspondence between concept and form. Cut off from the drama in which the others are already involved, but definitely the only one ready to spring into action at a word of command, he is a magnificent specimen of the great professional sport of the time: war. The hardness of this aesthetically superb, almost animal face contrasts with the painful languor of the head behind and to the right, which is modeled with oriental overtones in the wavy beard and the folds of the turban. The upturned face is etched with marks of grief; in its composition there is no rigorous scheme but the wrinkles form freely in accordance with the spasm of emotion, while the features are transformed as if by a resurgence of Hellenistic pain. There are good constructional and formal reasons why this Nordic-Oriental foreigner

9

should appear in this particular part of the composition because, with the marked tilt of his head, he embodies the very opposite of the rigid, expressionless Kalmuck.

The central group [Plates 51-53], presenting a new thesis, abandons this kind of opposition. The two royal figures, one of whom is probably the King of Sylene, father of the princess, break down in their grief before the inevitable tragedy. Their faces become more human, refined, and pensive, for now—perhaps only now—they have become fully aware of the drama of the situation, and the Kalmuck fitted into the space between these two figures becomes an active, integral part of the group. Behind them, above and a little way off, the artist has placed a gallows with two hanged men dressed in rumpled, tattered coats of gray and pink. This motif is far from uncommon in early Renaissance Italian painting—examples are to be found in the circular *Adoration of the Magi* in Berlin and in Paolo Uccello's *Nativity* in the former Hospital of San Martino alla Scala. Here, however, instead of being isolated in space from the rest of the scene of action, the gallows motif looms over it and dominates it. The similarity of the red tones in the headdress worn by the Kalmuck on the left and in the hanged men's clothes could depend on more than chance, and could be intended to suggest a recent past of cruelty. The absence of enough space to create depth round the hanged men and so render them more distant, is here clearly intentional; the dumbfounded living figures, who can only feel disturbed and upset, are weighed down by a relationship which appears as a kind of fantasy. Thus there is no absolute contrast between the protagonists of the scene and the hanged men (in the *Adoration* and the *Nativity* already mentioned there is what might be called the absolute contrast between "the tragedy of sin punished, and the serene peace of redeeming Nativity"), but on the contrary a direct, perhaps even causal relationship which increases the sense of terror graven on the entire episode.

With its composed gravity the last group seems to add to this atmosphere of sin which becomes not only the symbol but also the pressing reminder of an experience that time will never be able to efface. This third stage of consciousness is embodied in two men of different ages, perhaps courtiers, but presented here as spectators and, virtually, judges of a reality that they absorb in full consciousness. They are shown in profile in accordance with the most widespread practice of portraiture, but they have the formal characterization, at once acute and vague, of Pisanello's portraits.

In the center foreground stands the main scene, now only remotely connected to the legend, for it has gone beyond all narrative content to become instead the symbol of that timelessness, rooted in both past and future, which establishes the atmosphere of the whole composition. As the basic element of the moment of climax, which is to be projected into the future, this group is cut off from the other parts of the painting—from the hanged men whose eyes stare blankly toward the opulent, mysterious city whose touches of red reflect the faded pink of their garments, and from the isolated group of knights—perhaps symbolizing present times—hemmed in by the rocks, among dark foliage and the nodding cluster of horses' heads. A complex emotion touches the central group, creating its indefinable quality: immobility and movement, decoration and refined elegance, anecdotal elements and thoughtful, aristocratic detachment, are all formally reconciled in the synthesis that unites different facts and qualities as pure ideas. Past, present, and future are thus incarnate in the three principal groups, but it is the last, outstripping the other two, which is illuminated by thought, so that it can overcome and cast off its own time and material situation.

Statuesque, adorned with rich robes the like of which could only have been conceived by International Gothic, the haughty princess in all her finery comes down from the castles to show off her beauty. The expression on her face, poised gracefully above her slightly inclined neck, would be as mute as that of a lady from Piero della Francesca's paintings, if Pisanello's determination to draw the head from life did not give the figure a hint of participation in the drama. This is one of Pisanello's least-characterized faces, in spite of the set of the lips, emphasized at the corners of the mouth. Though the lady is drawn with perfect style, she somehow does not achieve the substance of a Classical figure. She still lacks something, perhaps soul, and is impressive primarily because of her rich garments and carefully contrived preciosity. As a creature brought up in the sheltered, closed world of castles, in a world of fable, she cannot belong to real life, even when this real life is shown in its most tragic aspects.[4]

In this composition, however, not only the princess but every figure seems isolated, bound up in himself, engrossed in his own particular significance. The over-all effect would be completely divorced from outside feeling were it not for the pervading tone and atmosphere that create a general emotional climate and, as in Pisanello's other paintings, link the characters together. This link is achieved, not by rational construction, but by a magical fusion. Pisanello's work is pervaded by a fantastic, almost cosmic, and therefore mysterious unity that transcends the individual, a unity in which myth and anguish and mysterious apparitions finally join to dominate as an atmosphere that settles on the most disparate vital forms. This is perhaps what constitutes the most attractive achievement of Pisanello's art. In the full flood of the fifteenth century, when a new situation was imposing the absolute principles of geometrically harmonious construction, Pisanello preferred to create a unity neither of time nor space, but a universally more concrete and unifying harmony of thought and historical value; he placed his trust in a method more acceptable to his fancy, the general unity of feeling that in this case binds every individual motif in the expectant silence of anguish and moral upheaval. The romantic but real unifying function of the atmosphere and the unrest it contains, governs—and so, explains—the role of each element in the *Legend*. This is shown, for example, by the unforgettable, terrifyingly attractive form behind and to the right of the princess, in which a single magical apparition is forged out of a heavily caparisoned horse and the plume of a Kalmuck who holds a long spear in his misshapen hand. To accentuate further the general disorientation, two immense horses' heads peep in, whinnying, on the extreme right of the composition, implying that the procession continues beyond. At the top of the scene, castles, towers, and churches rise up on the other side of the arid, sparse hills, as a reminder, and recall another life. They seem far away, and the light reflected from their white tracery produces artfully contrived glimpses of fabulous symbolic images. We have no serene perspective, constructed in the Tuscan manner, framing a whole, eminently human and rational world. Instead, the painting is dominated by the interplay of phantoms, but always against a background of reality. Furthermore, these are not the phantoms that recur in terms of a straightforwardly unfolding narration; they spring up spontaneously from the clash between two civilizations that meet without one's capitulating entirely to the other.[5]

Though the animals are intended as breathing imitations of nature, they too, especially through their restlessness, become integrated into the indefinite universe of the scene.

To the left in a more open space, like a void separating the two principal scenes, a sailboat is outlined in full-blown curves on a mirror of greenish water; this motif follows a conception that is similarly realized in some landscape passages of fourteenth-century Sienese painting. On the other side of the pointed ogive of the chapel arch there is the monster, an enormous reptile[6] surrounded by a court of minor monsters, slaughtered animals, and other remains that suffice to arouse a reaction of considerable disgust. There is, however, little more, for this part of the fresco, in which the artist gives excellent proof of his ability as a draftsman, fulfills an essentially descriptive function and has nothing in common with the elevated sense of tragedy that emanates from the other half of the work. This sense of tragedy is assimilated, expressed, and idealized in the face of Saint George, the true center, both in form and content, of the composition. His appearance is ghostly; his slightly distorted face reveals how he suffers from the enforced contact of his higher nature—superior human nature—with the unrestrained, obtuse brutality that he knows can easily be conquered. At the same time, we can see his indifference toward the men crowded round him who, renouncing for once their supremacy of force, overcome their egoism and bow at the appearance of the fabled knight.

4 - STUDY OF FEMALE FIGURES AND ANIMALS - *Albertina* - Vienna

5 - STUDY OF A YOUNG MAN'S HEAD - *Louvre* - Paris

6 - MADONNA OF THE QUAIL - *Museo di Castelvecchio* - Verona

LA VERGINE ANNUNZIATA DALL' ANGELO
e sotto ai due pinnacoli laterali del fregio di contorno
S. GIORGIO E L' ARCANGELO S. MICHELE

Vittore Pisano, detto per Pisanello decorò di questo ammirabile a fresco
il monumento eretto dalla nob. famiglia di Brenzone in S. Fermo maggiore l'anno
1430. Se anche non islosse ancora ad uno de' lati il nome PISANVS, la purezza e la
soavità che spirano da questo dipinto non ne lascierebbero dubbio allora così non di-
pingeano che il Veronese Pisano e l'Angelico.

7 - THE ANNUNCIATION
(from an engraving by Pietro Nanin, published in 1864 in *Disegni di varie dipinture a fresco che sono in Verona*)

8 - THE ANNUNCIATION (*detail: An Archangel*) - *Church of San Fermo* - VERONA

9 - THE ANNUNCIATION (*detail: The Archangel Gabriel*) - *Church of San Fermo* - VERONA

He, in his turn, seems unhappy at the idea of performing a miracle. His face changes and hardens slightly, assuming a remarkably well-defined, many-faceted form, which stands out from the frame of loose, wavy hair. But a few locks of blond hair are not enough to make this dehumanized face angelic. We must think of the saint in terms of the typically medieval conception of fabulous and ghostly beings—good ones and bad ones—that filled the imagination of medieval man before he learned to break away from fixed images and flat planes, to enter a world more his own and more visible. With the dynamic tension of his figure dominated by his enigmatic expression, Saint George becomes the symbol of an imminent mysterious transition in the meeting of different ways of life. There is something macabre in this fascinating, compelling figure, which still bears traces of lethargy, of a forced awakening, of the anguish of returning to a world that once was his and now calls to him again. For this reason the figure of Saint George imposes itself as the central theme among the various motifs that run through the scene, whose general atmosphere, as we have said, takes on a symbolic rather than narrative quality. He makes himself the center of attention and, above all, of the emotional vibrations of every figure—fear, hope, trepidation, expectancy before an unknown happening. When the event takes place it is certain that the spell will be broken. But the moments before the loosening of the enchantment that binds men, things, and nature, were precisely what interested the artist, who pinned them down forever in this unforgettable synthesis.

It is tempting to interpret Pisanello's masterpiece as a representation of the decline of the Middle Ages. Formal and psychological elements could indeed lead to this conclusion. The misgivings of men whose background is formed of the ghosts of the past that was their world, the artist's refusal to open up new, deep space, the fabulous bygone splendor of garments and sumptuous colors that must originally have lent great brilliance to the painting, all support this theory. Moreover, several formal elements, prominently placed in the foreground,[7] bear witness to Pisanello's acquaintance with humanism and the Renaissance; he must have had time to mull over the experiences of his travels in central Italy before he painted the fresco. It should be remembered, however, that in confronting other correspondingly different forms and cultures, the artist showed a marked attachment to the world in crisis, though this may not indicate a well-defined choice on his part. And while the pale face of the knight is juxtaposed against the bulky horse, drawn and foreshortened with consummate skill, the entirely Gothic vision of medieval buildings wrapped in a crystal-clear light that renders their forms eternal reappears urgently, at the very moment when the night of inevitable decadence is thickening round these last gleams of light. By means of such dialectical oppositions, rooted here in the contrast between alarming forms that rise unreally out of the gloomy undergrowth and the vision of enchanting apparitions, Pisanello, with a dualism that presents the darker sides of a civilization even while saving its good qualities, pays homage to the poetry of Late Gothic culture.

PORTRAIT OF PISANELLO (medal) - *Bibliothèque Nationale* - Paris

THE LIFE OF PISANELLO

Famed and honored in his own time, Pisanello was widely discussed, for varying reasons, by his contemporaries, from the eminent humanists whose odes exalt his outstanding merits[8] to the Rectors of Verona who for political reasons labeled the artist, in their well-known "Descriptio," as "*Pisan pentor rebello.*"[9]

Two such contrasting verdicts created favorable conditions, right from the beginning, for the formation of an aura of romance around the figure of Pisanello. But it is precisely from the combination of those two different pictures, opposed only insofar as they reflect two divergent aspects of one personality, that the complex figure of the artist begins to take shape. Indeed, the position of privilege and fame which Pisanello undoubtedly enjoyed in no way excludes the possibility that the distinguished, cultivated artist committed himself personally to the struggles that continually shook the political life of the Quattrocento.

Pisanello's apparent double life—on the one hand, the celebrated painter and medalist *prudens gravis atque modestus*; on the other, the rebellious citizen who threw in his lot even with causes that went against the immediate interests of his native city—was for late-nineteenth and early-twentieth-century students[10] the main obstacle to forming a rounded picture of Pisanello the artist and Pisanello the man. The contrast appeared so striking that some scholars were even led to postulate the existence of two Pisanellos.[11]

This hypothesis could be justified by the fact that in the last few years the establishment of inventories of archives has forced us to reconstruct almost completely the life and activity of Pisanello. In fact, the documents published by Giuseppe Biadego established, as the first and most startling basic fact, that Pisanello's name was not, as had always been held, Vettore Pisano, but Antonio Pisano.[12]

This duality of names seemed to reinforce the suspicion[13] of the existence of two Pisanellos: Vettore, the great painter and medalist, a renowned genius of moderate opinions, and the other, Antonio, a subversive influence and a far less well-known painter, whose unique distinction was that of being mentioned in the documents discovered.

But it must be added that while Pisanello did sign some of his paintings (the San Fermo

Annunciation and the *Madonna with Saint George and Saint Anthony*, in the National Gallery, London) and his medals, he never gave his first name "*Pisanus pinxit,*" "*Pisanus pictor,*" "*opus Pisani pictoris*"—his signatures were always limited to the surname.

On the other hand, numerous documents have come to light mentioning an artist called sometimes "*Antonius Pisanus pictor,*" sometimes "*Antonius Pixanellus pictor,*" or more simply "*Pisanellus pictor,*" with occasional variations on the theme. No mention is ever made of a Vettore.[14] From this it is clear that the newly discovered documents, with their precise references to works and events in the life of one Antonio Pisano, merely complete the artist's biography, and any remaining doubts concern only the inexplicable origin of the name Vettore. But it may be that the error, which arose just under a century after the death of Pisanello, was due to a simple assonance between the inscription "*(opus) Pisani pictoris,*" which occurs on his widely known medals, and the name of the prominent Venetian condottiere Pisani Vettore, who died shortly before 1380.[15]

By November, 1395, Antonio Pisano had already been born to Puccio Pisano or Pucino di Giovanni, of Cereto, and Donna Isabetta, of Verona. The birth may have taken place in Pisa, but it is also possible that it happened in Verona. In any case, in that year Puccio di Giovanni made his will in Pisa, naming his son Antonio as sole heir and leaving him the impressive sum of six hundred golden ducats.[16]

So Pisanello was born before November, 1395; just how long before, it is impossible to say, perhaps only a few weeks, but perhaps some years.[17] In any case, Pisa, Puccio's native town, where the document was drawn up, ought to have had the registration of Antonio's birth as well; if then he went to Verona as a child, he would have received the nickname of Pisanello, the little Pisan.

All this would be beyond question if it were not for two things: first, the vast emigratory movement from Pisa to Verona in the fourteenth and fifteenth centuries,[18] certainly one of the reasons for the marriage of Puccio di Giovanni and Isabetta, which was probably celebrated in Verona,[19] and second, the fact that other Pisanellos are mentioned in Veronese censuses of the fifteenth century[20] and certainly they did not all receive the name because they were "little Pisans." Therefore the name Pisanello cannot be used as grounds for concluding that the artist's origins were in Pisa. What is more, some documents call him Pisano de Verona and others Pisano de Pisis,[21] and these names, for what they are worth, also combine to leave doubts as to the artist's city of birth.

We have no knowledge of his early childhood, which was presumably spent in Verona; probably his mother also lived there most of the time after her second marriage to Bartolo-

10 - THE ANNUNCIATION (*detail: Two Doves*) - *Church of San Fermo* - VERONA

11 - THE ANNUNCIATION (*detail: An Archangel*) - *Church of San Fermo* - VERONA

12 - THE ANNUNCIATION (*detail: The Virgin Receiving the News*) - *Church of San Fermo* - VERONA

13 - STUDY OF NUDES AND AN ANNUNCIATION - *Boymans Museum* - ROTTERDAM

14 - STUDY OF A LEG, FLOWERS, AND SQUID - *Louvre* - PARIS

15 - STUDY OF FIGURES - *Albertina* - Vienna

16 - STUDY OF FACES - *British Museum* - LONDON

17 - STUDY OF A DEER AND GOAT - *Louvre* - PARIS

18 - STUDY OF DOGS HUNTING GAME - *Louvre* - Paris

19 - STUDY OF DOGS HUNTING GAME - *Louvre* - Paris

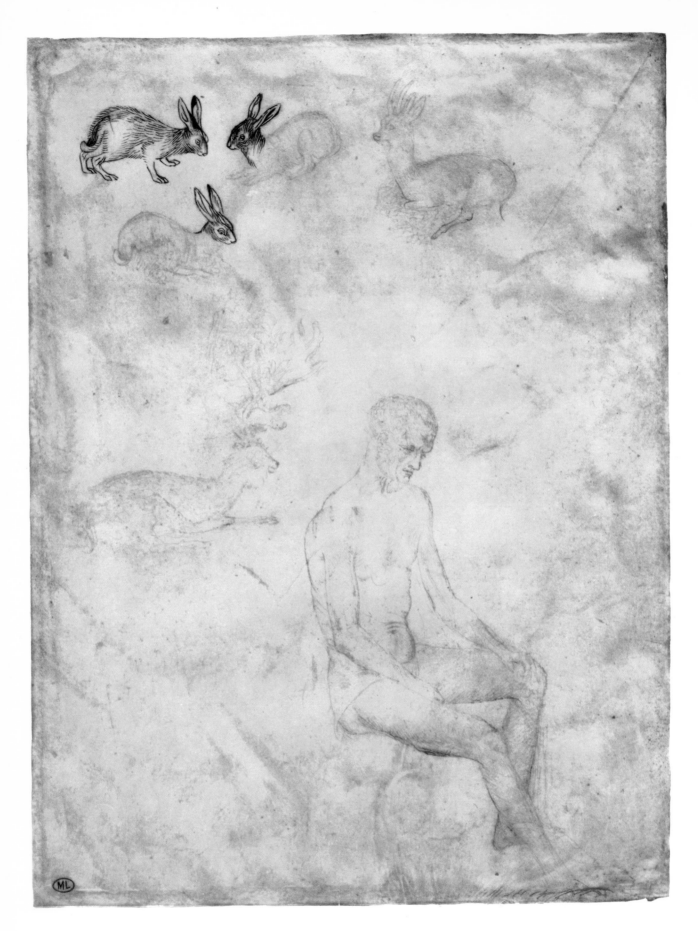

20 - STUDY OF A SEATED MAN, DEER, AND RABBITS - *Louvre* - Paris

21 - STUDY OF WARRIORS - *Lugt Collection* - PARIS

22 - STUDY OF A YOUNG MAN WITH A SWORD - *Louvre* - PARIS

23 - STUDY OF FIGURES IN A VAULTED ROOM - *Louvre* - Paris

24 - COSTUME STUDY - *Biblioteca Ambrosiana* - MILAN

25 - COSTUME STUDY - *Biblioteca Ambrosiana* - MILAN

26 - STUDY OF JESUS ADDRESSING A PILGRIM - *Louvre* - Paris

27 - STUDY OF A LEOPARD AND COLUMNS - *Louvre* - Paris

28 - STUDY OF A MANTLE - *Louvre* - Paris

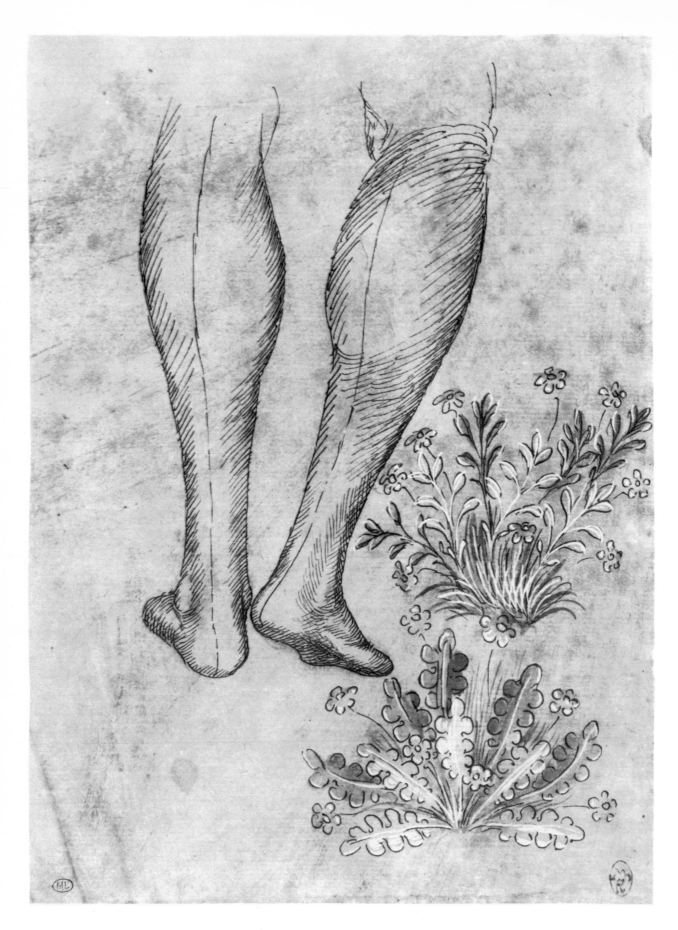

29 - STUDY OF PLANTS AND A MAN'S LEGS - *Louvre* - Paris

31 - **STUDY OF A TRUMPETER** - *Louvre* - Paris

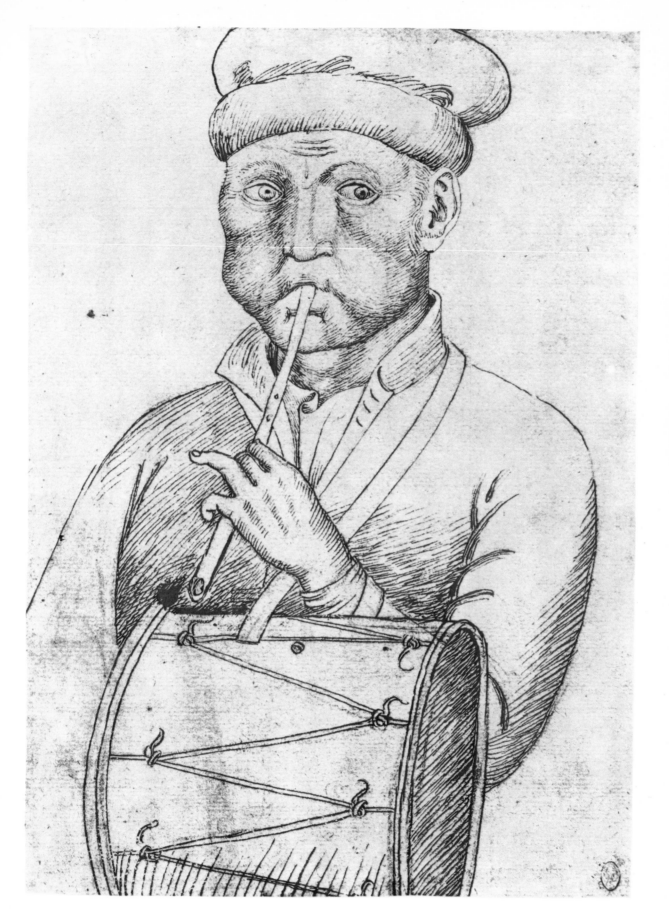

32 - STUDY OF A FIFE AND DRUM PLAYER - *Louvre* - Paris

33 - STUDY OF A CEREMONIAL SCENE, A TRUMPETER, AND MALE HEADS - *Louvre* - Paris

34 - STUDY OF A MALE PROFILE - *Louvre* - PARIS

36 - PORTRAIT OF THE EMPEROR SIGMUND - *Kunsthistorisches Museum* - VIENNA

37 - STUDY FOR A FLAGELLATION - *Biblioteca Ambrosiana* - Milan

38 - STUDY OF MALE NUDES, A SAINT, AND A RECLINING WOMAN - *Biblioteca Ambrosiana* - MILAN

39 - STUDY OF MALE NUDES AND A SAINT - *Museum* - BERLIN

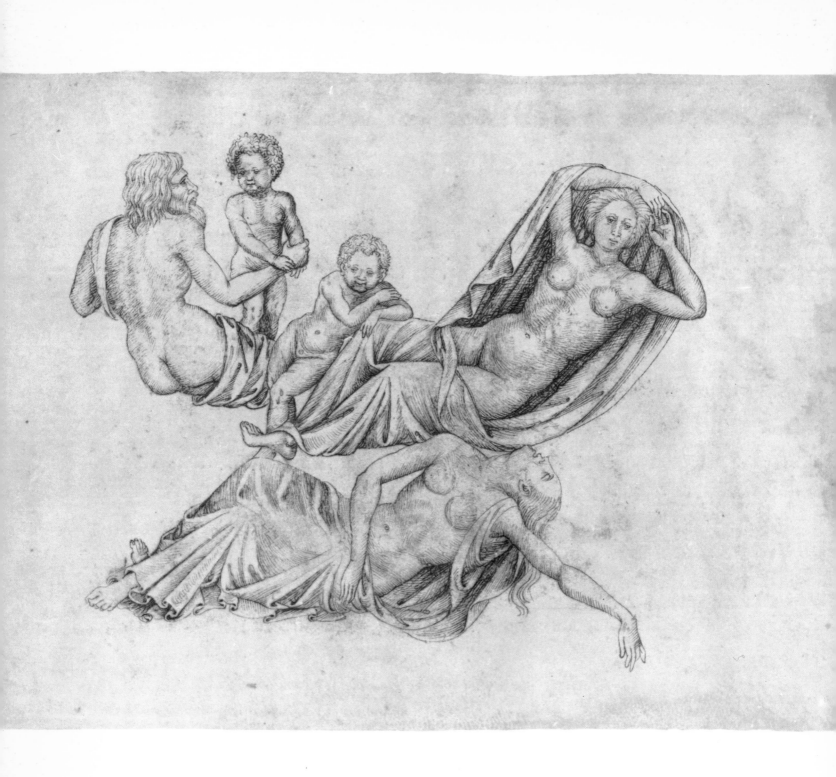

40 - STUDY FROM THE ANTIQUE - *Biblioteca Ambrosiana* - MILAN

meo de Pisis, and her third, to Filippo da Ostiglia, who was still alive in 1425, the year in which he drew up his last will and testament. The young Pisanello's artistic output tells us specifically that he lived in Verona for a long time and that he was familiar with the flourishing art of north Italy, especially with Late Gothic, which attracted him greatly and was later to find its highest, most coherent expression in his hands. This was the period during which he certainly had his closest and most frequent contacts with Stefano da Verona, and with all the various Nordic influences that penetrated into Italy, and that made their greatest mark on Verona, a convenient crossroads for travelers from France, Germany, the Tyrol, the Rhineland, and Bohemia. Pisanello stored up all these impressions while developing his technical mastery, thus becoming equally skilled in draftsmanship and in fanciful imagery.

And so, in the second and third decades of the fifteenth century,[22] we find him in Venice in the Palazzo Ducale, busy completing the frescoes left unfinished by Gentile da Fabriano. This was his first meeting with Gentile's work which, while it draws much of its vigor from the many sources of the International Gothic style, also bears conspicuous signs of a painterly, plastic sensitivity very different from the mobile pictorialism of the North—signs, moreover, of the new approach to modeling that was developing and establishing itself in central Italy. As the frescoes of Gentile and Pisanello were entirely destroyed in the disastrous fire of 1577, we can no longer even guess at the reactions of our northern painter to Gentile's work. But it is not unreasonable to imagine Pisanello arriving in Venice a full-fledged artist, very enthusiastic about his own artistic credo. This was the Pisanello who drew refined sketches destined later to take on more complex forms. While he did not disdain to experiment with Gentile's technique (see some of his rather heavy drawings of the Virgin) and was devoted to him for reasons that one suspects were essentially "chronological" rather than aesthetic, he reveals a discipleship that never went beyond a patient sharing of harness, born of necessity. If there were any influences between the two painters, it would seem that the elder received most of them.[23]

In 1422 Pisanello was residing in Mantua, although he is also mentioned as being in Verona. From then on began the close links with the court of the Gonzagas, who were to play such an important part in the painter's life. During this period his economic circumstances continued to prosper. Among other things, in 1424 his mother made over to Antonio the six hundred golden ducats left him by his father,[24] which she had been keeping for her son (who had not asked for them). In the legal document he is called *"pictorem egregium."* Indeed, Pisanello was sought after in all parts of Italy and universally admired; 1427 is marked by the celebrated ode which the humanist Guarino Veronese dedicated to him shortly after receiving a gift of a highly prized painting of Saint Jerome, now lost.

In addition to working in his own city of Verona during this period (the San Fermo *Annunciation* must have been executed around 1426), the painter was in Rome in 1431.[25] If he did not actually collaborate there with Gentile da Fabriano, as has been suggested,[26] he certainly continued the older painter's unfinished cycle of frescoes on the life of John the Baptist, in the church of San Giovanni in Laterano.

We must not exclude the possibility of Pisanello's having stayed in Florence on his way to or from Rome, and probably he repeated this visit during his later journey to Naples. It is more dangerous to reject this hypothesis than to accept it; the fact that we have no documents referring to a visit to Florence proves nothing more than the scarcity of our material. It is highly likely that so famous and cultivated an artist would have broken his journey, if only for a short time, in a city such as Florence whose artistic renaissance, then in full swing, must have been widely known beyond the narrow limits of the region. Whether or not Pisanello was won over by certain aspects of Florentine art is another side of the problem, which we shall examine in due course.

If Pisanello did stop in Florence on his return journey from Rome, he could have met, among other artists, Paolo Uccello, newly returned from the Republic of Venice. The two painters, artistically so alike in many ways, would have had the opportunity of getting acquainted and of exchanging opinions on the particularly decisive moment in history and art in which they were each playing a far from unimportant part. Vasari says[27] that in Florence Pisanello painted the story of the pilgrims in the Temple Church (destroyed in 1530 when Vasari was barely nineteen years old). But it must be stressed that apart from this evidence, in all likelihood inaccurate, no document or reliable source mentions any work executed by Pisanello in Tuscany; this fact cannot be ignored. However, in spite of this lack of evidence, it would be exaggerated to exclude all possibility of contacts, however vague, between Pisanello and Florentine circles, especially since this period, as we have seen, is one of the most obscure in the life of the painter, and one about which it is impossible to make categorical statements. As far as the visit to Rome is concerned, Vasari supposes that the painter went there for the first time in 1420 with Gentile, at the invitation of Pope Martin V.[28]

Certainly the similarities, if only in working methods and not in style, between the two painters, which date from Gentile's period in the Veneto, could confirm the hypothesis of a long-standing collaboration, so that an invitation extended to Gentile would almost automatically have included the young Pisanello.

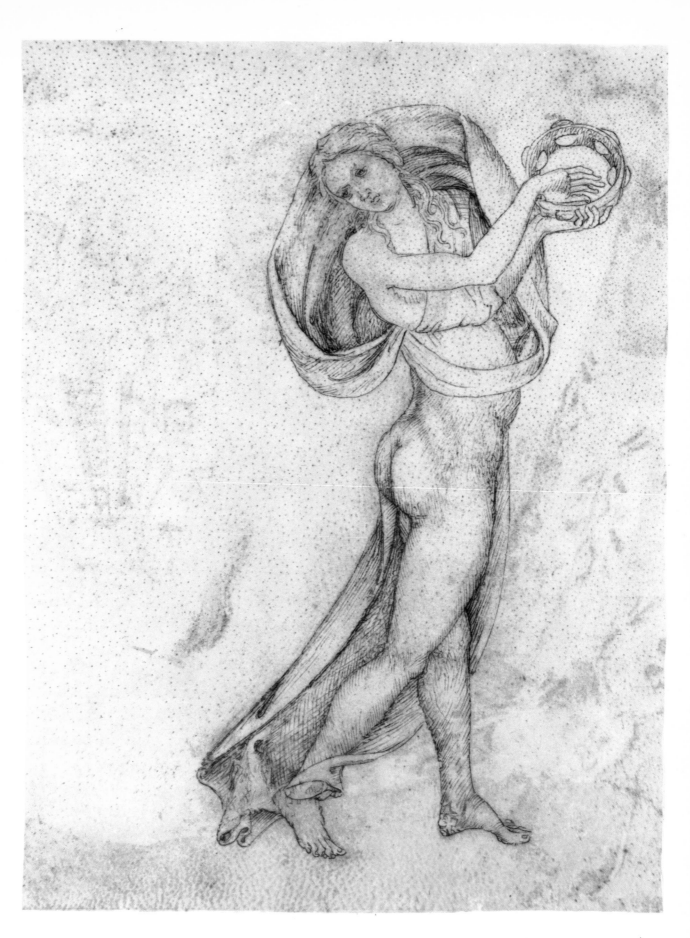

41 - STUDY OF A DANCING FIGURE - *Ashmolean Museum* - OXFORD

42 - STUDY OF AN EMPEROR'S HEAD - *Louvre* - Paris

43 - STUDY OF A WINGED BULL - *Louvre* - PARIS

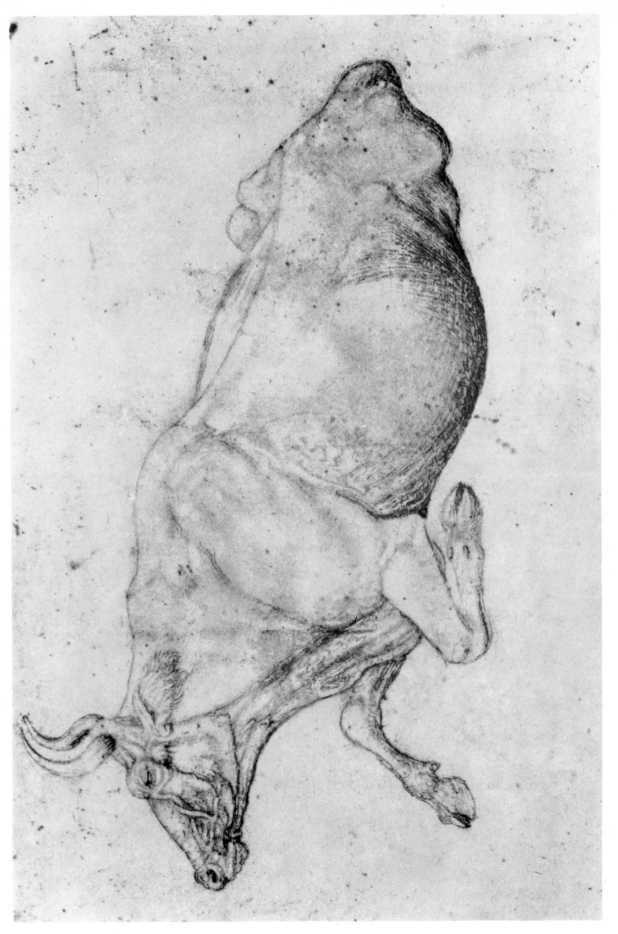

44 - STUDY OF A RECLINING BULL - *Louvre* - PARIS

45 - STUDY OF A HORSE - *Louvre* - PARIS

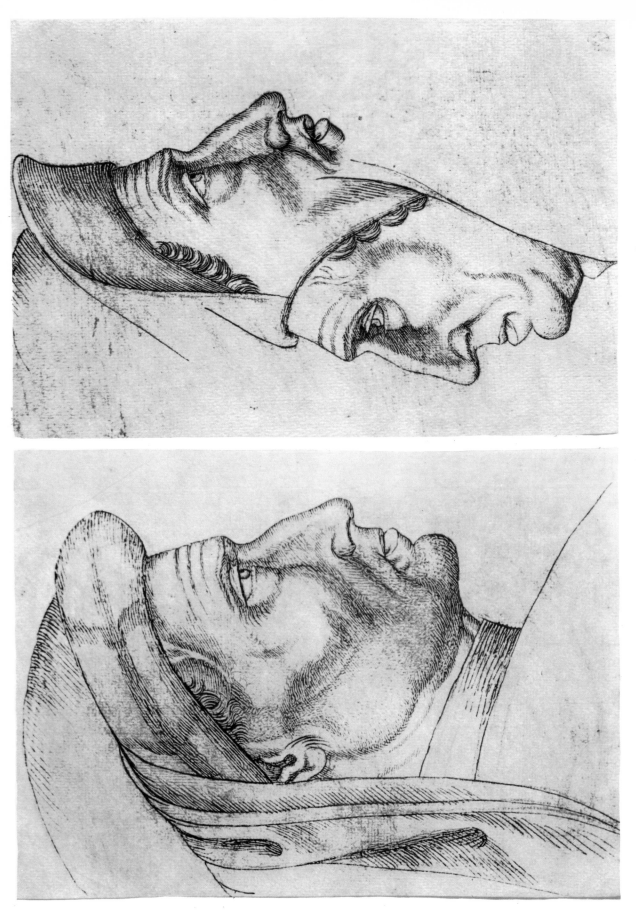

47 - STUDY OF A YOUNG MAN TAKING OFF HIS DOUBLET - *Louvre* - PARIS

48 - STUDY OF A WARRIOR - *Louvre* - PARIS

And as usual Vasari would have confused us further, if we did not actually know[29] that in 1420 and the following year Gentile could not have gone to Rome (and therefore, neither could Pisanello, as he would then have been working in "collaboration" with Gentile).

As has been pointed out, however, it is by no means impossible that Pisanello may have worked on the San Giovanni frescoes a few years before 1431,[30] since when Gentile died in 1428 he left his painting equipment to Pisanello,[31] who must therefore have been with him in Rome in that year.

And it was in Rome, rather than in Verona, that the Classical world was revealed to Pisanello. As we shall see, he assimilated the values of this world in a highly personal way.

He arrived in Rome—in exactly what year hardly matters—fresh from the active atmosphere of the northern courts and conscious of belonging to a distinguished artistic tradition that by then had imposed itself over the greater part of Europe.

Though he could have glimpsed vestiges of Classical civilization in other parts of Italy, in Rome he saw it in its natural setting and through the spectrum of works of art of unparalleled greatness. He was receptive to all the examples he saw, but especially so to the Grecian elements, whose influence was to make a profound impression on him, predisposing him toward the subtle sensibility that was later to inform the astonishing rhythm of his medals. Pisanello worked in Rome until July, 1432: payments made to the painter for the frescoes in San Giovanni in Laterano are recorded in documents of 1431 and 1432.[32]

He broke his return journey in Ferrara, where he presented a painting of the Virgin to Lionello d'Este,[33] and in August, 1433, he returned to Verona, where he stayed with his mother and other members of his family in the San Paolo quarter of town. Presumably it was during this stay in Verona, which lasted until 1438, that Pisanello painted his masterpiece in the church of Sant'Anastasia. *The Legend of Saint George*, a work of catharsis par excellence, proclaims the artist's maturity and marks the transition from the broad Late Gothic culture to the Helleno-Classical discovery of a pure, but by no means static, world alive with a certain elevated, resigned melancholy.

A decade before, probably about 1424, Pisanello had already painted in the Castello di Pavia, "skies colored with the finest azure, wherein were set diverse sorts of animals in gold... most beautiful figures representing hunts and fishing and jousting," to use the words of Stefano Breventano.[34]

At that time Pisanello, not yet possessed by his fascination with classicism and taking his cue from courtly fables, was busy painting very competent anecdotal pictures which he enriched with a complete freedom of expression and an inexhaustible number of naturalistic details. It is thus possible that some of his many drawings of animals, hunting scenes, and flowers may have been intended for the celebrated lost frescoes in the Castello di Pavia.

During the fourth decade of the century Pisanello was a particularly assiduous visitor to the courts of the Gonzagas in Mantua and the Estes in Ferrara. In February, 1432, the artist sent a servant ahead of him to Ferrara with a painting of Julius Caesar,[35] Lionello d'Este's favorite writer, as a gift for the prince. This was probably to celebrate Lionello's marriage to Margherita Gonzaga.

Then in 1438, after spending about four years in Verona, Pisanello arrived in Ferrara for the famous Council called in Italy by Emperor John VIII (Palaeologus). Here he executed the Emperor's portrait in what can be considered his first medal (providing the Filippo Maria Visconti medal dates from 1440 and not from 1431[36]). Considerations of style make the later date seem more convincing. Six years after his return from Rome, shortly after completing his great work in Sant'Anastasia, Pisanello began to change the style of his art in another outstanding cycle, which took concrete form in his work as a medalist. In the medals, formal refinement develops in step with a new but entirely personal vision of reality. This reality is now spiritually transformed by a smooth harmony, in accordance with a humanism that resides not in the expression of absolute power, but in the fact that it is victorious (in the ethical and aesthetic sense) over a situation that is exceptional yet contingent (the humanist-Renaissance innovation).

The year 1439 was marked by Pisanello's greatest success at court in Mantua, where he was in close contact with the Marquis Gianfrancesco Gonzaga. The Marquis included him in his "household," although this still did not prevent him later on from denying the painter certain recompenses due him. It is also in this year that we have the first glimpse of Antonio Pisano's political activity. In November, 1439, after the bitter defeat inflicted by the Venetian army under the command of Francesco Sforza, one Niccolò Piccinino, a captain in the service of Filippo Maria Visconti, managed to escape from the fortress of Tenno where he had been imprisoned; with Gonzaga's blessing, he drew up a plan for the assault of the city of Verona, then under Venetian rule. In the night of November 16-17, the Marquis of Mantua's troops entered and sacked the city. However, three days after this conquest, the approach of Venetian troops was enough to put Piccinino and Gonzaga to flight, and the city fell once more into Venetian hands.

According to some documents[37] Pisanello was with the Marquis of Mantua and took part not only in the siege, but also in the sack, during which, however, he did all in his power to avoid excesses.[38]

49 - THE LEGEND OF SAINT GEORGE (*detail: A Kalmuck*) - *Museo di Castelvecchio* - Verona

Nonetheless, in the house of the lawyer Andrea della Levata, the father of Pisanello's brother-in-law Bartolomeo,[39] the painter "plotted evil," to use the expression of the Rectors of Verona in the famous "Descriptio" they sent to the Council of Ten two years later.[40] We have not enough information to interpret exactly this "plotting evil." In the same way it is difficult to uncover the motives that impelled Pisanello to take part in the sack of his own city. In fact, when hostilities broke out, the Venetian Republic ordered all its subjects residing in Mantuan territory to return home; Pisanello was among those who did not obey this injunction. His behavior can be explained either by the fact that he had to complete certain commissions (apart from other work, he was engaged in painting a room in the Ducal Palace in Mantua, which was destroyed in 1480[41]), or by the danger of being in a town threatened with siege, where the painter enjoyed nothing comparable to the protection lavished on him by the lord of Mantua. He could, however, have maintained a neutral or passive stand. The fact is, though, that he chose to take part in the siege and conquest of his own Verona, a dominion of that Venetian Republic against which he so often had occasion to fulminate.[42] Since this war between the little states and minor lordships could hardly avoid taking on the appearance of a civil war, with all the consequent factions and partisanships, we should not be shocked that the painter, for reasons we do not, and for this study need not, know, should have thrown in his lot with the faction opposed to the Venetian dominion. He may well have had a grudge against Verona—where he nevertheless showed his contempt for all forms of violence throughout the sack.

This "plotting evil," as his enemies defined it, in the house of his relatives must be taken to mean plotting against the interests of the then established Venetian regime, that is, in favor of an active Veronese faction which hoped to realize its plans with the help of Gonzaga and Visconti. In this case Pisanello's behavior appears completely justified by his partisan position.

Toward the end of 1439, after his city had passed back into Venetian hands, Pisanello was once more in Mantua, where he stayed for a few months before resuming his travels around the cities of northern Italy.

In 1440 he was in Milan, where he testified, along with other witnesses,[43] in a memorial intended to record for posterity the facts and events that led up to Piccinino's and Gonzaga's conquest of Verona and their subsequent defeat.

It may well be that it was not till after his return to Mantua that the artist cast the medals of Niccolò Piccinino and Gianfrancesco Gonzaga. Among other things the tumultuous events preceding his return obviously would not have left him time enough for the meticulous prep-

21

aration of the work; moreover, stylistic considerations suggest that the medals were executed in the second half of 1440, that is, after Pisanello's return from Milan, where he struck the Duke's medal.

Shortly after, in the early part of 1441, the artist was in Ferrara, where the famous contest for the portrait of Lionello d'Este[44] took place between Jacopo Bellini and himself. Niccolò III, young Lionello's father, judged the contest to have been won by Bellini. The winning portrait is lost, so that we cannot compare the merits of the two works, but considering Pisanello's greater courage in portraiture, the traditional interpretation of this strange verdict seems justified: the father of the ugly Lionello rejected the Pisanello portrait (now in Carrara), which was overflowing with realism, in favor of the work by the Venetian painter, who had presumably idealized the boy, or at least had not concentrated on his defects, as the spirit of inquiry had led Pisanello to do.

In August, 1441, Pisanello traveled from Ferrara to Mantua on a trireme.[45] As he had contracted some debts in the latter city in that year,[46] the artist's financial situation could not have been so comfortable as it had been a few years earlier. No doubt this was a consequence of the political events in which he had taken part. Although Pisanello lived on a fairly lavish scale, the relative expenses could not have weighed too heavily on his budget, since, as a member of the prince's household, he certainly lived at the court's expense. Besides, he had few family liabilites, first because his mother, as the widow of three well-to-do men, enjoyed a certain prosperity, and second because he had no wife to maintain.[47] In the numerous documents referring to his life and family, no mention of a wife is to be found.

It is true that Pisanello had a daughter, Camilla, born about 1429 and married to Jacopo Turtois de' Martinengo in Verona in 1448, but this was almost certainly a natural daughter, brought up by her mother and paternal grandmother and therefore not a cause of much financial worry to the artist. In any case, even if Pisanello had had to contribute generously toward the maintenance of his family (his mother, to whom he was very much attached, his daughter, and probably also her mother), this could not have been a burden to the most famous artist of his time, sought after by monarchs and illustrious personalities.

The precarious financial position in which the artist often found himself may therefore be attributed to the too irregular and perhaps inadequate rewards he received at the courts of Ferrara and Mantua.

Mantua above all: the Marquis's replies to explicit requests for money are very revealing. In a letter dated 1443, Gianfrancesco Gonzaga tells Pisanello, then in Ferrara, that he has no means of sending him the sums in question,[48] while in a later letter (March 11, 1444), similar

50 - THE LEGEND OF SAINT GEORGE (*detail*) - *Church of San Giorgetto* (formerly in the Church of Sant'Anastasia) - VERONA

SANTVS·GIORGIVS·

51/52 - THE LEGEND OF SAINT GEORGE - *Church of San Giorgetto* (formerly in the Church of Sant'Anastasia) - VERONA

53 - THE LEGEND OF SAINT GEORGE (*detail*) - *Church of San Giorgetto* (formerly in the Church of Sant'Anastasia) - VERONA

in content, Gonzaga declares candidly, though not without a note of hypocrisy, that "we shall see if it is possible to make some provision for you; if we can, we shall, and willingly, for it is in our nature always to satisfy those who deserve anything from us."[49]

On the other hand, in 1441, when Pisanello had already contracted debts, the Marquis must have given his consent without too much deliberation, for a hundred golden ducats were delivered to the painter.[50]

In any case, whatever the causes of Pisanello's financial difficulties may have been, it is significant that in 1448, on the occasion of his only daughter's marriage, he made over to her a dowry consisting only of a piece of land with two houses in the San Paolo district;[51] not a very valuable gift, but perhaps all that remained to him after the stormy happenings of 1439. Even then, he made the gift by proxy, for at the time he was living in Ferrara, and his absence from Verona at Camilla's marriage may have been due to an imperative and ever more pressing need for work.

In 1441, the judiciary phase of Pisanello's political activity had begun. In July of that year, his name appeared in the already quoted "Descriptio" of the Rectors of Verona, on the list of exiled Veronese guilty of having followed the Marquis of Mantua. Then, in 1442, after a petition from the community of Verona, he was granted, along with the others, permission to return, provided he first went to Venice to ask for pardon in person. After he refused to comply with this condition, the magistrates of the Most Serene Venetian Republic proposed that the tongue of "*Antonium dictum Pisanum pictorem de' Verona*" be cut out in the Piazza San Marco, to punish him for having spoken against the Republic of Venice, as had Gonzaga. But on the same day (October 17) the Council of Ten rejected this proposal, contenting itself with confining the painter to Venice and forbidding him to dispose of his goods.[52]

On November 21 of the same year, probably soon after the death of his mother Isabetta, who was dead by the 13th of the month, Pisanello decided to present himself before the Council of Ten. Three months later the Council permitted him to go to Ferrara to attend to his interests; however, he was forbidden to go as far as Mantua or Verona, that is, to the two cities in which he was politically compromised.

In February, 1443, then, Pisanello went back to Ferrara; it was just at that moment that the Marquis of Mantua, officially ignorant of the Venetian sentence, asked for news of the real reasons why the artist stayed away from Mantua and preferred the city of the Estes.[53] When he realized the implications of the various clauses in the Council of Ten's deliberations and foresaw that thenceforth it would be virtually impossible for the artist to establish himself in Mantua, he continued to refuse Pisanello's requests for money. Indeed, in a letter of November, 1443, he even hastened to claim the return of a " picture on canvas on which is portrayed Our Lord."[54]

In 1444, in the letter of March 11, already quoted, Gonzaga made further promises, but we do not know how far these were honored, for the Marquis died shortly after.

In the meantime the artist struck a medal, dated MCCCXLIIII, for the marriage of Lionello d'Este, while in the following year he executed a painting for the summer residence at Belriguardo, receiving fifty golden ducats as payment for the latter work. It was perhaps at this time, in Rimini, that he cast the first medal of Sigismondo Pandolfo Malatesta.

In 1447, though living in Ferrara, he spent a little time in Verona,[55] and maybe also in Mantua, to execute the astonishing medal of Cecilia Gonzaga. If he was able to go to the two forbidden cities, he must by then have been granted complete freedom of movement.

In 1449, Pisanello, realizing a project he had been elaborating since 1444, was working in Naples,[56] where he struck the medals of Alfonso of Aragon and Inigo d'Avalos. From then on the documents concerning him are silent. It appears, from other documents in which he is mentioned, that he died in 1455, and it is certain that he was already dead in 1456.[57] Where? Some great city between Naples and Verona, perhaps even one of those two towns; we cannot tell for certain.

54 - THE LEGEND OF SAINT GEORGE (*detail: The Hanged Men*) - *Church of San Giorgetto*
(formerly in the Church of Sant'Anastasia) - VERONA

THE PAINTINGS

Many excellent artists, endowed with considerable technical skill and genuine inspiration, figured among the interpreters of the Late Gothic art which burst forth in a last great flowering during the end of the fourteenth and the beginning of the fifteenth century; they were, however, motivated more by the force of tradition than by the introduction of a fresh new spirit. Gothic art became more and more rich and rarefied, exploiting every means to produce startling effects, and embarking on a broad exploration of the diversified aspects of nature (this was perhaps its principal merit), so as to assimilate even the most disparate elements of reality on the same plane without concrete opposition or antithesis.

However, the world that produced Late Gothic art had halted in its course. Its process of development could be considered at an end, and the artist who chose to devote his time and energy to Gothic automatically limited himself to the penetration of an already formulated reality, without pursuing the innumerable hidden reasons for its existence—reasons which, once exposed, could have led to a new orientation in the evaluation of man and of nature. Thus the artists of Late Gothic were working with a world which was over and done with, precisely while another world was quietly preparing the way for the Renaissance. Since they clung so to tradition, it is hardly surprising that they sometimes seemed almost to immobilize themselves in renunciation. Falling into melancholy, they then gradually surrendered, after which—and only after which—they were definitively swept away by Renaissance humanism. Yet the Gothic tradition was so firmly rooted in certain ineradicable values that not only did it not disappear, but in fact it helped strengthen the famous current of pantheistic naturalism. This current, developed particularly among the northern artists of the fifteenth century, was to find new force in the Italian art that appeared in the last years of the fifteenth century and the first of the sixteenth, and that was already far removed from so many concepts of the early Renaissance.

The main opposition to Late Gothic was to be found in Tuscany, where the transition to new ideas took place more quickly, though even there the resistance to these new ideas was far from weak in Florence and Siena. Nevertheless, Tuscany provided the most fertile field

25

for the art of the Renaissance, not only because of the local artists' natural tendency toward abstract geometrical construction, but also because of particularly favorable social and cultural conditions. Meanwhile, the change took place more slowly and along somewhat different lines in northern Italy, and artists as un-Gothic as Giusto de' Menabuoi or Giovanni da Milano, who had long breathed the air of Tuscany, could still keep a characteristic personality. This personality was interwoven with the unmistakable language that placed it in the world of the North—in a culture, that is, aware of having become a true civilization, drawing its life from a tradition that had become a historical fact. Since the value of this tradition was beyond doubt, it could view innovations, not as miraculous revelations, but as potent, valid creative forces, and appraise them coolly, rejecting any unwanted features. It is for this reason that in northern Italy—in Lombardy, Venetia, and even Emilia—the Renaissance advanced gradually at first, instead of exploding with the immediacy and the characteristics revealed in Tuscany. In northern Italy it had to proceed slowly, making allowances for the particular demands and situations that impeded its absolute victory, and it often had to be assimilated, at least in part. The opposition between the two cultural currents, the one forged out of tradition, the other springing from Renaissance humanism, reached its most critical moment in the first half of the fifteenth century. While on one side stood Florence, proud of the importance of the new discoveries, though even there "Masaccio and Paolo Uccello were the two poles embodying the twin temptations of painting,"[58] on the other side was much of north Italy, headed by Venice, Verona, Milan, Modena, and Ferrara, where the arts, though by no means languishing, were showing a momentary weakness, a decrease in creative inventiveness.

It is precisely in the context of this critical phase of fifteenth-century art that Antonio Pisano must be placed. It was then that non-Florentine art gained unhoped-for vitality through this artist's work, perhaps exclusively through it. Indeed, Pisanello succeeded in elevating Late Gothic art to the inalienable status of an essential culture; his mind ranged from the enchanting rhythms of Hellenistic modeling to humanist awareness, from the lyrical naturalism of northern Italy to the tortured expressiveness which had come from beyond the Alps and had taken vigorous root in Italy, more precisely in Emilia.

All these situations and factors combined to form his extraordinarily complex art. Thus, if we isolate Pisanello in one, or as more often happens, two of these contexts (Late Gothic culture and humanism) we can make no real contribution toward an understanding of his stylistic sources and development. It is essential to bear in mind all the elements, including the influence of Hellenic aestheticism, which composed the artist's personality. His elevated poetic vision led these component factors into the realm of things that exist in time, but which time cannot separate, far less destroy; on this plane they are fused together as key concepts in the harmony of form, to act as a spiritual and aesthetic catharsis.

Rather than symmetry, form—the intuitive grasping of the essential by means of an *a priori* construction—constitutes Pisanello's harmony. It is the expression of the essence of things in a harmonious relationship: harmony between what is and what was, harmony between lasting values that can only lead to the discovery of others through this harmony.

Stefano and Altichiero, who were respectively the propagator of the Gothic revival in Verona at the end of the fourteenth century and the most distinguished representative in north Italy of the Giotto-oriented Tuscan tradition, are indicated as masters of Pisanello; his art can be considered as depending on these two main sources in every other one of its elements, in the elegant grace drawn from French painting and miniatures, the agitated discursiveness of Nordic artists, or the serene harmony of Classical creations. We must therefore consider how far each of these two painters influenced the younger artist.

Pisanello's first works bear the stamp of Stefano's influence. The *Madonna of the Quail*, the *Madonna Enthroned* which is more often questioned when attributions are discussed, and the signed fresco of the *Annunciation* in San Fermo all reveal a Pisanello decisively oriented toward the graphic stylization of Gothic, fascinated by the naturalistic decorative idiom of the international movement and attracted by the soft cadences of the French school. At that time in Verona all these characteristics were combined in Stefano's art where the rhythms were built around exaggeratedly boneless figures. Incarnating some strange puritanism, he magically spirited bodies away, dematerializing them beneath rich courtly garments; no other artist until Botticelli was more obsessively fascinated by a sophistication of line that seldom permitted the plastic solidity maintained and favored by the Sienese Gothic painters themselves. It is therefore natural that Pisanello's youthful work should seem to draw its main inspiration from Stefano. Even the Lombards did not possess Stefano's vaporous elegance and flexibility, which were to be reflected, though in a different way, by Antonio Pisano. The mannered Michelino da Besozzo himself does not reach Stefano's level; the works of Stefano da Verona seem made "from thin air, the drawing is so light," while Michelino's "have heavier forms and less lyrical inspiration."[59]

However, already in Antonio Pisano's first compositions, there is something that distinguishes his work from the elegant but tense work of his master. Decoration and graphic effect, which were almost ends in themselves for Stefano, are replaced in Pisanello's work by a more sustained, coherent pictorial discourse. This reveals a more profound meditation on the

27

subject of inspiration and on its conceptual symbolism, from which there stems a greater formal consistency; the painter's attempt to reinforce and revalue Late Gothic, injecting it with new strength, is then shown clearly.

Later we shall discuss at length this second element, the most difficult to isolate if one does not follow the usual practice of considering it as the natural point of union between a declining Gothic style and a rising Renaissance classicism. In fact, it does not seem to have come directly to Pisanello from any other artist. It must then be admitted that we are here confronted by completely personal, original creation: an intuitive sense of the eternally new values contained in a temporary state of the culture of the time—in Pisanello's case, International Gothic—combined with an awareness of the burning individual need to revalue this state. The revaluation could not be achieved by introducing elements foreign to the state but by using its already inherent values, the naturalistic harmony combined with an expressiveness which is of a very refined elegance and yet concrete, though in a spiritual rather than a physical way. This unique intuition is what sets Pisanello's art apart from the superficial Rhenish and watered-down Bohemian expressiveness, the detailed concreteness of the Lombards, or the pressing alienation of the Tuscans.

Thus Altichiero, whose northern formation did not preclude Tuscan affiliations, could not have lent Pisanello a regenerating strength. The current started by Giotto, which went on to inspire Turone, Avanzo, and Altichiero, in whose work free inventive fantasy is balanced by the imposing volumes of the figures, could not have found a receptive subject in the young Veronese painter. Indeed, the movement may have struck him as particularly obsolete and even monotonous because of its slavish imitation of Giotto. Besides, in the formative years of his career he still knew nothing of the renewal going on in Tuscany, which was to be affirmed in the work of Masaccio, with all the decisive consequences entailed.

Pisanello, then, could hardly avoid working on the basis of courtly Gothic, and in particular of the Gothic represented by Stefano da Verona, with whom he felt a strong affinity, in a cultural climate which certainly gave him much of the grace and refinement that constitute one of the most attractive aspects of his work as painter, draftsman, and medalist. He unswervingly maintained this close bond with the latest period of pure Gothic, despite the fact that nearby Padua was dominated by the frescoes of Altichiero and Avanzo in the Chapel of San Giorgio, and the same artists had recently completed their celebrated murals in the Great Hall of the Palazzo di Can Signorio in his own Verona.[60] The most that one can reasonably suppose is that Pisanello saw the medallions of illustrious men painted between the arches of the Loggia di Can Signorio, and found inspiration in them for his medals.

Among Pisanello's numerous paintings, a few are signed; others have been attributed to him with more or less validity.

Of the pictures that can be attributed to him, the *Madonna Enthroned* [Plate 1] in the Palazzo Venezia Museum, is a work of the painter's early youth. Stefano's graphic narcissism pervades this widely discussed painting, which already shows Pisanello's rethinking of Stefano's compositional procedures, and his considered resolve to go beyond them. The novelty of terminology in the language of the painting is barely perceptible, but the general discourse is bound together in a far closer synthesis, so that it might be said that the work marks the point of transition from the vague sweetness of Stefano's art to more vibrant rhythms. The flowing fall of the garments, which in Stefano's more archaic *Madonna and Child* [Fig. 1] in the Colonna Gallery is abandoned, too deliberately loose, and seems to drop mechanically, is more controlled in the Palazzo Venezia *Madonna*. Innovation and originality in this painting are shown most of all in the solid under-layer which supports and lifts the sinuously curved bands, and in the Virgin's face where Stefano's serene, fulfilled expressivity is replaced by an expression of more melancholy resignation.

Stefano's influence is still visible in the *Madonna of the Quail* [Plate 6] in the Museo di Castelvecchio, which is nevertheless more rhythmic than the Palazzo Venezia painting and livelier in the undulations of its motifs. The single long curve of the body continues the wave of negligently flowing blond hair, and reappears more heavily along the ermine edging of the cloak, already seen in the *Madonna Enthroned*. It frames the dreaming but real face of an individually portrayed girl, who has none of the insipidity of a Masolino Virgin and still less of the serene happiness radiating from the works of Cristoforo Moretti.[61] The beautiful, sympathetic figure holds the Child in her elegant, mobile hands, so that He stands upright and forms an opposing element to fill the space left by the curve of her mantle. The famous quail is at their feet on the ground, where other birds and flowers enliven the space round the Virgin's cushion.

Pisanello's naturalism here begins to take on a consistent form, but at the same time, the differences between it and Stefano's naturalism—best seen in the *Madonna in the Rose Garden*—are revealed. While in Stefano's work every enlivening element seems imprisoned in the intricate rose garden as mere decoration in the fantastic tapestry against which the two main figures are flattened, in Pisanello's painting there is an invigorating breath of nature awakening, and the figures themselves, more freely posed, show their enjoyment of it; even the angels holding the crown, who are reminiscent of Stefano, are here more lively and attentive.

And the angel of the *Annunciation* [Plates 7-12], the first signed work of Pisanello, executed in fresco above the Brenzoni tomb in the Church of San Fermo in Verona, is one long sustained vibration. It is purely and simply a masterpiece, the first full synthesis of Pisanello's complex of poetry.

The angel appears in a flow of rhythms and Gothic harmonies underlined by unconscious impulses that disturb and move this oval face in an almost pagan manner. He bows low in an enchantingly narcissistic pose, holding a branch of lilies in front of him. His gaze and head are turned downward while the air plays through his hair and uncovers his bare neck. The wings, dazzling sheaves of gold, form a crown for this rare creature, who might almost be designed to symbolize beauty reveling in itself. But the most striking thing here is the complete absence of conventional religious piety: any familiar intimacy or touch of sentiment would be utterly foreign. The angel comes from some fabulous world reserved for initiates, unknown to all outsiders, and he reveals this in the elusive, indefinable expression of his face and the rich, enchanting appearance of his entire figure. Below, two doves flaunt their pink and white and blue feathers, while at the back, beyond the mountain that rises, echoing the curve of the wing, there are still higher mountains crowned with fantastic castles, a forerunner of the landscape which Masolino, perhaps drawing on his impressions of northern countries, was soon to conjure up in Castiglione Olona.

On the right, in a setting of unambiguously Gothic architecture, sits the Virgin wearing the traditional embroidered cloak. This figure seems to owe less to Stefano than to Gentile, whose Virgins, from the Verona Madonna to the one in the Perugia Pinacoteca, show marked similarities to this work. However, even in this case of greater affinity, the difference between the two painters is pronounced.

A few years before he painted the *Annunciation*, Pisanello had worked with Gentile in the Ducal Palace in Venice on the execution of a large fresco; he was very likely engaged on this work in his own right and not merely as assistant to the older painter. We have already pointed out the probable stylistic relationship between the two painters. It must not be concluded that Gentile had a decisive influence on Pisanello; indeed, Gentile's archaic style, still redolent of Giotto and Byzantium, owed its life essentially to its cosmopolitan decorative richness and does not seem to have left any appreciable trace on Pisanello's genius. Gentile, who must also have been a talented draftsman, may perhaps have helped restrain Pisanello's still Stefano-oriented hand, temporarily moderating its too unbridled excesses of fantasy. But it could be better argued that, on the contrary, the main influence was exercised by the younger, more gifted man. This hypothesis should not be excluded, any more than the other which proposes Pisanello's collaboration in Florence on the *Adoration* [Fig. 8] by Gentile.[62] A few figures in the Florentine *Adoration*, particularly the group on the right, foreshortened in an attempt at expressionism, might justify such an assumption, if, here too, Gentile's irrepressible calligraphic sense did not hinder the manifestation of a true inner state of pathos and anguish, so ruling out the possibility of any basic collaboration with Pisanello. Though the work is in the mainstream of Late Gothic art, the inheritance of Giotto makes its weight felt; this is shown by the manner in which some faces, though conventionalized, are distorted and set into unmistakable elongated almond shapes. Naturally, here we are dealing with residual influences, for we are far from the poetry of Giotto, just as Pisanello's poetic sense has yet to reveal itself. If Pisanello actually collaborated on this Florentine painting, his presence could be adduced from the three figures behind the youngest of the Magi.

However, it seems that the expressionist elements inserted in Gentile's work should not be considered the fruits of the artist's own imagination, nor should they be equated with Pisanello. It would be more convincing to derive them instead from the fresco cycle executed shortly before in the Bolognini Chapel in the Basilica of San Petronio in Bologna where there is an abundance of superficial expressivity which assimilates elements from Giotto. And this style must have made no small impression on Gentile, the provincial painter from the Marches who had soared to the heights of Late Gothic and now suddenly found himself face to face with the unexpected visions of a demoniac spiritual brother of Bosch. Their impression must have been all the stronger as Gentile was by nature predisposed to gentle beauty and paradisiacal splendors.

It is precisely when one considers the San Fermo *Annunciation* that the differences in style between Pisanello and Gentile show themselves most strikingly; the Virgin, though fixed in a pose of devout resignation, reveals the individuality of a human presence. All conventionalities are discarded in the composition, while the face shows the pathos of Pisanello's thoughtful world. The expression is attentive and the subtly emphasized eyes are the discreet channel for emotion; the hair falls negligently, as in the *Madonna of the Quail*, while the opening of the cloak exposes a soft tunic that blends with the living flesh.

The architectural elements are Gothic at its most flamboyant, foreshortened to frame the scene; a little dog stands rather inappropriately on the floor, detracting somewhat from the mystic atmosphere of the moment. In the center, above the door where the angel waits outside Mary's house, the symbolic tiny Christ Child comes down from heaven, in accordance with the traditional naïve convention.

Finally, encased in medieval silver armor, the archangels Raphael and Michael stand above

31

to complete the ensemble. The former, on the left, is handsome and strong, bursting with life; the other forsaken, melancholy, and abstracted, his incomprehensible expression emphasized by the serpentine twining of the wavy hair round his spellbound face.

Still further above, behind the slender architecture soaring to the sky, the golden stars of the universe gleam against a background of purple.

After the *Annunciation*, the next documented works of Pisanello are the lost frescoes of San Giovanni in Laterano, followed by the Sant'Anastasia frescoes in Verona. These consisted of *The Legend of Saint George* (described in the first chapter), the lost *Saint George Replacing His Sword in Its Sheath*, and, also destroyed, the *Saint Eustace* beneath which, according to Vasari, was written "the name of that Pisano." Among these frescoes, the high artistic level of the *Legend* singles it out as a work entirely conceived and executed by the master. If he called on helpers, it was for other scenes, now lost; this could be attested to by the *Arms of the Pellegrini Family* [Plates 90, 91], parts of which might be from another hand, perhaps that of Bono da Ferrara, one of Pisanello's pupils.[63]

The tempera painting *The Vision of Saint Eustace* [Plates 120-122], in the National Gallery, London, is generally placed in the same period as the Sant'Anastasia frescoes. This dating is often justified on the grounds of certain affinities of line between the figures in the painting and those in the *Legend*; others hold that the subject treated is similar to that of the lost frescoes in Sant'Anastasia. These, however, are not conclusive reasons and cannot provide a sure dating, especially as the affinities in question are not substantial, for the animals in the *Vision* reveal a more mature elegance of style than do those in the *Legend*. Second, while both the lost fresco and the London tempera painting had Saint Eustace as subject, they treat two different episodes in his life. In fact, the fresco did not depict the Vision, but a moment when the saint was caressing a dog "piebald brown and white"; nor can it be supposed that some admiring patron invited Pisanello to repeat the episode from the fresco in a painting. Because of its maturity of style and refined construction, we hold that the work can be dated about 1440, that is, when Pisanello, after realizing his greatest poetic creation in *The Legend of Saint George*, was setting out to polish his style, a task which was paralleled by his activity as a medalist.

And indeed the *Vision* seems to be the work of a fine carver. The colors, fawns and browns, and dark greens, relieved only by the yellow coat and the blue turban of the horseman, glow darkly over a bronzelike surface, barely scratched to suggest rocks and ravines and to render hares and other animals with scintillating suavity.

Here Pisanello conveyed marvelously well the atmosphere of a mountainous, wooded land-

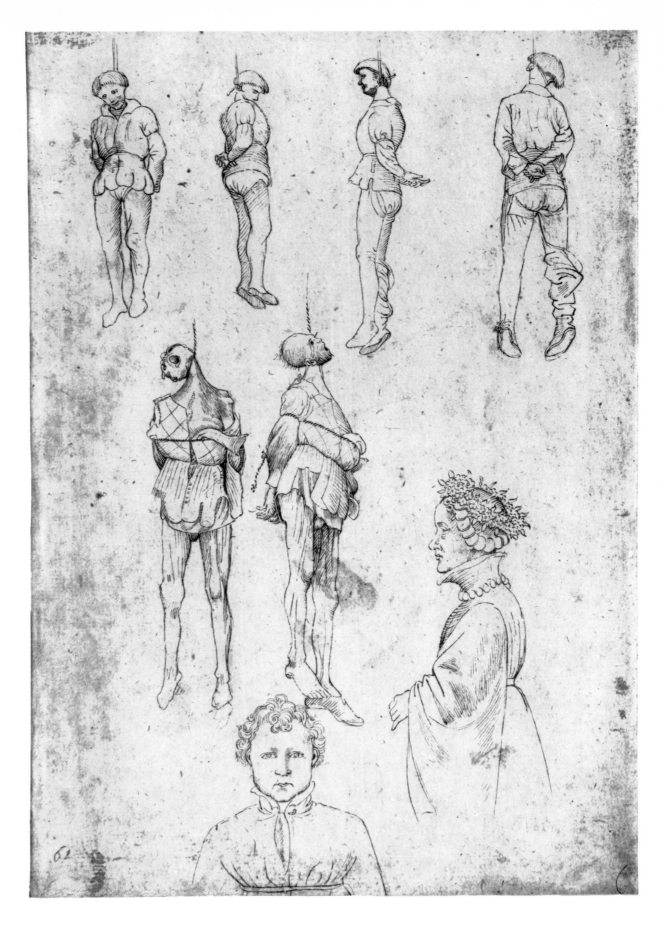

55 - STUDY OF HANGED MEN, A LADY, AND A BOY - *British Museum* - London

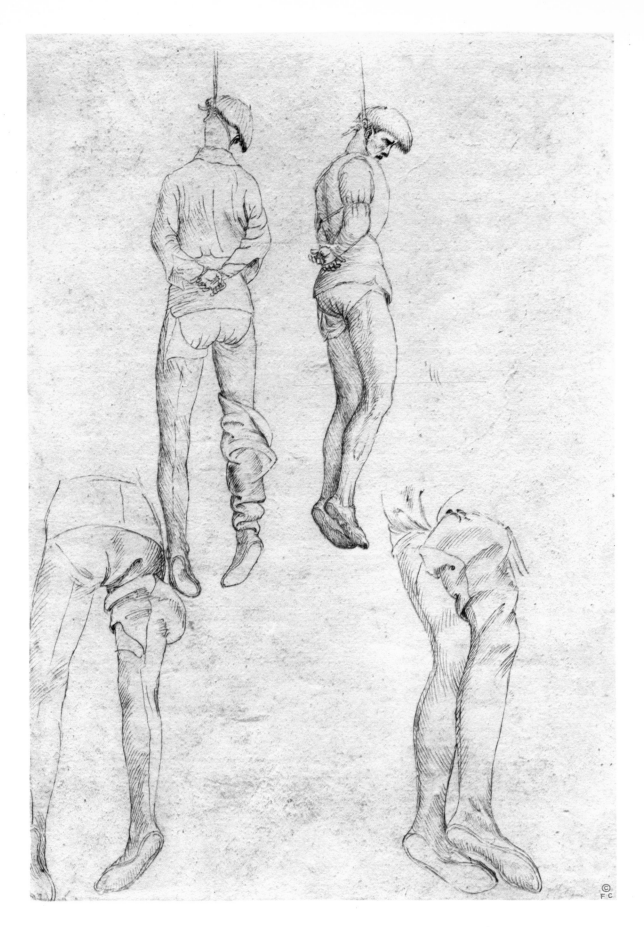

56 - STUDY OF HANGED MEN - *Frick Collection* - NEW YORK

57 - STUDY OF HEADS AND AN ARCHER - *Louvre* - Paris

58 - STUDY OF A MAN'S HEAD - *Louvre* - Paris

59 - THE LEGEND OF SAINT GEORGE *(detail)* - *Church of San Giorgetto*
(formerly in the Church of Sant'Anastasia) - VERONA

60 - THE LEGEND OF SAINT GEORGE (*detail*) - *Church of San Giorgetto* (formerly in the Church of Sant'Anastasia) - VERONA

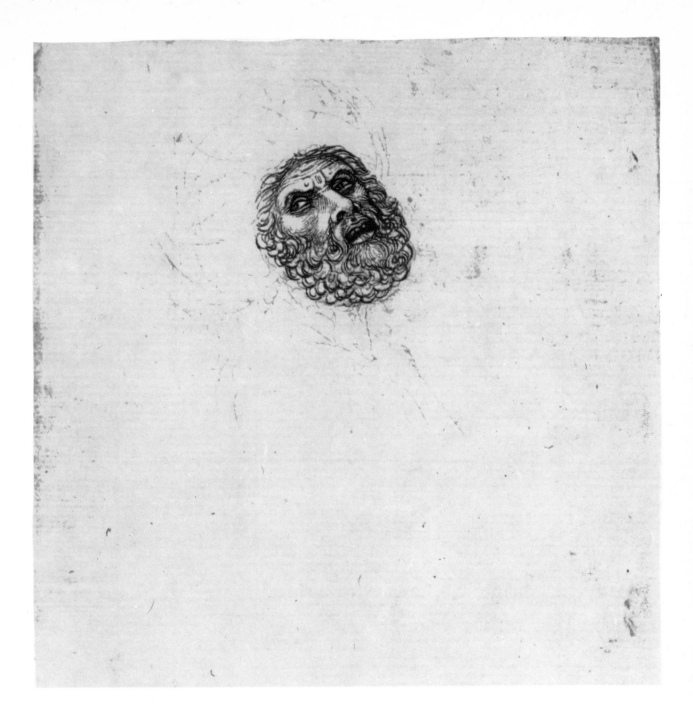

61 - STUDY OF A HEAD - *Louvre* - PARIS

62 - STUDY OF A YOUNG MAN'S HEAD - *Galleria Estense* - MODENA

63 - STUDY OF A HORSE - *Louvre* - Paris

64 - STUDY OF A WOMAN'S HEAD - *Louvre* - Paris

65 - THE LEGEND OF SAINT GEORGE (*detail: The Princess*) - *Church of San Giorgetto*
(formerly in the Church of Sant'Anastasia) - VERONA

66 - THE LEGEND OF SAINT GEORGE (*detail: Saint George and the Princess*) - *Church of San Giorgetto* (formerly in the Church of Sant'Anastasia) - VERONA

67 - STUDY OF A WOMAN'S HEAD - *Louvre* - Paris

68 - STUDY OF A WOMAN'S HEAD - *Louvre* - PARIS

scape, where shadows are accomplices of that medieval sense of the *fabuleux* that saw fantastic works of magic in all nature's more esoteric aspects. And there is indeed something magical about the sudden apparition, like so many will-o'-the-wisps, of all these animals, some of which can scarcely be distinguished from the dark background of the scene; space becomes flattened and its very flatness shortens distances, even in time. There is no longer distance to separate the horseman or the animals or the divine apparition from one another; the animals seem to spring up suddenly and are all placed in the foreground, as if they had been pushed forward by stage machinery. Each one is in its proper element, the stag on the path, the herons in the sky, and the swans on the water, but they all remain on the same plane, and Pisanello has taken care to avoid creating depth, even by false perspectives. Instead, he had the idea of representing the fable—very appropriately in this case—in a dreamlike atmosphere: the saint, the animals, the wood, and the apparition then form a unique whole, the particular whole that is indispensable to insure the survival of the mythical nucleus of the fable, here expressed visually as a hallucination.

The contrast between the motionless shadow that wraps the scene and the horse's lively trappings provides yet more support for the theory of the apparition, which, once glimpsed, causes a complete breakdown of all spatial and temporal relationships. However, we are not in the presence of figures painted in a more or less stately vein with the sole aim of setting them off prominently in geometrically divided space; instead, we are faced with an example of naturalistic exaltation of living creatures, insofar as they are all symbols of irreducible entreaties which the artist expresses by pushing their "spatial communion" to its extreme limits. Finally, it must be noted that the crucifix reflects no supernatural light; as if to comply with the painter's wishes, it does not send out conspicuous flashing rays that would have disturbed the uncanny calm of the scene. The saint, richly costumed on his imposing horse, which might almost be a product of the Renaissance, stops in awe before the apparition while his hound looks around at him in curiosity. Another hound, further down, carries on his hare hunt undisturbed; one feels that if the apparition were to withdraw even a little it would disappear and everything would return to the original planes and the normal dimensions that the eye perceives.

Because of its daring conception of space as a two-dimensional façade, with depth only a secondary factor to heighten the fantastic vision, this painting can be considered as one of the finest achievements of Pisanello's maturity.

The same period, though it is impossible to establish exactly how long before or after, produced the painting in the National Gallery, London, *The Apparition of the Virgin to Saint*

George and Saint Anthony [Plates 146-47 and 150]. The static atmosphere plays a major part in this painting, as does the construction of the figures, in particular that of Saint George. Much of the coloring has been altered by later retouching and restoration, yet the simple architecture of the composition and the contrasts between the principal tones combine to proclaim the value of this rare panel signed by Pisanello.

The atmosphere, as we said, has an unusual function in this painting, deriving mainly from the relationships of contrasts between the blaze of the apparition (which has an equally luminous counterpart in the figure of the knight), the intense darkness of the background, and the immobility of the figures. This immobility seems to stem from a suddenly frozen movement which allows depth to open up in the center. The landscape is closed by a wood so dark it establishes the distance between it and the foreground. Here we have the Flemish naturalistic procedure of conveying the distance between different planes by a contrast of light; only here the closest figures are the most brightly lighted and the space between the tree trunks, right in the center of the painting, is barely hinted at in the shadow of twilight—or dawn?—that dominates the scene. In this way Pisanello avoids the Flemish style of airy infinity, which a Van Eyck would have rendered with retreating planes of gradually increasing luminosity; in the *Apparition,* though the elements are all marshaled together, the front planes assume the greatest life and are sharply separated from the others. Thus the painter creates a vertical backdrop, recalling the *Vision* but presenting less two-dimensional interest, on which the remaining elements are placed as a naturalistic residue, serving to condition and in a certain sense to define the characters. It is also unusual that instead of favoring the opening of a space that could have situated the moment and temporality of his conception, whether empirically, in the Flemish manner, or, as the Tuscans did, metaphysically, the artist should have preferred to avoid any "opening" of the kind, which might have diversified the individuality of the figures beyond their real essence, even with a simple hint of open space. This is a fundamental point in Pisanello's poetics. Through his inimitable pictorial language, the artist shows himself more attached than ever to the immediate moment, the particular historical moment, beyond which he glimpses a new world in which everything is to be remade. This position might appear reactionary if we did not know the precise value Pisanello attached at the same time to Gothic naturalism as a "harmonious union and participation." However, it must not be forgotten that this did not preclude various manifestations of the tormented expressionism which the particular, critical cultural moment produced in him. Thus we see how, faced with a period of regression in the world he inhabited, he opposed it by an elevated language, a language of "harmonious vitality," just as some artists of the early

69 - COSTUME STUDY - *Musée Bonnat* - Bayonne

70 - COSTUME STUDY - *Musée Condé* - CHANTILLY

71 - COSTUME STUDY - *Ashmolean Museum* - OXFORD

Renaissance tried to react with the formal means at their disposal against a situation that was equally reactionary, albeit for different reasons.

There is nothing surprising, then, about the strange atmosphere which in the *Apparition* mingles relaxed serenity and repressed anxiety, static postures and naturalistic expressions, or about the grotesque Saint Anthony, as wrapped up in his own predicament as any Bruegel figure, with his personality reflected in the archetypal weightiness of the robe that enfolds his squat body. There can be no cause for shock in the Mother and Child group, in which the swirling rhythmic waves and spirals of the clothes are at one with the immediacy of the apparition, nor in the two ghostly horses' heads which project against the blue background on the right; nor even in the breathtaking figure of Saint George himself, weighed down with armor yet still highly elegant as he stands among the coils of the dragon. The saint is left expressively undefined, as are so many of Pisanello's characters. Instead of being represented plunged in thought, as he usually is, as if to attribute to him heaven knows what feats of heroism, he remains simply the plastic embodiment of an aristocratic set of ideals that cannot easily be identified with aesthetics or with inner fulfillment duly acquired, abstracted but still defined in lyrical terms.

The painting is not governed by any precise law; its expressive force is maintained by an atmosphere which, while preserving the acute naturalistic rhythms of the figures, transports some of them to a level of metaphysical dignity and elegance.

Pisanello's presence at some of the most famous courts of Italy was undoubtedly not the least of the reasons for his activity as a portrait painter. However, while the personalities he immortalized in his medals are unquestionably authentic (since the artist's signature figures on the work itself),[64] with the painted portraits the situation is rather different. First, none of the painted portraits attributed to Pisanello are signed, and, second, they show differences among themselves in certain elements of morphological structure which are always more or less constant in the medals.

The portraits unanimously attributed to Pisanello are that of *Lionello d'Este*, in the Accademia Carrara, and the *Portrait of a Lady*, in the Louvre. Among the numerous others assigned to him, we hold that he was probably responsible for the *Portrait of a Lady* in the National Gallery, Washington, and the *Portrait of the Emperor Sigmund*, in the Kunsthistorisches Museum, Vienna.

The *Portrait of the Emperor Sigmund* [Plate 36], only recently attributed, but the first chronologically of Pisanello's surviving portraits, is also one of the most controversial because of the Bohemian traits that have been detected in it. Indeed, the morphological-figurative details that have been adduced as evidence[65] for ascribing or not ascribing the work to Pisanello have a certain importance, but they are not sufficient to determine a definitive attribution or exclusion. A certain affinity, purely linear and poetic, exists between this work and the face of Saint George in the *Legend*: in both cases the lines forming the eyes show a certain looseness of the upper lid, which meets the lower one heavily, and the sad, half-closed position of the mouth could also point to a common source of inspiration. Further, the fine strokes of the beard and hair could well recall Pisanello's sinewy drawing. It is not possible to make precise comparisons between the decoration of the garments of the two figures.[66]

While one may attach great importance to this straightforward comparative material, it would be foolish to neglect the thesis which draws parallels between this painting and certain works of Bohemian painters.[67] Indeed, when one compares the portrait with the *Head of an Apostle* executed by a Bohemian artist of the fifteenth century [Fig. 13], one cannot fail to notice immediately a certain community of style in the two faces. The eyes and mouths are again the determining features for such comparisons, yet on closer analysis fundamental differences become clear and the particular calligraphic approach of the Bohemians becomes evident.

The weakness of the arguments favored by both theses is the fact that morphological details, though their fundamental importance is undeniable, must always play a secondary role when difficult problems of attribution arise. In such cases it is necessary to refer, first and foremost, to the artist's poetic repertory, which is the most essential aspect of his personality. In fact, although in every separate moment of creation each artist expresses something unique, something he has never before said in this particular way and will never reproduce exactly, nevertheless each of these moments in which the artist's poetic acts take on material substance is dominated by a determined characteristic bound up in the individual, in some ways constant and immutable, "inspiring line" that shapes the inimitable creative activity of the artist himself. Now, morphological terms are for the most part governed by a certain technical experience—that is, by a material factor not always subjected to poetic criteria; the *raison d'être* of poetics, on the other hand, is to be found in the sentimental and intellectual capacity of the man himself, or in contingent but unique historical situations. And there can be no doubt that in many cases poetic values are more revealing than technical or morphological details.

Though figurative morphology is necessary for building up poetic discourse, it can never be

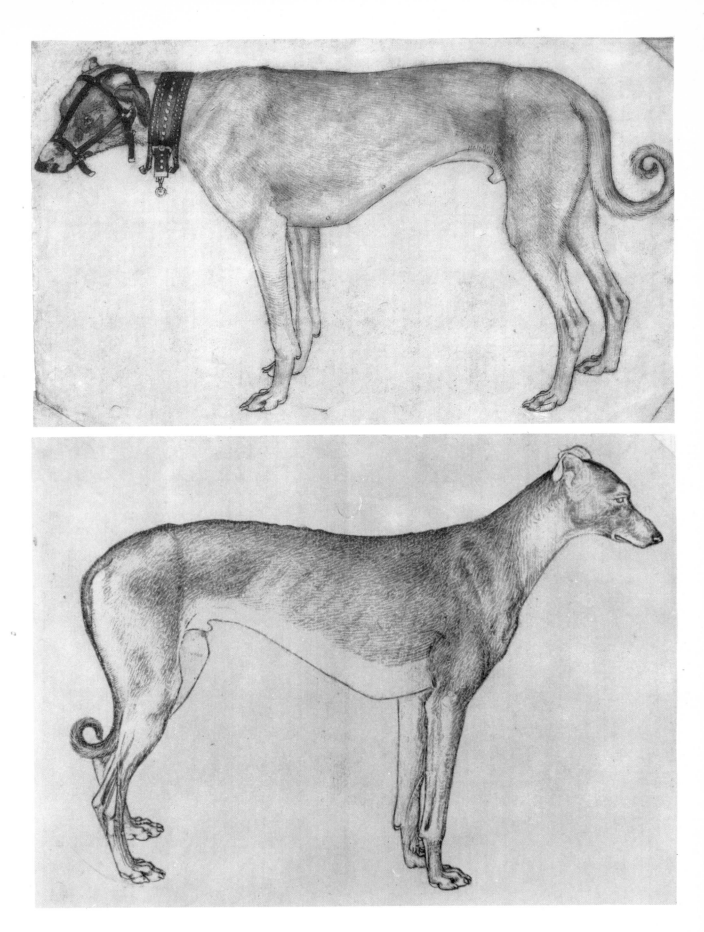

72 - STUDIES OF DOGS - *Louvre* - PARIS

73 - STUDY OF CRANES - *Louvre* - PARIS

74 - THE LEGEND OF SAINT GEORGE (*detail*) - *Church of San Giorgetto* (formerly in the Church of Sant'Anastasia) - VERONA

75 - THE LEGEND OF SAINT GEORGE (*detail: Saint George*) - *Church of San Giorgetto*
(formerly in the Church of Sant'Anastasia) - VERONA

76 - THE LEGEND OF SAINT GEORGE (*detail*) - *Church of San Giorgetto* (formerly in the Church of Sant'Anastasia) - VERONA

77 - THE LEGEND OF SAINT GEORGE (*detail*) - *Church of San Giorgetto* (formerly in the Church of Sant'Anastasia) - VERONA

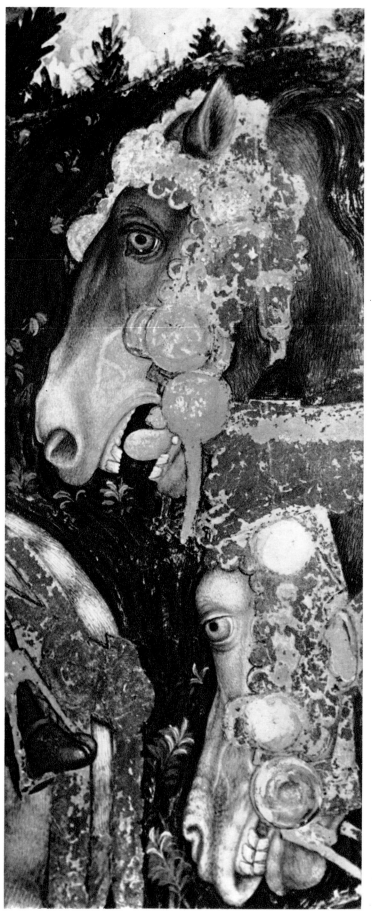

78 - THE LEGEND OF SAINT GEORGE
(*detail*) - *Church of San Giorgetto* (formerly in
the Church of Sant'Anastasia) - VERONA

79 - THE LEGEND OF SAINT GEORGE (*detail*) - *Church of San Giorgetto* (formerly in the Church of Sant'Anastasia) - Verona

80 - THE LEGEND OF SAINT GEORGE (*detail*) - *Church of San Giorgetto*
(formerly in the Church of Sant'Anastasia) - VERONA

81 - THE LEGEND OF SAINT GEORGE (*detail*) - *Church of San Giorgetto*
(formerly in the Church of Sant'Anastasia) - VERONA

82 - THE LEGEND OF SAINT GEORGE (*detail: The Dragon*) - *Church of San Giorgetto* (formerly in the Church of Sant'Anastasia) - VERONA

74 - THE LEGEND OF SAINT GEORGE (*detail*) - *Church of San Giorgetto* (formerly in the Church of Sant'Anastasia) - VERONA

75 - THE LEGEND OF SAINT GEORGE (*detail: Saint George*) - *Church of San Giorgetto*
(formerly in the Church of Sant'Anastasia) - VERONA

76 - THE LEGEND OF SAINT GEORGE (*detail*) - *Church of San Giorgetto* (formerly in the Church of Sant'Anastasia) - Verona

77 - THE LEGEND OF SAINT GEORGE (*detail*) - *Church of San Giorgetto* (formerly in the Church of Sant'Anastasia) - VERONA

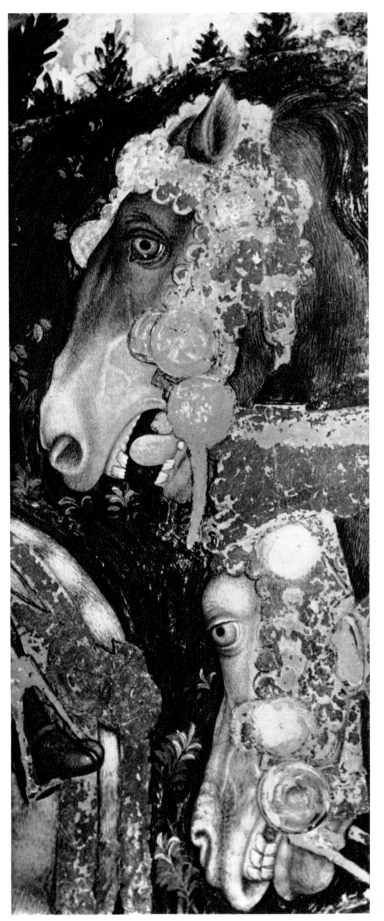

78 - THE LEGEND OF SAINT GEORGE
(*detail*) - *Church of San Giorgetto* (formerly in
the Church of Sant'Anastasia) - VERONA

79 - THE LEGEND OF SAINT GEORGE (*detail*) - *Church of San Giorgetto* (formerly in the Church of Sant'Anastasia) - VERONA

80 - THE LEGEND OF SAINT GEORGE (*detail*) - *Church of San Giorgetto*
(formerly in the Church of Sant'Anastasia) - VERONA

81 - THE LEGEND OF SAINT GEORGE *(detail)* - *Church of San Giorgetto*
(formerly in the Church of Sant'Anastasia) - VERONA

82 - THE LEGEND OF SAINT GEORGE (*detail: The Dragon*) - *Church of San Giorgetto* (formerly in the Church of Sant'Anastasia) - VERONA

counted more important than the reasons that determine poetics. Otherwise there would be a risk of confusing artistic personalities, similar in certain terms of their vocabularies, but differing widely in the particular ways they use these languages to express their poetic worlds. By attributing a dominant role to morphological considerations, one would run the risk of falling into absolute materialism, just as one would be lost in the emptiness of absolute idealism if poetic expression were not sustained and nourished by particular, historically contingent cultural elements that contribute decisively to molding the artist's personality.

The *Portrait of the Emperor Sigmund* reveals a vague quality, which we find both in Bohemian painting and in various of Pisanello's works. However, it seems to possess the poetic qualities of the latter, especially in the intimate, truly spiritual reality, which is revealed in all its richness through the imperceptible channels of Pisanello's forms, with the nonchalant realism that is always printed on the faces depicted by the master.[68] The portrait is not a profile, but neither is it a completely frontal view;[69] the pose follows a diagonal line running from left to right away from the observer, along the shoulders and the headdress that frames the face of the seventy-year-old emperor. In spite of his age, the sitter still shows vitality in his lively eyes, with their underlying melancholy, and in his half-open mouth. The style is elevated and realizes a timeless synthesis of a complex individual life, not least by its manner of disposing forms in space.

The *Portrait of a Lady* [Plate 104] in the Louvre (Ginevra d'Este, Margherita Gonzaga, or some unknown lady from a North Italian court) already shows signs of maturity in Pisanello's pictorial and portrait style. In this work we see the fusion of Gothic grace and splendor with a classically sustained meditation. They are blended in a long reverberation of chromatic shadings which develop in dry tones and half-shadows to project the subject even further into the unknown, profound essence on which her eye, as if attracted by an unreal world, is fixed. The irregular, asymmetrical movement of the background, teeming with flowers, butterflies, and foliage, accompanies the slow separation of the subject from immediate reality. Apparently a decorative motif, this hedge, with its play of kaleidoscopic shapes, acts to accelerate the figure's dissociation from the world that originally possessed her, so that she surrenders herself with surprising ease to the hypnotic song that holds her enthralled. She forgets everything, her entranced face grows pale, the ghost of a smile shows her joy, but it is as if she sees nothing now, and all her ribbons and cords and embroidery, her silks and pearls, not only do not "lyrically magnify her"[70] but cannot even awaken her vanity to recall her to life. She is irrevocably caught by a summons from beyond earthly existence. The long curve of her neck continues up to the oval of her elaborately dressed hair; the over-all flow of the lines seem to emphasize the subject's slow detachment from the world.

We are a long way from other fifteenth-century portrait painting, even from the school of Uccello, which could have much in common with this work. In fact, while in Paolo Uccello's portraits the subjects, in their psychological abstraction, are obviously pursuing a highly spiritual but none the less immediate end, in Pisanello's work the definition of individuality is equated with some metaphysical imperative that invariably conditions the subjects. Pisanello makes his characters show the anguish of existence as well as the joy of spirituality attained. For this reason he often has recourse to the enchantments of simple, fabulous exaltation.

The *Portrait of Lionello d'Este* [Plate 117], probably the one executed in the contest with Jacopo Bellini, is perhaps Pisanello's most controversial work. The prince's humanist attitude is evident. The features are idealized (which would seem to contradict the hypothesis, perhaps not without foundation, that Alfonso selected the Bellini portrait because it was the more "handsome" entry in the contest) and so interpreted as to capture the inner nature that made Lionello famous as an enlightened and cultivated ruler.

But before one has finished admiring the purity of line that makes the work so classical and yet so personal, as in some Renaissance masterpiece, a few red flowers break in to interrupt the vision. They spring up at the foot of the picture and follow the main lines of the composition: two are placed along the strong curve of the chest, while another is introduced in the arc formed by the bare neck and the back of the head, which is pitilessly depicted in its elongated egg shape. As with many other flowers and animals in Pisanello's works, and particularly in a portrait, these flowers do not at first sight seem to have any plausible justification— not even in the Late Gothic taste for fanciful decoration. But here more than elsewhere, perhaps, Pisanello definitely intended to convey a message with this simple decorative device, so naïve and almost superficial at first glance: by juxtaposing the human figure with elements taken from nature, he was trying to fix the limits of his subject, preferring not to leave him in dominating isolation against a formless background. Thus framed, Lionello appears calm and on the point of smiling; spiritualized, though not cut off from the world, his gaze is firm and confident. His neck is long and elegant, his jaw strong below the mouth and chin, his ear stands out almost in relief, while the chromatic reality of every detail is suffused with metallic shades that give intense life to this enthusiastic young man, in love with beauty and happy in his love of it.

38

83 - THE LEGEND OF SAINT GEORGE (*detail*) - *Church of San Giorgetto* (formerly in the Church of Sant'Anastasia) - VERONA

84 - THE LEGEND OF SAINT GEORGE (*detail*) - *Church of San Giorgetto* (formerly in the Church of Sant'Anastasia) - VERONA

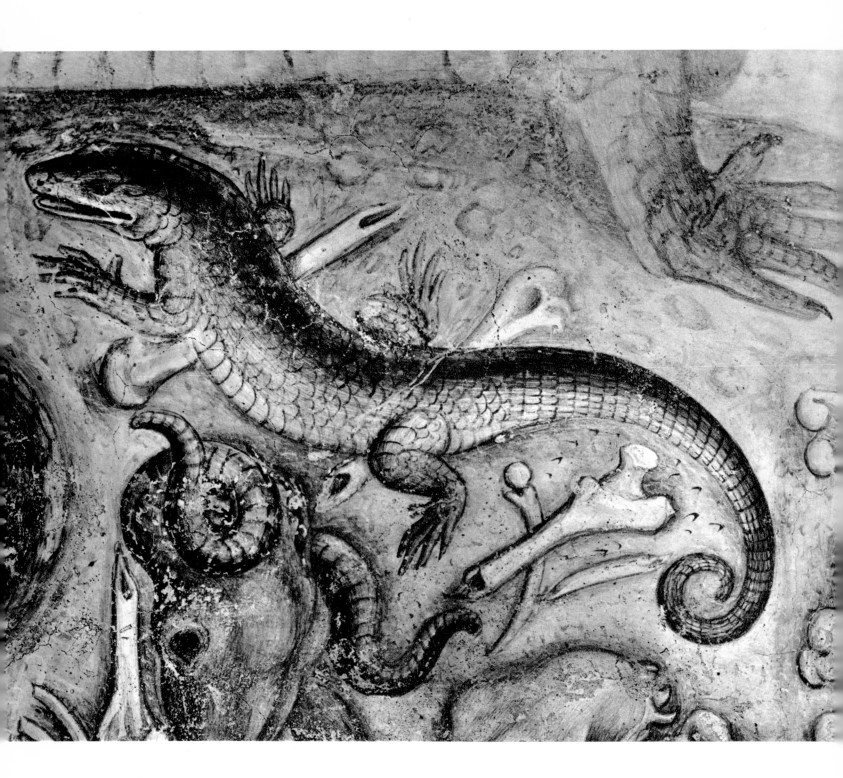

85 - THE LEGEND OF SAINT GEORGE (*detail*) - *Church of San Giorgetto* (formerly in the Church of Sant'Anastasia) - VERONA

86 - STUDY OF A WOUNDED LIZARD - *Louvre* - Paris

87 - STUDY OF A MAN IN A TURBAN - *Louvre* - Paris

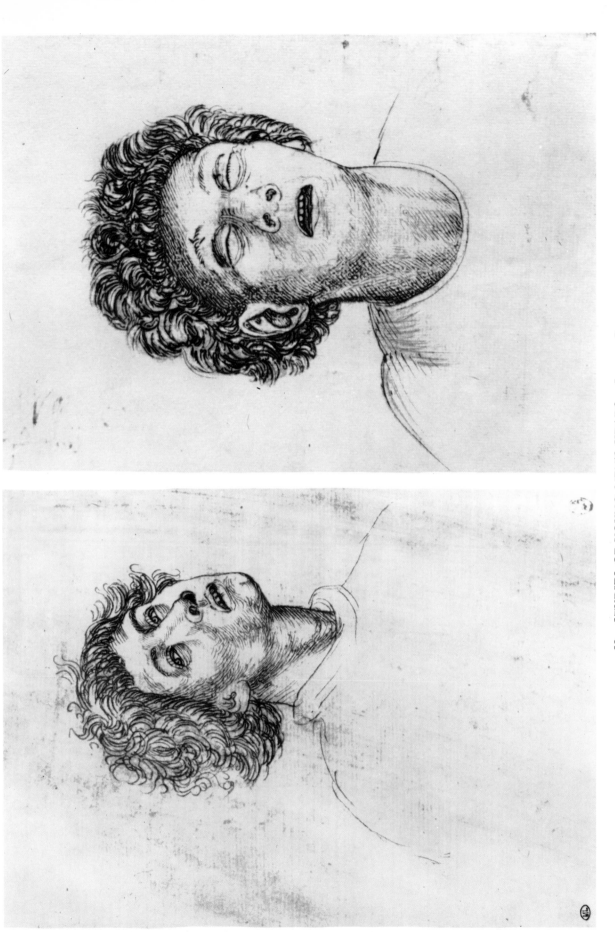

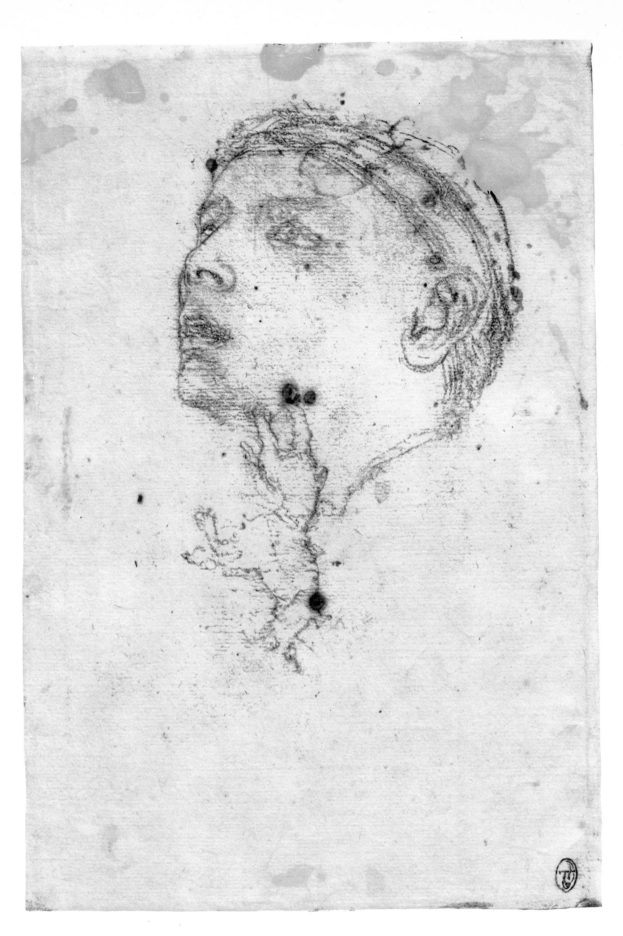

89 - STUDY OF A YOUNG MAN'S HEAD - *Louvre* - PARIS

90 - ARMS OF THE PELLEGRINI FAMILY - *Museo di Castelvecchio* - VERONA

91 - ARMS OF THE PELLEGRINI FAMILY (*detail*) - *Museo di Castelvecchio* - VERONA

Tawny colors predominate, as in the portrait of the Emperor Sigmund. Again the background is dark green and the tunic, in damask according to the fashion of the time, is decorated with dull yellow. The eternal flash of life that pervades this work makes it beyond dispute by far the finest of Pisanello's portraits.

Pisanello shows his perfection of style once more in the *Portrait of a Lady* [Plate 137] in the National Gallery, Washington. The features resemble those of the Louvre *Lady*, though the subject is older, so she may have been an elder sister or some close relative.

From the little we see of the long neck escaping above the embroidered collar, we imagine it to be identical with that of the other; the hair is similarly dressed, but somewhat longer, to allow the jeweled headdress to be twined sumptuously around it. The dark-blue gown is very rich and adorned with jewels,[71] following a taste widespread in northern Italy, and it lies heavily on a body whose three-quarter position sets a more solemn pose. The curves of the mouth are emphasized, but only slightly: in this the work resembles the Lionello portrait rather than the Louvre painting. Although the lines of the nose and chin, certainly faithful to the model, may seem too marked, the shadow which diagonally crosses the corner of the mouth, and the convexity of the forehead continued up to the headdress, are typical of Pisanello. To these main characteristics must be added the oblique set of the eye, which is very unusual and not, as has been suggested, similar to many far more realistic Burgundian portraits, and which gives the gaze its barely perceptible firmness.

The gaze—and so the expression—is lost in the midnight of the dark-blue background. The spell is already cast and there is no need for outside forms around the subject. Everything is pinned down forever, and the gold ornaments, the damasks, silks, and jewels form a single piece with the flesh, whose pink-tinged pallor makes one shudder. This sensation is all the more intensified by the contrast, always dear to Pisanello, between the smoothness of expressively bare flesh and the richness of ceremonial finery. A sinister light falls on this figure, so that she seems a sort of tightrope-walking priestess irremediably cut off from her own human reality.

THE MEDALS

Pisanello the painter has already revealed the basic features of his poetic style. As happens with every advanced stage of an art—in this case, Late Gothic—the complex language of an individual artist turns out to have numerous sources. Among these can be detected an insistent element which appears frequently in Pisanello's major works and distinguishes itself from the others by creating, often through some hint of discord, an atmosphere of harmony and nonchalant abandon that sometimes leaves the onlooker perplexed by the exotic nature of its origins.

In fact, whenever the composition seems on the point of showing a weakness in construction (as in the *Legend*) a sudden upheaval occurs, and an overflowing emotional harmony binds everything together and transports the mind beyond the realm of ordinary relationships into a new dimension of being and feeling. When the relation between primary and secondary themes leads to a hybrid structure (as in the *Apparition*), atmosphere intervenes to minimize or even overcome this opposition by embracing elements that up till then would have been incompatible. In cases where flat, tapestrylike composition (as in the disconcerting *Vision*) risks degenerating into sheer decorative miniaturism, the phantom element darts out once more to dominate the vision, unify it, and set it in order, though conceding it only a provisional reality. Again, a smoothness of relationships extends over the *Annunciation*, as in the portraits; always rhythmic, it gives new value to the Gothic placing of details, endowing them with an individual life, which is no less concrete than the busy, reforming life of the early Renaissance. On the contrary, this Gothic life is perhaps more universal and so, more valid, when viewed in absolute terms.

Therefore, the basic principle of Pisanello's art is contained in the thematic construction of these harmonious relationships, which he grasped quickly and intuitively. It is precisely in this harmony that the mind, in its act of comprehension, can perceive forms that exist on the unreal level of timeless space, in which the existence of either social or religious idols can no longer be justified, and each individual act draws its importance from the eternal motivations that are inherent in existence and being.

92 - MEDAL OF JOHN PALAEOLOGUS
Bibliothèque Nationale - Paris

93 - MEDAL
OF FILIPPO MARIA VISCONTI
Castello Sforzesco - MILAN

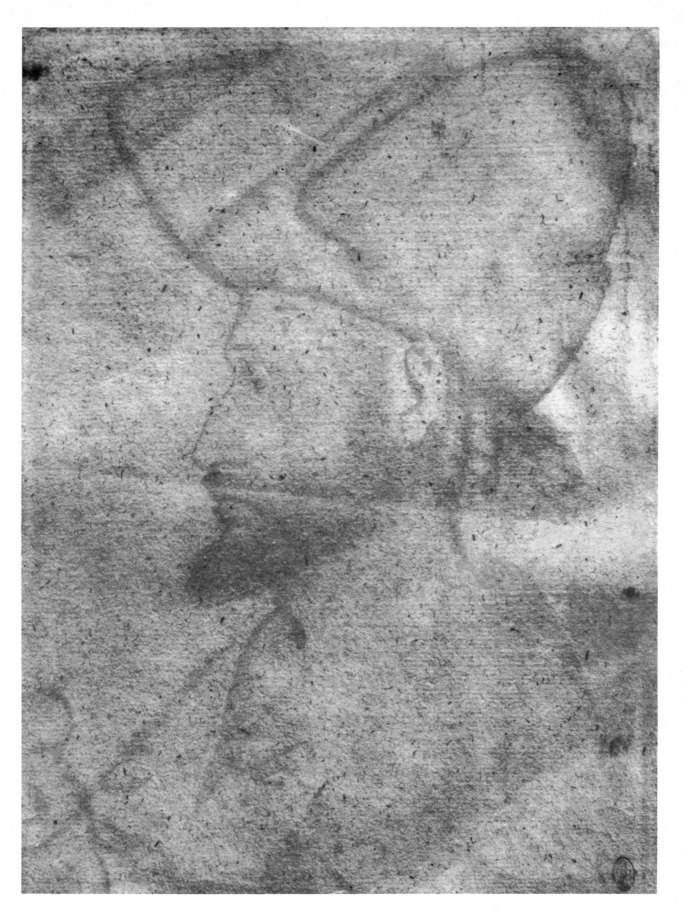

94 - STUDY FOR THE MEDAL OF JOHN PALAEOLOGUS - *Louvre* - Paris

95 - STUDY OF FIGURES - *Louvre* - Paris

96 - STUDY OF FIGURES WITH A CUFIC INSCRIPTION - *Louvre* - PARIS

97 - STUDY OF A MAN IN A TURBAN - *Louvre* - Paris

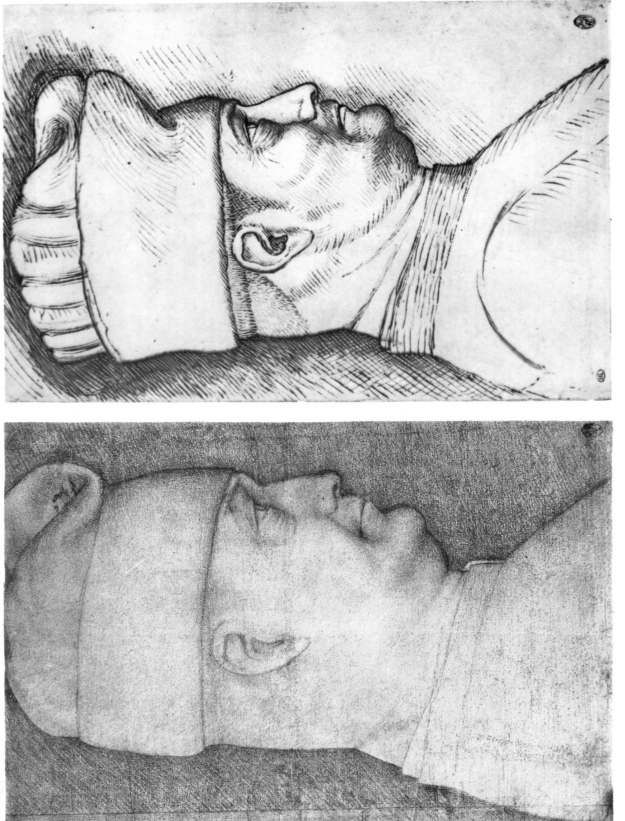

98 - STUDIES FOR THE MEDAL OF FILIPPO MARIA VISCONTI - *Louvre* - PARIS

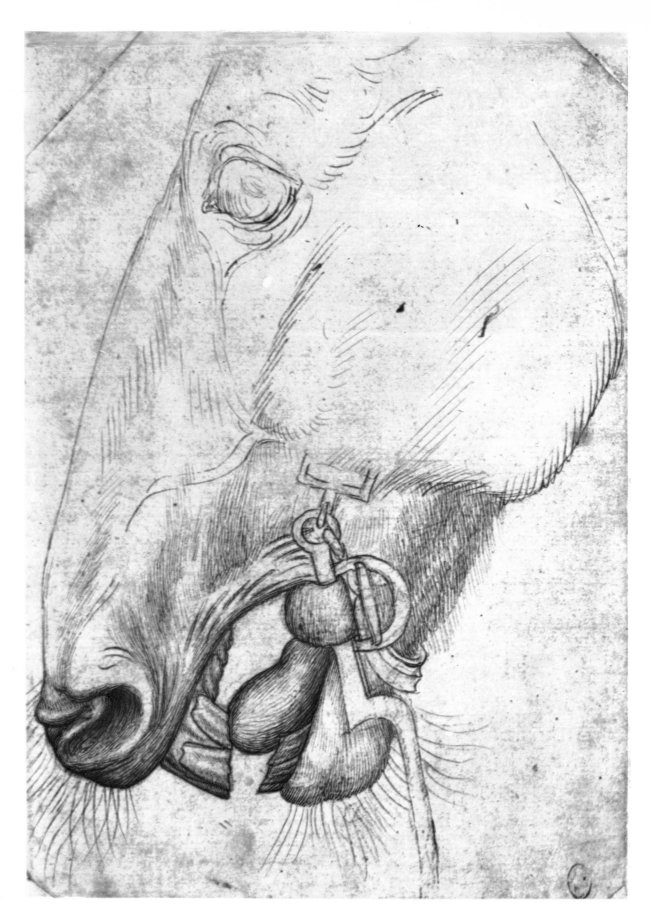

99 - STUDY OF A HORSE'S HEAD - *Louvre* - Paris

100 - STUDY OF A HORSE'S HEAD - *Louvre* - Paris

101 - STUDY OF A MAN'S HEAD - *Louvre* - PARIS

102 - MEDAL
OF GIANFRANCESCO GONZAGA
Museo Civico - BRESCIA

103 - MEDAL OF FRANCESCO SFORZA
Castello Sforzesco - MILAN

104 - PORTRAIT OF A LADY - *Louvre* - Paris

This subtle but vital regulating flux pervades all Pisanello's work. It is evident, sometimes in the over-all conception of his masterpieces, sometimes in the isolated tremors that give life to his "naturalistic" subjects, or again, in the strong characterizations that still invariably hint at ghostly impressions defying immediate perception.

The essential feature of Pisanello's poetry is the musicality of his rhythms, the harmonies of concrete relationships. Whether he entwines convulsive Late Gothic lines or uses static humanistic modeling, whether he arranges expressively hatched and marked forms or with his indefatigable skill as a draftsman assembles tough broken strokes or long smooth curves, Pisanello never fails to relate his art to some irrepressible existence beyond the objects. While he may not always enrich this existence, he always dominates it, and expresses it most of all in the form of atmosphere, the manifestation of some invisible, underlying force that is usually reluctant to be seen: amorous attraction freely displayed, anguish-stricken states of mind, surrender, and so on, ad infinitum. All the "nature" that the artist conceives seems directed toward one single aim.

Certainly medieval fantasy sharpened his perception in such intuitive processes, while the discoveries of the early Renaissance encouraged the unfolding of his fundamentally Classical compassion. In this respect he is a child of his time. However, it was exclusively through his intellect that he perceived, with what we may consider unique power, a metaphysical yet not unreal complex of truths.

From the very beginning of his career he must have possessed this faculty, which enabled him to penetrate, not so much the essence of things—for the essence after all is already a defined condition—but rather the flux and reflux that govern the life force. However, this ability was certainly heightened after his visit to Rome, where he came into contact with Greek and Hellenistic civilization.

Pisanello had the good fortune to arrive in Rome at the moment after the torpor of the Aragonese occupation, when an important reawakening was taking place in the city. At this time, under the pontificate of Martin V, who summoned Gentile and Pisanello to Rome to execute frescoes in San Giovanni in Laterano, many examples of Hellenic art were being discovered.[72] There can be no doubt that the sensitive northern artist was deeply struck by these discoveries—literally discoveries—and the impression they made was in time to influence many of his works.

This influence seems to show particularly clearly in his medals: in the harmony that dominates them, in the handling of volumes so that the play of light and shade settle caressingly on certain motifs which radiate a strange mystical force reminiscent of some Greek sculptures.

These works cannot be called Classical in the word's usual sense. Classical, which in the early Renaissance was taken to mean a proud monumentality and proportion, simply does not exist here. Instead we have the Grecian melody, the Greek and Hellenistic thrill interwoven with painfully sensual overtones, blending with the Gothic naturalism and the acute penetration native to Antonio Pisano.[73]

There are various hypotheses about the origins of Pisanello's medals, but these are valid only if the factors which caused him to embark on this new activity are taken into account. It is agreed that the artist may have seen the Burgundian medals of the emperors Heraclius I [Fig. 17] and Constantine IV,[74] executed toward the end of the fourteenth century, and have found in them a stimulus to portray some of the more prominent figures of his time. Nevertheless it is difficult to accept the idea that his medal-making depended on such fortuitous causes. It is easy to detect, for example, the archaic quality of the medal of the Emperor Heraclius; there is no soft gradation of tones, and, on the contrary, a rocklike hardness hinders the development of sculpturally harmonious modeling. Besides, we cannot say for certain whether or not Pisanello knew this medal.

However, it is beyond doubt that he was familiar with the medallions in the loggia frescoes of Can Signorio in Verona, where the mark of Classicism, though of a still cold Roman variety, is visible. There is an interesting quality in these lively figures set in their four-lobed frames; in particular, the medallions of emperors, though strongly inspired by their Roman precursors, have a structural completeness and a clarity of line that show the outstanding potentialities of pre-Renaissance art in Verona. We therefore hold that the placing of these portraits, calculated to achieve an effect of nobility, must have made a considerable impression on Pisanello and encouraged him to make his own splendid medals. The reasons for his delay in casting the first one, which was not done until 1438, were probably inconsequential.

The arrival in Italy in 1438 of the Emperor John VIII (Palaeologus) provided the most favorable conditions for launching Pisanello's career as a medalist. The emperor's great prestige fully justified the creation of a new medal dedicated to him, and Pisanello carried out the work so astonishingly well that, before long, lords and princelings were vying with one another to be immortalized by the artist's new skill.

But it must not be forgotten that by 1438 Pisanello had already been in Rome and undergone a noteworthy transformation. The memories of what he had seen there became more and more evident in the polishing of his plastic sense. From his first medal to his last, one can trace this gradual process of refinement along the lines suggested by Greek influences. The development in quality of the medals always seems channeled in this direction: though

42

the Palaeologus medal and that of Inigo d'Avalos have the same basic aim, there is a considerable difference between the two works. From a modeling whose simple, understated flow shows it to be hardly detached from the traditional stereotypes of the Middle Ages, one arrives at the aesthetic conclusion of the d'Avalos medal, which can be considered perfect in all respects.

Pisanello's medals have already been described and catalogued from every angle;[75] the present study is concerned with exposing some points of style, with particular reference to the poetic language of the artist. Elements of fourteenth-century courtly medieval art, above all in the overemphasized contours that exaggeratedly outline the motifs, are still present in the *Medal of John Palaeologus* [Plate 92], the first struck by Pisanello. The harmonious calculation of proportions, which was to become one of the outstanding features of later medals, is already manifest as a distinguishing factor. The likeness of the emperor is crowned by a hat with its brim folded into sharp points, the longer of these balancing the emphatic point of the beard. The concave space thus set out frames the inscrutable Eastern face, while the high, ribbed crown of the hat rises clear to the edge of the medal, as if to push beyond its bounds. However, each form, though composed of extremes and not yet modeled with refinement, has sufficient space in the narrow circle, in which every element has light, movement, and rhythm. On the reverse side, the whole seems to have been sacrificed to a too instantaneous impression of the scene, so that the necessary harmony between elements is lost: for example, the legs of the horse on the left are drawn in perspective, while the other horse and rider have the awkwardness of any archaic Romanesque carving. The mountains in the background, so carelessly executed, bear full witness to the charming clumsiness of Pisanello's first essay as a medalist.

But a mere two years later, with the *Medal of Filippo Maria Visconti* [Plate 93], the artist begins the masterly series that shows his full possession of all the means necessary for modeling portraits and symbolic scenes. The Visconti medal proves conclusively that Pisanello has discarded once and for all the predetermined archaic models that might have fettered his hand. In the portrait of the Duke of Milan, the pictorial fluidity of contrasts in light and shade, which is most pronounced in the soft folds of the headdress, is combined with an exceptional skill in portraiture to make the work particularly effective in revealing the sanguinary nature of this tyrant, "mad and fierce, whose effigy breathes bloodthirsty stupidity mingled with the sentiments of a dolt."[76] The reverse side is bathed in a fantastic atmosphere, similar in some respects to that which pervades the *Vision of Saint Eustace*. Yet here, partly in compliance with the demands of the spatial frame, the formal discourse is associated with elegant lines of movement, running principally along the two transverse planes formed by the two horses, placed side by side in slanting positions, their hoofs barely touching the ground. At the same time the relationship between the areas of high and low relief takes on something of an atmosphere of quiet unbalance, first in the individual forms and then in the entire work, so that references to isolated details become totally unpredictable and are in the long run subordinated to Pisanello's cosmic outlook.

To credit Pisanello with a consciously ironic approach to contemporary society would perhaps be going beyond the artist's original intentions. While he did view the world with a certain note of irony, as can be seen from time to time and for which there is contemporary testimony,[77] nevertheless he did not adopt a fundamentally critical position, as did another painter of the time, Paolo Uccello. In no case does Pisanello's irony acquire the Tuscan aggressiveness found in the works of the Florentine painter. Pisanello does not by any means idealize his characters, but neither does he systematically portray them in their least edifying attitudes; he tends rather to capture them in action, and not to judge them. Thus, without forcing his means of expression, he leaves the spectator the task of drawing the appropriate conclusions from an objective representation of life.

However, when he executed the *Medal of Gianfrancesco Gonzaga* [Plate 102], which shows the Marquis as a wan, dried-up old maid of a man, it seems unlikely that he was trying to render a particularly precious service to the lord of Mantua. From a formal point of view the portrait is unexceptionable, with its coherent vertical relation of the elongated lines of the chest and the fanned-out folds of the hat (though the composition gains little from the centrally placed inscription which breaks into the figure's isolation). On the reverse side, the structural relationships are considerably better than before, especially between the two horses (the right-hand one reappears in the medal of Novello Malatesta), and the artist's observation, slightly obscured by the ghostly air that so often surrounds his reliefs, is sharply revealed in the ceremonious attitude of Gonzaga and the caricatured pose of the page.

The penetrating, psychologically oriented inquiry that obviously went into the making of the Gonzaga portrait contrasts with the approach in the *Medal of Niccolò Piccinino* [Plate 109, top], where the execution of the subject is more loosely defined. Piccinino was a friend of Pisanello at the time of the foray into Verona, and the mercenary's figure is visibly ennobled to suggest his natural ability as a leader, expressed here simply by the contemptuous, tightly closed lips. The artist chooses to infuse his friend with detached strength, underlined by the shadows that fall on his face, which is slightly tilted in accordance with the grammar of movement that becomes increasingly characteristic of Pisanello's medals. Here this repertory of movements

44

105 - STUDY OF A PROCESSION AND A LANDSCAPE - *Louvre* - Paris

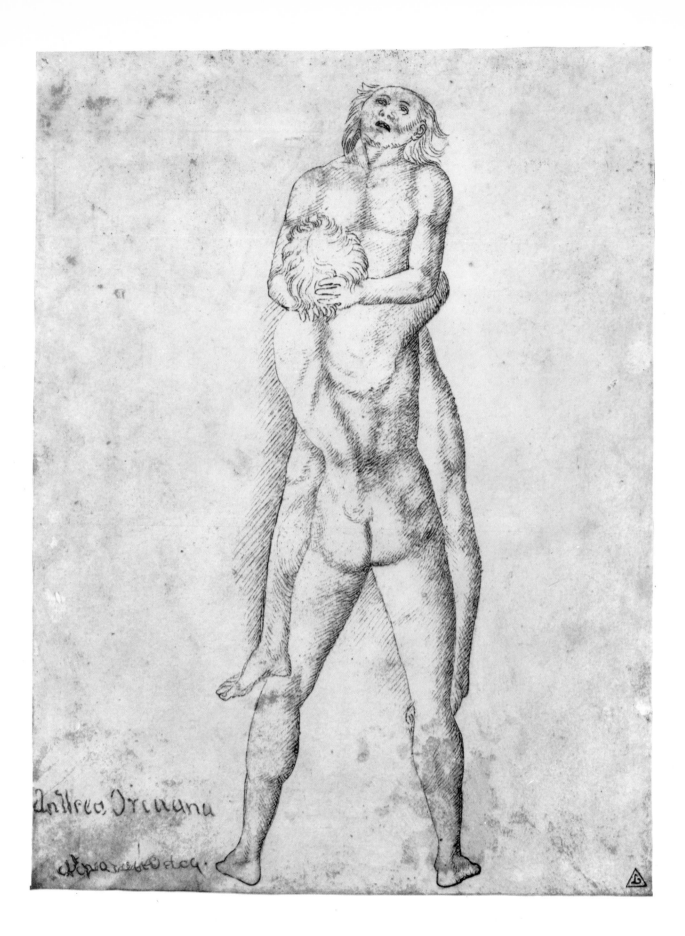

107 - STUDY OF MALE NUDES - *Boymans Museum* - ROTTERDAM

108 - STUDY OF A MALE FIGURE - *Louvre* - Paris

shows its effectiveness in isolating the face within the space enclosed by the inscription. Precisely through the tendency of relief toward abstraction, which this movement renders only just visible, the head is transformed into a symbol of the lot of man, as if by magic. Even making all the appropriate reservations about formal differences, one cannot help drawing a parallel between the deep scores of the face in this magnificent portrait and those on the fresco medallion of Gordiano Antonio in the Can Signorio Palace. An element, new by comparison with preceding medals, appears on the reverse; the motif, a griffin suckling two infants, has no narrative content and has become purely symbolic.

This symbolism is still more striking on the fine reverse[78] of the *Medal of Francesco Sforza* [Plate 103], where the objects are assembled as if in a still life, connected quite gratuitously by metaphysical contrasts of light: the whole is dominated by the majestic, demoniac horse's head. The elements are flawlessly related, and the arrangement of the various parts in space is fine and chaste. On the other face, the portrait of Sforza shows a rather slack construction, while in the facial features and elsewhere the relief, through a weakening of pictorial traits, does not rise to the stylistic heights of the Visconti and Piccinino portraits.

In 1443 the series of *Medals of Lionello d'Este* [Plates 109-116] begins. There are six of them, with as many different allegorical motifs on the reverse faces, some of which are genuine masterpieces of style and poetry. The obverse of each medal portrays Lionello at one moment of his career as a humanist prince, passionately in love with beauty, yet never able to forget his illegitimate birth. A gradual process of refinement can be traced through this cycle of medals: if not refinement in style, then certainly in the sitter's actual psychology. The first medal, whose reverse carries the three-faced head, has been interpreted[79] as showing a personality that hardly fits our image of Lionello. The crudely carnal features and the tensely drawn outlines may indeed reveal sensuality and a lust for power, but we feel, on the contrary, that the prince was portrayed with profound psychological insight, perhaps even too detailed, but not emphasizing these supposed traits that in fact were foreign to Lionello. The artist's aim was rather to pin down the unhappiness of the prince's condition, and the face does show both a sadness and a frustration that fit well with Pisanello's usual melancholy approach to emotions.

Little by little, however, the medals show the young man's face becoming increasingly spiritual. It is as if they reflect the maturing of the sitter's nature: the pictorialism which at first gave tangible form to the face disappears, yielding to a gradually intensifying and, in some ways, liberating luminosity. Nevertheless, this is not the light proper to Renaissance Classicism. The medals do not have the clearly delimited bands of radiance that seem to reflect as many rationally formulated ideas, nor is there any of the metaphysical light which dissolves nature in its attempts to escape from it. Here, instead, the light imposes itself as the basic factor from which stems an exquisitely delicate plasticity that progressively eschews overtly psychological overtones and tends rather to record, in its continually perfected rhythms, the gradual process of refinement of a human nature.

We, who see only with human eyes, may prefer the first of these images, in which Lionello's true self is revealed, and a certain sense of anguish filters through. However, in the last medal, struck on the occasion of his marriage, the style of the portrait is probably more elevated, the various elements are more harmoniously related, the spaces are more open and the bust fits into the general composition like a precious stone in its setting. Yet we must not look for fundamental stylistic differences between the first and last medals; while the last is distinguished by its more consistently rational forms, the first loses nothing by the pathos it radiates.

The reverse faces of the six medals merit particular attention, for in them we can trace virtually all the essentials of Pisanello's art as a medalist. The reverse bearing the three-faced head [Plate 109], though not free from rather strained rhythmic experiments in the side motifs, has something of the quality of a bas-relief, where the main themes are accentuated in a striking atmosphere of light that grows and fades felicitously.

The plastic factor is even more striking in the reverse with the sail [Plate 114], but here it follows conventions almost Roman in inspiration: these facilitate the division of space into layers, either through the slanting composition of the whole or through the prominence given to the two bodies which, while clearly flesh and blood, are materially as lightly sketched in as symbolic apparitions.

The reverse adorned with canephori [Plate 111] already shows the suppleness of a Grecian plastic sense, serene, elegant, and precious in its carefully modulated reliefs. The decorative theme of the two tilted baskets filled with branches which overflow onto the carriers' shoulders, contrasts beautifully with the flawless rhythm of the two naked bodies, carved with a certain expressive softness. The great refinement in the two dish motifs which flank the composition accompanies, as it were, in a minor key, the modeling of the bodies.

But the juxtaposition of human body, nature, and objects is even more successful in the masterly reverse with the nude and the vase [Plate 113]. Here the roughly suggested rocks support the vase and the broken anchor to form a purely decorative background for the relaxed yet vigorous body of a young man, whose countenance recalls the mythical heroes of ancient Greece. The superbly elegant modeling and the perfect rhythms of this medal give an exact idea of an essential aspect of Pisanello's style.[80] His conception is neither Gothic nor truly Renaissance; once more, Grecian harmony appears, with its relaxed gravity and refined elegance. Perhaps Cellini himself, in later times, did not remain indifferent to such an example.

The reverse with the lynx [Plate 115] has a simple but graceful motif whose impact stems from the piquant placing of the restless, velvety beast, the wind-blown scarf, and the extravagant, inclined pillow. In the last medal of Lionello [Plate 116], the reverse, with its wealth of elements, is governed by a sense of proportion that can hardly be matched elsewhere. The lion, the winged cherub holding the scroll, the symbolic pillar, the mountain, and the eagle constitute a whole that covers the medal to the edge, and is simply perfect. The refinement of plastic modeling here reaches its summit, thus enhancing the symbolic effect; each of the various elements is bathed in a clear light which, blurring naturalistic traits, fuses them all into a vision to serve the purposes of the symbol.

Humanist and medieval Gothic traits are combined in the *Medals of Sigismondo Pandolfo Malatesta* [Plate 133], especially in the one with the standing warrior (top). The portrait of Malatesta is conceived along a solid vertical axis, though the slight movement which distinguished the Piccinino portrait is not absent. This more rigid pose seems intended to exalt Malatesta's strength and power, but Pisanello, whose task here is not, as it was with the Visconti medal, to display absolutely negative ethical qualities, tends to elevate the subject by concentrating on the pervading details of the sitter's personality. Thus the emphatic set of the tightly closed lips denotes willpower and determination undeterred by obstacles. At the same time, the highly developed feeling for light and shade softens the face, drawing a veil over the eyes to hide untold resources, while the hair falls over the head to cast a deep shadow on the long, elegant neck. The humanist approach permeating the portrait is completely absent on the reverse, which is rhythmically irreproachable yet rather comical because of the dominantly heraldic tone. The contrast between the formal and material perfection of the portrait on the obverse and the awkwardness of the figure shut in its armor—or perhaps only of the empty armor—on the reverse is too strident not to seem grotesque. On the other medal the portrait of Malatesta is less spontaneous but fits more comfortably into the circular space which is broken just beneath the bust; in the general area afforded by the frame, the features project with such naturalistic violence that the metallic nature of the medium is excessively exploited in the modeling. On the reverse, the representation of the mounted soldier encased in armor shows yet another example of Pisanello's irony, here pushed so far that it almost turns the scene from a symbol into a simple anecdote.

The medium stands out again in the *Medal of Novello Malatesta* [Plate 134], but with caressing harmony, not only in the portrait, where the Oriental-Egyptian profile head seems bewitched, but also in the reverse. Here all is glowing light; the modulation of every element is musically conceived, and the calm foreground composition of the knight embracing the cross is particularly effective emotionally.

Pisanello's distinctively acute powers of penetration are shown in a new, more concise constructive synthesis on the reverse of the *Medal of Ludovico Gonzaga* [Plate 138], where symbolic and decorative requirements hardly assert themselves before being subjected to a stricter conception of form. Similarly, the portrait on the obverse is drawn with composed calm, though the general conception is not one of Pisanello's most fortunate.

The medals so far examined used mainly Gothic and antique Classical motifs, which Pisanello liked to combine for their gentle, humane characteristics, translating them into a delicate range of faint lights and shades which sprang from his lively pictorial sense. Even the Renaissance humanist aspects, bursting out here and there, are always conditioned by the predominant Gothic and antique elements.

In 1447, shortly before he left northern Italy, Pisanello executed the *Medal of Cecilia Gonzaga* [Plates 139, 140], one of his finest works and the only one dedicated to a woman. Although the girl's features recall the Louvre portrait, a very different atmosphere surrounds the face on the medal and gives it greater purity of structure. The lady in the painting, with her rather far-away expression, is content to surrender herself to the magical bewitching echo, the indefinable but pleasant call she hears; on the other hand, the girl in the medal is portrayed in a moment of extreme spiritual grace, with nothing to separate her from the world but her complete self-forgetfulness. The impeccable modeling and the vaporizing white light accentuate the slight turning of the figure inward toward herself, so that at the very instant when she enters a new world—which, if not actually human, is at least the world of a human dream—she seems to forget and abandon her body. It remains very elegant, petrified in a pose of melancholy renunciation, while the head trembles on the long neck, weighed down by the elaborately dressed hair which forces the profile forward into a more intensely sublime expression.

The convergence of spiritual abstraction, formal perfection, and profound sadness in Cecilia's medal affords a better opportunity than most for understanding how far Pisanello was inspired by Grecian art. This is perhaps more evident on the reverse face of the medal, where all the elements—the mountains, the unicorn, the girl, and the crescent moon—combine in their flawless relationship, and most of all in their stirring plastic relief, to form a stupefying whole.

Standing out against the waves of the rest, the figure of the girl, with her loose hair and half-naked body, the distant expression of her profile, and her gaze lost in the infinities of another world, seems derived from a Greek Venus.

It is difficult to decide at which rarefied peak of his creative powers Pisanello conceived such a masterpiece. There can, however, be no doubt that the medal of Cecilia Gonzaga shows him in a fortunate state that enabled him to straddle the Renaissance and to unite without anachronism two eminently real, yet different, well-defined worlds: the Grecian and the Gothic.

One of Pisanello's most daringly synthesized compositions is to be found on the reverse of the *Medal of Vittorino da Feltre* [Plate 144, top], in which the symbol has absolute value in its own right, with no reference to the sitter's personal attributes. The pelican, symbolizing humanity, love, and union, is shown feeding its young;[81] they form a closely knit group in the circular space, so that the artistic language takes on an ethical quality. However, the formal relationship between the central group and the surrounding inscription leaves something to be desired, since the excessive number of words is suffocatingly heavy. On the other hand, the portrait of Vittorino displays an elevated humanist conception of the man: represented with generous modeling harmoniously arranged and bathed in an atmosphere of calm, he becomes the true prototype of fifteenth-century society, devoted to the disciplines of literature and learning.

A wholly different atmosphere pervades the *Medal of Belloto Cumano* [Plate 145], another humanist immortalized by Pisanello. The elegant portrait, with its studied vertical pose and the balance between its various parts, is one of the artist's most successful; however, it is not devoid of an undercurrent of caricature. This is hinted at by the ostentatious verticality, the serious expression of the face, and above it the ornamental dome of the beret which offsets the loosely falling hair, with its almost feminine coiffure. On the reverse, which must be numbered among Pisanello's most accomplished plastic achievements, naturalistic spareness seems to yield momentarily to the pleasure of pure formal elegance, pure harmonious relations of content and line between the elements. The whole composition, from the inscription's widely spaced lettering which spreads around the edge like a constellation, and the few lines that suggest the ermine on the roughly indicated ground, to the tree stumps that close the central portion, is a succession of pure forms—the artist attains this through the continued perfecting of his exceptional graphic gifts.

The last medal commissioned from Pisanello before his departure for Naples was the *Medal of Pier Candido Decembrio* [Plate 144, bottom], which, viewed from the standpoint of stylistic polish, can be considered halfway between the Vittorino da Feltre and Bellotto Cumano medals. While it does not have the humane tenderness that radiates from the portrait of Vittorino, Decembrio's figure is still the result of the same close scrutiny that is obvious in the Cumano medal; its main feature is the naturalism of the facial details, and the pronounced fidelity to the physique of the original. Yet, as happened every time Pisanello represented human beings, the subject is shown with all his particular physical characteristics thrown into relief and at the same time he is projected onto another level, where his unique individuality is once and for all defined. The open book on the reverse of the medal establishes an exact parallel between Decembrio's figure and his intellectual capacities; this symbolic synthesis is mirrored in a happy synthesis of forms, so that the book is linked to the rock on which it rests.

During his stay in Naples, Pisanello struck the three *Medals of Alfonso of Aragon* [Plates 153, 154, and 158]. All executed within a short time, they nevertheless present fairly important differences. The portraits show a gradual progression from an acute psychological examination of Alfonso's inner self to a more rigid definition of his personality, which falls into complete harmony with the symbolic motifs used. So, in the medal whose reverse bears the eagle rearing up, proud and haughty, to dominate its victims, the monarch of Aragon shows a swaggering arrogance, and Pisanello was no courtly diplomat in giving him such a likeness. But then, in the *venator intrepidus* (fearless huntsman) medal, Alfonso's figure takes on new proportions, while everything seems purified in the atmosphere created by the bare verticality of the bust with the crown below. On the reverse, the lively scene of the boar hunt has a mythological flavor. This mythological flavor is naturalistic and is shown in the chiseling of the two animals, whose light, graceful lines are the surest proof of the work's authenticity, joined to the Classical conception of the agile nude. This young man is to be found several times in some of the artist's most beautiful medals, which could lead one to suppose that Pisanello was still inspired by the same model. The portrait executed for this medal was repeated by Pisanello in the elegant plaque of the *Portrait of Alfonso of Aragon* [Plate 157].

In the last medal dedicated to Alfonso [Plate 158], the punctuation of space is more rhythmically balanced, though the various relationships do not seem to gain by this. The portrait is less individually defined, colder and more commemorative; though the arrangement is well supported by the inscriptions, it has a certain rigidity. On the reverse the modeling is rough; because of this, it has been suggested that Pisanello was not able to complete the work.[82] The hypothesis is further borne out by the existence of a drawing for another medal dedicated to Alfonso, which is not known to exist in medal form. This would confirm the

109 - MEDAL OF NICCOLÒ PICCININO - *Museo Civico* - BRESCIA;
MEDAL OF LIONELLO D'ESTE (reverse with three-faced head) - *British Museum* - LONDON

110 - MEDAL OF LIONELLO D'ESTE (with canephori) - obverse - *Bibliothèque Nationale* - PARIS

111 - MEDAL OF LIONELLO D'ESTE (with canephori) - reverse - *Bibliothèque Nationale* - Paris

112 - MEDAL OF LIONELLO D'ESTE (with nude and vase) - obverse - *Bibliothèque Nationale* - Paris

113 - MEDAL OF LIONELLO D'ESTE (with nude and vase) - reverse - *Bibliothèque Nationale* - Paris

114 - MEDAL OF LIONELLO D'ESTE
(reverse with sail)
British Museum - LONDON

115 - MEDAL OF LIONELLO D'ESTE
(reverse with lynx)
Museo Civico - BRESCIA

116 - MEDAL OF LIONELLO D'ESTE
(reverse with lion and winged cherub)
Castello Sforzesco - MILAN

theory that Pisanello suddenly left the court of Naples without finishing his work there. The medal, with the relief of a triumphal procession on the reverse face, still has an importance of its own because of the unexpected structure of its spatial relationships. For the first time, Pisanello abandons construction on receding planes in illusory perspective, and while one can hardly speak of scientific, linear perspective, it is impossible to ignore the particular arrangement on two horizontal planes, which thrusts the lower forward by a play of perspective and similarly projects the rear plane backward in depth. There are evident links between this work, unique in Pisanello's output, and the *Triumphs* in the diptych by Piero della Francesca in the Uffizi, Florence [Fig. 22]. The meeting of these two conceptions (that of Pisanello on one side, concretely exploring a new field of inspiration, and of Piero on the other, passively accepting some traits of northern naturalism) must be placed mainly between the "opening" hinted at by Pisanello and the Flemish-inspired brushwork, more evident than ever in the Uffizi triumphal scenes, that Piero always seems reluctant to discard. Yet when Piero used only the Renaissance structure of perspective, he invariably subjected the scientific module and the exaltation of unique individuality to a concept of form so elevated that it transmuted his material into absoluteness, thus exorcizing his obsession. Probably he saw Pisanello's medal and later took it as a model for his two paintings.

While still in Naples, Pisanello created one further masterwork in the *Medal of Inigo d'Avalos* [Plates 159, 160]. The portrait of Inigo is similar to Paolo Uccello's two Olivieri portraits (in the National Gallery, Washington, and the Rockefeller Collection, New York) and to the anonymous *Portrait of a Young Man* (Musée de Chambéry), not so much because of the characteristic clothing as for the poetic interplay of lines and forms in space. The young man's face is absorbed in a timeless infinity. The pale plasticity of the reliefs owes nothing to atmosphere; here there is only a pure plastic sense, pure dazzling light which mutes the life of the modeling. This in turn dissolves into the looseness of the cloth which escapes from the headdress and, tucked into the jacket, forms a melodious cascade of curves behind the dreaming, motionless face of Inigo d'Avalos, whose gaze is lost in the infinite, perhaps in the infinite cosmos symbolized, within its circular frame on the reverse, by water, mountains, and stars.

THE DRAWINGS

It can be seen that there is a direct relationship between the complexity and sincerity of the conceptions embodied in an artist's work, and his personality. The explanatory expression of a concept or a sentiment, however formally sophisticated, can never equal poetically the restrained movement of a classic work or the tumultuous but always compressed content of a product of expressionism.

The richer a work is in "noneloquent" reality, the more it fascinates and interests, because "noneloquence," whether it is projected in Classical or expressionist terms,[83] always presupposes the working of a more profound poetic sensibility. Indeed, once the existence of such reality has been understood and grasped, it seldom bursts forth in all its richness at once; instead, it surrounds itself with an aura of mystery and so leaves greater freedom of interpretation to the onlooker. Its value remains immense, precisely because every true work of art is made up of open revelations and, at the same time, oblique implications, known realities, and others that, although unknown, are nonetheless existent.

The means employed obviously adapt themselves to the individual circumstances; the important thing is that an otherwise inexpressible idea be revealed through the form used. There are artists who, at the precise moment when a painstaking inquiry into a particular reality finally gives their language concrete form, also penetrate into a sphere removed from the object under consideration, thus endowing it with richer inner meaning.

Pisanello is one of these men. His means, far from being ends in themselves, exhibit these two ways of considering reality, these two viewpoints which merge in his work, perhaps for the first time in the history of art in modern times. Each of Pisanello's works shows not only the definite outline of a particular object, but also the widest possible range of potential motivations contained in that object. From this point on, it is a question of establishing how and where the object's basic way of existing is most manifest.

We have pointed out elsewhere how in the work of this Late Gothic artist, who lived in what was already a Renaissance era, means which are minutely detailed yet not mere craft find their natural place in creating an atmosphere of a certain indeterminateness and universality.

117 - PORTRAIT OF LIONELLO D'ESTE - *Galleria dell'Accademia Carrara* - Bergamo

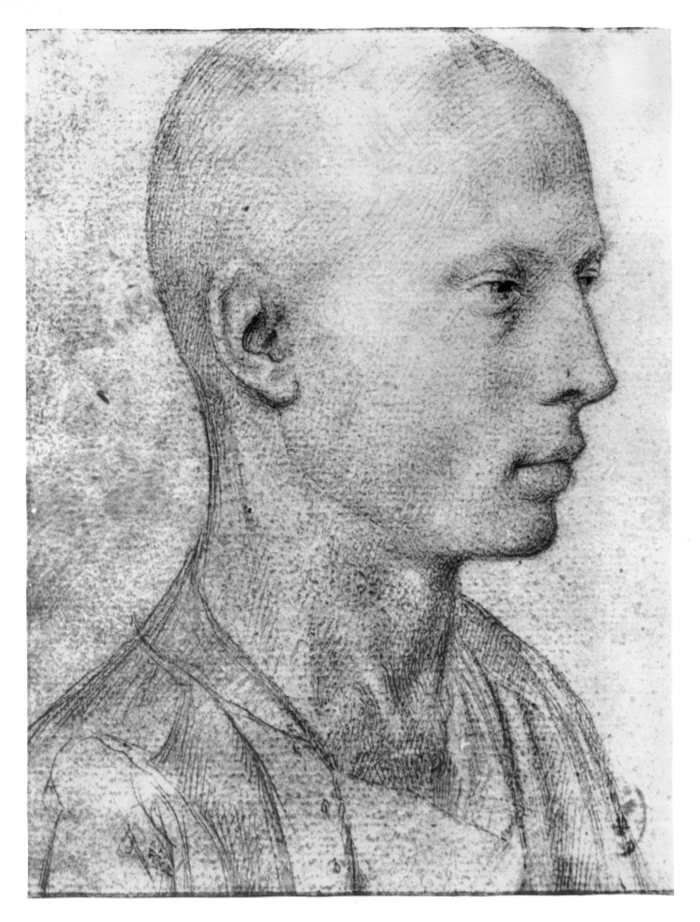

118 - STUDY OF A YOUNG MAN'S HEAD - *Louvre* - Paris

119 - STUDY OF A BOY READING - *Louvre* - PARIS

Pisanello was a master of every technique and a born manipulator of forms; a man gifted with profound insight into the souls of his sitters; and a narrator of natural events on the highest level. His art and craftsmanship led him to cover every aspect of nature and the world of man. This tendency toward analysis and at the same time toward a comprehensive synthesis, though already present in no mean measure in his paintings and medals, is seen most clearly in his drawings. Indeed, it is as if two tendencies run through Pisanello's graphic art: one linear, anchored to the crisp outline, and the other, more specifically intuitive, showing in those rough sketches for which Pisanello seems to have had a marked predilection. In fact, his greatest achievement in the art of drawing is in these rough sketches. The very linearism of some of his drawings which could be related to Florentine theory, assumes a special aspect, for it, too, is as spontaneous as the technique of the rough sketches. It is basically a darting linearism, not an end in itself; it springs forth too immediately to be considered a rebellion against either the schematically defined graphic procedure of the Florentines or the over-minute definition of the Late Gothic artists.

If, then, we imagine Pisanello dragged into the quietly glowing though not yet white-hot dispute that during and after the fifteenth century marshaled in one camp the partisans of drawing as pure line (an objective outlining of the subject), and in the other the theoreticians and enthusiasts who saw in drawing an expression of the work's fundamental qualities rather than a simple delineation, we shall see that Pisanello adhered to the latter school of thought. The reason is clear.

At that time, the current problem was to decide whether drawing, as the first material expression of the artistic impulse, should be assigned only the scientific, exclusively instrumental role of the simple line demarcating contours[84] and spaces in accordance with precise rules likely to facilitate the better realization of the work of art, or whether more complex functions should be attributed to drawing as the first sign of the rich (albeit only potentially) vision of the artist's poetic world.

Moreover, acceptance of one or the other point of view was not simply a question of a certain "technical" manner of realizing forms, but implied adherence to one of two different, and in many ways opposed schools of thought about apprehending reality. The polemical difference between these two currents of thought on the art of drawing was not, then, dictated by chance, but can be inserted into the framework of a dialectic that provided a stimulus to artistic creation from the late fourteenth to the early sixteenth century. The difference between these two tendencies was not merely academic, but concerned two different conceptions of the work of art itself. Renaissance art, in its first expressions (though not in all, for they were marked by various tendencies), is too absorbed by the scientific nature of plans that promised to create a new reality, and by the relative enthusiasm aroused by this situation, to concede much importance to the sketch. The sketch, with all its undetermined, incomplete elements, is rich in vast possibilities for development, and therefore in a sense is opposed by definition to the scientific geometrical method.[85]

This was a categorically established situation, whose contradictions were soon to become evident. It prevented Renaissance theoreticians, who were absorbed by the harmonious geometrical precision of the work of art, from realizing the true importance of the sketch or rough drawing, in the modern sense.[86] Even Piero della Francesca, a fanatic for theorems of perspective, who succeeded in overcoming the burdensome dualism of his time by raising every living form to a transcendental plane, saw in drawing no more than "the outlines and contours contained in the object." And indeed his drawings are conceived without any possibility of further development, without hidden lights, since light and real form could come only after the "definition" of the drawing, when the artist could operate in another sphere.

However, warning signs appeared at the very birth of this dualism, and attempts were soon made to conquer it; even some Tuscan theoreticians realized the difficulties entailed in assigning only a preparatory, schematic function to drawing. Basically, the warning heralded the same contradiction that early Renaissance Tuscan art faced when it claimed to have elevated the spatial perspective drawing to the status of an inviolable rule governing the work of art.[87]

The line that can be traced through the theoretical stands taken by Leon Battista Alberti, Brunelleschi, and Piero della Francesca, and that connects the most significant Tuscan art of the fifteenth century, at least as far as graphic representation is concerned, differs greatly from the one rooted in Gothic pantheism, which barely touches Ghiberti and runs through the artistic struggle of the entire century, right to Leonardo. The first is based on the scientific, geometrical conception of drawing, often linked to precise mathematical rules, as the artist's "preconditioned" field in which he must construct his work.[88] In this case the drawing, though chronologically the first stage, has only secondary importance, its main role being restricted to the outlining of forms according to the demands of contours or the fixed rules of linear perspective. Where the drawing might have assumed independent artistic importance, an intrinsic value of its own, and so a poetic and critical function, pure rationality in the form of a technical and material law had to fulfill a role of immediacy contrasting with the rigorous reformulation of the diagram itself. It must be stressed that the two conceptions

120 - THE VISION OF SAINT EUSTACE - *National Gallery* - LONDON

121 - THE VISION OF SAINT EUSTACE (*detail*) - *National Gallery* - London

of drawing clearly reflect the contrast between Late Gothic poetics and Late Gothic and Flemish naturalism on the one hand and, on the other, the poetics cherished by the new Tuscan art for the exact proportions that determined the molding of forms in space. For this reason the rigidity of the Tuscan working diagram was better served by a more rational, mathematical drawing that *indicated* outlines and "definitively" set out the situation without leaving room for alternative interpretations of the object: by a drawing whose function remained secondary, though it had to be executed impeccably; by a drawing dependent on precise rules, the same rules that risked creating the academicism of the purely diagrammatic drawing.[89]

For the other school, the art of drawing has greater independence and more precise individuality, so that Ghiberti could declare that " the sculptor's competence is as great as his skill in drawing; the same can be said of the painter," thus assigning to the drawing an essential and poetic value.[90] On this other footing, graphic art assumed pre-eminence and, liberating itself from the laws that governed the diagram, progressively imposed itself as an independent value. Developing further the sketch rather than the finished work was to be recognized as embodying the culminating moment of artistic intuition and fulfillment, so that the drawing, thought of as a sketch and not merely as a working diagram, could also be considered as a complete work of art.[91]

Such was the general atmosphere in which Pisanello carried on his great activity as a graphic artist. It has been noted, and will be better shown later, that he never seems to have needed to follow the technical rules of fifteenth-century art, nor to identify his humanism, which he nevertheless felt intensely, with the exclusive, tyrannical variety—formally conditioned by the laws of perspective—that was then current in Florence.

The importance of his drawings, therefore, is all the more striking when they are viewed in the light of the two dialectical trends that marked the development of graphic art in the fifteenth century; these trends can be summed up, respectively, as the conception of the drawing as a sketch, already a work of art, and the theory of drawing as a mere linear diagram. In fact, for Pisanello drawing is not only a means but also a language in its own right. For this reason he can be considered the father of modern drawing.

Pisanello's drawings, which have survived in great number and are now spread among various museums and private collections,[92] cannot be classified according to precise criteria and thus cannot be attributed to determined periods of the artist's activity. The diversity of style, the variety of subjects treated, and in many cases the difficulty of relating the drawings to painting, constitute too great obstacles.

The technique and style of this imposing corpus of graphic work present a continual intermingling of elements which appear sometimes in the greater part of the drawings, sometimes only in a few. When it seems that the insistent recurrence of various motifs could justify their being used as factors on which to base a precise judgment, they suddenly prove to be absent from some other drawing which for sure stylistic reasons cannot be denied the artist. Moreover, though these same stylistic grounds can facilitate the work of attribution, they do little to resolve doubts over chronology. For example, while we find light, sinewy strokes or penetratingly sharp insight in the best, most mature sketches, nothing precludes our finding the same characteristics in drawings that can be assigned with good reason to other periods. In short, it is an arduous task to try to find one's bearings in the labyrinth of attribution and chronology that must be faced by the student of Pisanello's drawings. Perhaps the best way to solve these problems is to avoid taking too absolute a stand in cases where the thin line separating the sure from the unsure leaves only probabilities as a basis for judgment.

The poetic range of Pisanello's graphic world is enormous: it is enough to remember that the largest collection, the Vallardi Codex, contains drawings reminiscent of Stefano, others that are close to Lombard art, and others again which have a clear affinity with the art of Leonardo. Such stylistic complexity, which enables Pisanello's graphic output to embrace both the fourteenth-century modes of Stefano and those, yet to appear, of Leonardo, presupposes a correspondingly complex range of conceptions, capable of assimilating devices from the recent past and others destined to mature in the future.

Yet Antonio Pisano possesses a personality and a temperament that guide us through the maze of stylistic differences presented by the vast corpus of drawings. In fact their strength is shown by their ability to isolate themselves clearly from any stylistic "manner" and so to constitute themselves solidly round a poetic and ideal nucleus.

In other words, this artist has an outstanding capacity for pinning down the intimate nature of every being, for perceiving the moment in which the being lives most fully, with every last strand gathered together. By a few signs, strong lines, or loose, unfinished strokes, he states clearly how the subject is transformed in the flow of fantasy, and appears in its essential nakedness. This is a singularly sublime empirical process in which the particular case is considered only in those of its parts which prove effective on the level of absolute values. So it is this lightning dash to the heart of things which constitutes the most personal characteristic and the main guarantee of the authenticity of Pisanello's drawings.

Purely with a view to providing some orientation, but without wishing to exclude the possibility of further precise reference to particular moments in the artist's career, we can divide

122 - THE VISION OF SAINT EUSTACE (*detail: Saint Eustace*) - *National Gallery* - LONDON

123 - STUDY OF A HORSE AND RIDER - *Louvre* - Paris

124 - STUDY OF A HARE - *Louvre* - Paris

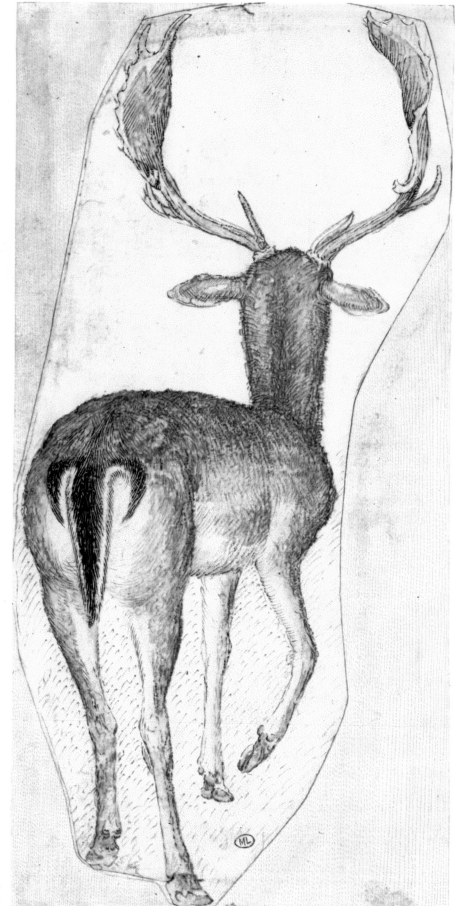

125 - STUDY OF A STAG
Louvre - PARIS

126 - STUDY OF A DUCK - *Louvre* - Paris

Pisanello's graphic activity into eight main periods:

1. Stefanesque-Gothic period (drawings clearly influenced by Stefano but already containing some stylistic innovations).

2. Period of the *Annunciation* (a few drawings stylistically related to the celebrated fresco).

3. Courtly Gothic period (drawings executed over a fairly long period. They have some bearing on all of Pisanello's activity and can be classed with other drawings, placed in various well-determined periods. Nevertheless it seems plausible that the most significant specimens of this hypothetical cycle were produced during the time from the end of the Stefano period to the period of the *Legend of Saint George*).

4. First Classical period (drawings derived from the first impressions of Classical art received by Pisanello, mainly in Rome).

5. Period of the *Legend* (drawings related to the Sant'Anastasia fresco; during this period a profound transformation took place in the artist's personality and style).

6. Period of the portraits and medals and second Classical period (in which Pisanello's highly developed plastic sense affirms itself, while his Classical inspiration becomes further refined).

7. Period of the *Apparition* and the *Vision* (drawings presumably related to these two paintings).

8. Last period (characterized by a more indeterminate style, yet still worthy of consideration from the poetic angle).

A drawing of the *Madonna Suckling the Infant Jesus* [Plate 3] should be assigned to the first period; it shows Stefano's influence, especially in the treatment of the drapery, though it already exploits a more detached and at the same time more complex construction of the image. The controlled lines combine to build a harmonious form, while the quivering life unique with Pisanello can be seen in the doe, which is drawn with mature and polished style heralding the artist's most important drawings.

A sheet with *Studies of the Madonna, Animals, and Demons* [Plate 2] gives rise to considerable doubt as to its author, for the links with Stefano are so evident that they could justify its attribution to him.[93] However, after closer examination of the two Virgins, one notices the absence of Stefano's disembodied fluidity and the broad outlines he uses to give life to his subjects. These two figures already have their own clearly defined personalities, especially the upper one, which anticipates the San Fermo *Annunciation*. The animals, with the darting movement typical of Pisanello's work, show a strong vital force: while the camel can be compared with the one in Stefano's *Adoration*, the pelican feeding its young is the same that Pisanello was to use in the Vittorino da Feltre medal. By virtue of its residual allusions to

Stefano, this drawing can be placed in the period immediately preceding the *Annunciation*. In the *Study of Female Figures and Animals* [Plate 4], in the Albertina, which belongs to the same period, the difference from Stefano's procedures is even more clearly shown; it is here, if anywhere, that Pisanello inclines toward the artistic culture of Lombardy. One may well suppose that he had contacts with Lombard art; its unsophisticated Late Gothic devices had a beneficial but not decisive influence on him.[94]

When Pisanello set to work on the renowned fresco in the Church of San Fermo, his style was already free from outside influences, and was developing along its own characteristic lines. Through a reaction—not, however, polemical—against Stefano's influence, his strokes become lighter and lighter, sometimes scarcely visible, and their vibrating tension tends to bring the inner life of things to the surface. Nonetheless, his hand is not yet completely emancipated, so that the transition from conception to execution is not always managed with perfect harmony.

Thus the *Study of Nudes and an Annunciation* [Plate 13], in the Boymans Museum, shows the turning point between Pisanello's initial graphic activity and the successive development which hinges on his first Classical experiments. The structure of the naked figures relates this drawing stylistically to other nude studies in the Ambrosiana, which will be considered later; but in this drawing the bodies are rather stiff,[95] though the superb execution of the thick masses of hair contrasts with this, while the *Annunciation* sketched at the top alludes to a manner close to Pisanello's, but not his own.[96] On the other hand, the *Study of a Young Man's Head* [Plate 5]—perhaps of an angel, for it is similar in style to the archangel seen in profile in the San Fermo *Annunciation*—is very much the work of Pisanello, exquisitely so, one of the peaks of the master's graphic art. Pisanello here marshals his strokes with consummate technique and succeeds in linking the various elements by hair-thin lines to produce finely shaded *sfumato* passages. The face, constructed with scrupulous gentleness, at one with the space it occupies, presents a mild and at the same time occult appearance.

Another drawing that must be classed in this period is the *Study of a Leg, Flowers, and Squid* [Plate 14], elegant, harmonious, and varied, with a spontaneous line, saturated with pictorial sense in the intense dark zones. There is an extraordinary vibrancy in the unfolding and open flowers, an irresistible impulse to open out into life; to achieve this, the line is more agitated and surrounded by smaller strokes that set the direction of the movement. The naturalistic and pictorial effect of the squid is perfect, while the leg, bent with studied elegance, seems to establish harmony between the other scattered forms.

After this brief outline of the first arbitrarily defined period of Pisanello's graphic work, which began under the influence of Stefano and was then strengthened by borrowings from Lombard art, the time has come to move into the courtly world that is more strictly Pisanello's. As has been pointed out, the productions of this phase cannot be fixed precisely in time, but they all hang together because of the unmistakable quality of their penetrating language. But before examining this large cycle of drawings, mention must be made of some other works, especially of a *Study of Figures* [Plate 15], one of the most famous works attributed to Pisanello, which was executed at exactly the moment of transition between this and the following, more advanced phase. The line expresses the calm atmosphere in which the artist's fantasy still moves; the smaller strokes are placed with precise care and accuracy, outlines are traced with an almost naive simplicity, especially in the two female figures on the left, though the isolated face to the upper right predicts the more profound insight of the *Legend*. Line, figuration, everything shows allegiance to Gothic and, at the same time, to Lombard art. The Lombard influence can be seen in the ordered dignity of the composition, in the luminous polish of the surfaces, and in the general spellbound immobility. However a new, classically inspired element appears: the elegant élan of the structures, the hinted inner inquiry revealed with expressive calm.

Two very fine drawings, the *Study of Faces* [Plate 16] and the *Study of a Seated Man, Deer, and Rabbits* [Plate 20], can also be included in this group. In these drawings the Late Gothic element is ennobled by a surer placing of the lines, while expression seems filtered through slight half-shadows, especially in the drawing of the two faces, where the features peep out cautiously and reluctantly. In the other study the pensive, seated male nude, lightly sketched in, is swallowed up by an obsessive sadness, while behind, like ghosts, figures from the beloved world of nature reappear.

Antonio Pisano was accustomed to observe everything that happened in and around the courts of Italy, with which he had the opportunity of close and frequent contact. He followed great events and everyday happenings, watched and took part in battles and triumphs and processions; he penetrated into the most private corners of castles where he observed courtly life with its treacheries and intellectual elegances, saw feasts and hunting expeditions and entertainments, and was stimulated by everything that passed before his eyes. His fancy immediately transformed these scenes and their actors and, seizing them in their most essential moments, immortalized them through the elegance and preciosity of his art. His art furthermore provides an ample source of documentation on this aristocratic society, whether dominated by princes or warriors or led by humanists, and on all the various ways of life and expression that gravitated toward it. Some studies of this type can be grouped together in the period which we have called "courtly Gothic." Though Pisanello, as is well known, spent all his working life in courtly circles, the drawings under consideration here present certain special points in common which other works, even those treating courtly themes, do not possess. These lack the freshness and spontaneity of execution that mark his earlier works, and do nothing to convey the artist's enthusiasm for the throbbing movement surrounding him. The most striking, fluent, and shrewd drawings of this period are the ones which, after the artist's liberation from Stefano's influence, reach right to the last phase, without particular reference to specific cycles like the medals or the *Legend*. While formally they are less accomplished than many, they are still among the most interesting of Pisanello's works. Here are a few examples.

In the parks and villas and hunting reserves Pisanello was able to observe every sort of animal and plant, and he took to portraying them with almost the spirit and interest of a scientist; however, his scientific interest is focused less on the "anatomy" of things than on their vitality.

This lively interest is manifest in the *Study of a Deer and Goat* [Plate 17], finely colored and exquisitely drawn and shaded. Above all, in the upper animal, which is placed like a precious ornament on a barely visible horizontal plane, the torso, through the contrast with the whites of the background, acquires a relief and elegance that are particularly well concluded by the fine, slim legs.

In two studies of *Dogs Hunting Game* [Plates 18, 19], Antonio Pisano shows certain links with Lombard art. The influence of Giovannino de' Grassi has been traced in these drawings, especially in the one highlighted with watercolor. It has even been held that the colored drawing is by a member of the Lombard School[97] and that the black-and-white drawing by Pisanello derives from it, but there is no conclusive reason for not attributing the color study to Pisanello. In both, the line is rapid and the free movements dart across the page with none of the heaviness and rigidity often found in de' Grassi's otherwise elegant drawings [Figs. 10, 11]. Nor can it be said that the airiness created by movement, though more labored in the colored drawing, should provide grounds for not attributing the work to Pisanello. In fact, it is evident that coloring accentuates the material nature of figures in a drawing; from this alone we can explain the differences, though slight, between the two stylistically very close studies.

Much is revealed about Pisanello's activity at this time by his *Study of Warriors* [Plate 21], which shows men fighting furiously with every means at their disposal. The rapid strokes betray Pisanello's hand, which then is obvious, on the lower right, in the larger figure of a

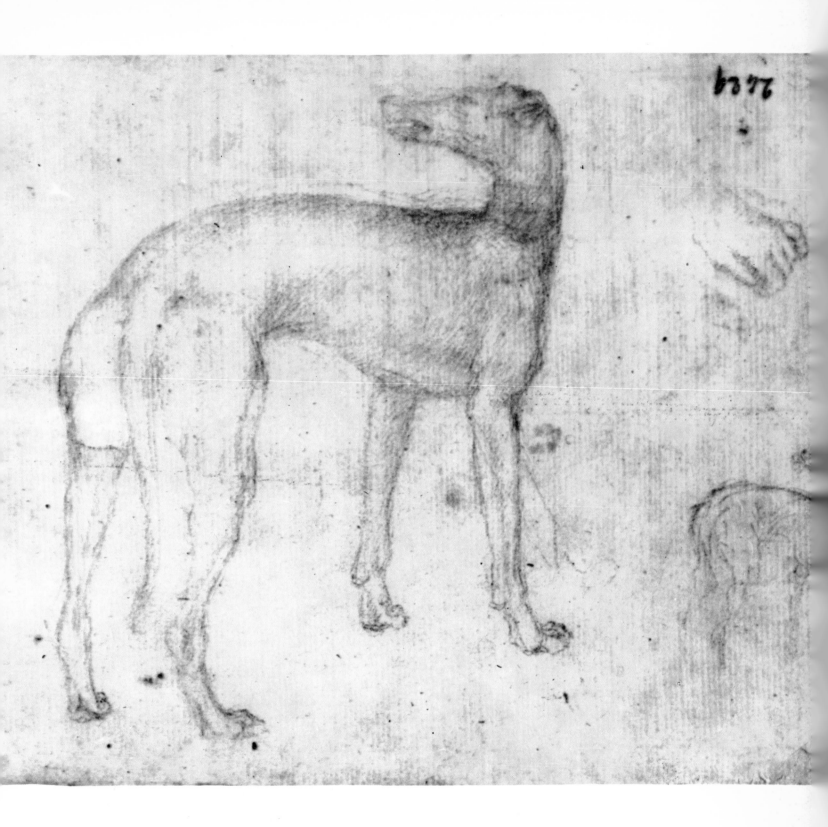

127 - STUDY OF A DOG - *Louvre* - Paris

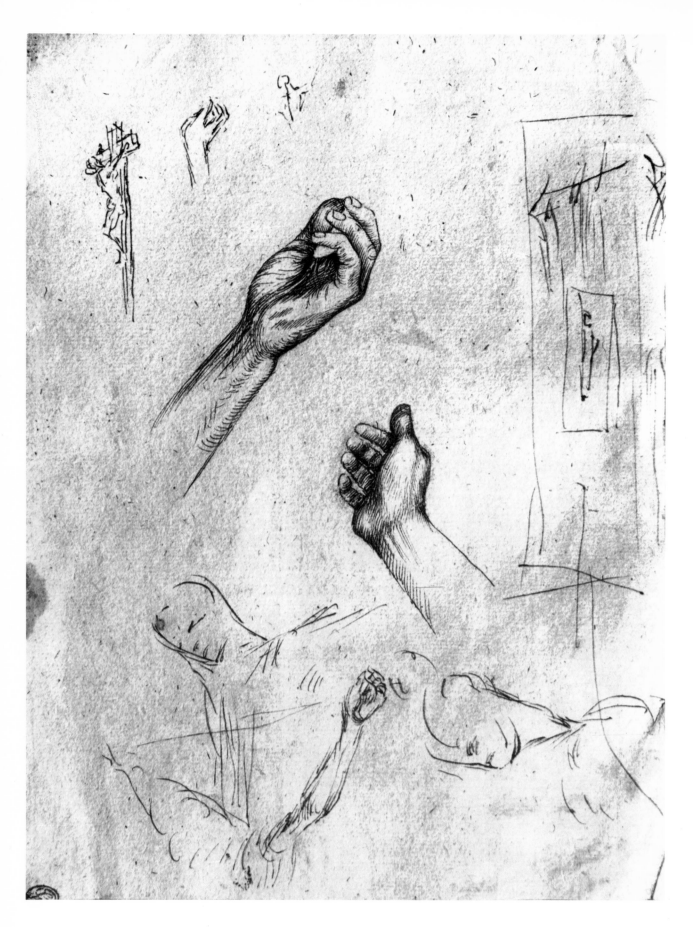

128 - ASSORTED STUDIES - *Louvre* - PARIS

man who is hurriedly pulling up his hose. There is an interesting composition of trees in the center: an analogous arrangement is to be found in the painting of the *Madonna Appearing to Saint George and Saint Anthony* [Plate 146].

In the *Study of a Young Man with a Sword* [Plate 22], the technique is enriched by the greater breathing space left between the strokes in the general structure of the composition. Besides, the subject is a very unusual one: the figure, though clad in the soft garments of a page, is holding a long, heavy sword—a sight that does not often occur in reality. This shows Pisanello's interest in drawing for its own sake, often without reference to particular facts. The study seems to confirm the hypothesis[98] that there is not necessarily any relationship between the drawings and paintings, but only occasional dependence. It must then be supposed that the artist sometimes used drawings or parts of drawings which had been previously executed without any precise aim in view.

In a *Study of Figures in a Vaulted Room* [Plate 23] the room is protracted like a long gallery and introduces us into the world of palaces and the sumptuous life that was led in them. The high arches contrast with the straight lines that stretch back on the floor in a daring perspective, creating an atmosphere of icy, mysterious solitude. This atmosphere is all the more effective as, by comparison, the courtiers appear minute and clumsy, moving like marionettes in their heavy, ostentatious clothes, sketched in by a clever hand with an acute impressionistic sense.

Once we arrive in this mysterious, fabulous court, the spectacle which Pisanello, always ready to set down what he saw, unfolds before our eyes is long and continually enriched with new sights. Costumes fascinate him for their own sake, for their aesthetic appeal, and also for their ceremonial function which tends to stifle the wearers. His amusement at pompous garments can be seen in some of his most personal drawings. One of these, a *Costume Study* [Plate 24] in the Ambrosiana is particularly significant. It is like nothing so much as the show window of a men's shop, with rich slashed suits, capes, hats, and to complete the selection, a young warrior at the upper right, resting in a suit of armor. The strokes are rapid, as the immediate nature of the impressions must have demanded, and it is not improbable that Pisanello collected most of these images at once, jotting down their main characteristics at one sitting, while the warrior and the reptile, probably heraldic themes, could have been executed before or later. It must be noted that the costume themes grouped here are further developed in Pisanello's later work, as is shown by other of his drawings which have points in common with this one, notably another *Costume Study* [Plate 25], also in the Ambrosiana. A costume from Plate 24 is repeated in one of the Louvre drawings, *Study of Jesus Addressing a*

Pilgrim [Plate 26], in which the theme is shown with a more stylized elegance in a purely decorative figure. Throughout the whole composition the pen strokes are more careful, more studied and, one might almost say, intended to create pictorial effects through a more relaxed language. The drawing has not the speckled writing of the preceding sketches, but it has the polish often attained by Pisanello, here perfected by slenderness of line and gentle contrasts. Finally, the theme of a cape seen from the back, also in Plate 24, is repeated more effectively in *Study of a Mantle* [Plate 28], where the slight curving of the lines magnificently renders the softness of the fur and material and the downy consistency of the garment as a whole. The combination of chiaroscuro effects and nonchalant short strokes in this drawing shows a greater mastery of style and presages the more refined and more competent sketches that appear in the last period of the artist's career.

Many studies of architecture, masks, and embroidered cloths can be explained not only by Pisanello's continual thirst for experience, but also by fortuitous happenings that may have impelled him to treat rather exceptional subjects. Indeed, it is probable that Pisanello, who participated in the complicated life of the courts for a long time, was charged with the "stage design" for festivities and entertainments, and that it was with this end in view that he prepared these architectural decorations, parts of costumes, and fantastic masks. This group of drawings is fairly rich and is included in the Vallardi Codex, where the series of studies of ships with dragons, columns, and other decorative motifs does, however, leave some doubt as to its real authorship.[99]

Two drawings that can be placed in this particular group are a *Study of a Lion Mask and Architectural Motifs* [Plate 30, left], in the Louvre, and a *Study of Masks, Feet, and Sandals* [Plate 30, right], in the Boymans Museum. The two drawings, whose execution is very polished, have many points in common, especially in the control of the line, which is released in an intricate flow of curves. In the Louvre, drawing, the Gothic nature of the architecture, in spite of the cruder relationships of its volumes, leads to the architectural elements in the San Fermo *Annunciation*, while the lightly suggested curved lines of the lion's head foreshadow the stylized creations of the artist's most mature phase. However, the drawing in both studies tends less toward abstraction and has more in common with the impressionism of the study of a mantle just mentioned. The most striking characteristic of the Boymans drawing is the silky smoothness which gives shape to the wild beast's mask and the human one; the sphinxlike abstractedness of the latter recalls the portrait of the Emperor Sigmund. The feet roughed in above represent a first attempt at similar studies that Pisanello was to execute later in perfect elegance of style.

This period of Pisanello's production also includes a colored *Study of a Leopard and Columns* [Plate 27], whose graphic refinement springs mainly from the chromatic transparency of the architectonic motifs and the execution, almost miniaturist in its care, of the leaping wild animal.

The sheet of *Plants and a Man's Legs* [Plate 29] can also be referred to this period, in which are grouped drawings, ornamental motifs, and costumes. In this study, the rapid strokes follow one another almost spirally to sketch in the hose and to determine the direction of movement. They contrast with the small masses, more decorative pictorially, of the two plants which are rendered with such diversity of tones that the lighter parts stand out brilliantly. The graceful elegance of the parts, harmonizing with the masterly general execution of the whole, makes this study one of the most significant in the artist's whole output.

Some sheets closely related to courtly life, which form a more or less independent group, have been variously attributed to different periods of Pisanello's career, while their authenticity has not passed uncontested. It would seem that the drawings, often retouched with quills, were carried out by a heavier hand than Pisanello's; this can indeed be observed in the three examples reproduced: *Study of a Trumpeter* [Plate 31], *Fife-and-Drum Player* [Plate 32], and *Ceremonial Scene, a Trumpeter, and Male Heads* [Plate 33].

In the first two, the thickening of the line suits the caricatural intention of the drawings. Indeed, it is difficult to imagine how light, slender strokes could have conveyed the coarse awkwardness of the trumpeter. Only Pisanello's acute sensitivity could do justice to this subject's dullness and stupidity as he performs his part with the same automatic gestures seen in the other musician with the drum, where the short, hatched strokes emphasize the puffed-out cheeks. A similarly psychologically profound inquiry, moving toward abstraction but still faithful to the subject's innermost reality, makes itself felt in the third study, which was certainly executed later than the other two. Pisanello here shows himself master of his medium: the style gains in variety and complexity, and progresses from the simple strokes of some passages to the tempestuous concentration of expression in the largest figure. From the top sketch, which can still be equated with some lavish ceremony and contains motifs still close to Pisanello's first language, we pass to the coiling strokes of the head on the left. These are too urgent for precise placing, so that tension is built up and finds its outlet in the trumpeter's head. This is the moment when Pisanello's art decisively throws off the outside influences—which had nevertheless made it what it was—to concentrate on a different, more severe expression and a more carefully thought-out construction.

Shortly after his return from Rome, Pisanello was asked to demonstrate his abilities on the occasion of the Emperor Sigmund's visit to Italy. Perhaps the two *Male Heads* [Plate 35], outstanding for their delicate execution and their sharp expressivity, are sketches of two members of the emperor's retinue. On the other hand, no drawing can be related to the emperor's portrait in the Vienna Museum [Plate 36] (similarly, it is impossible to find drawings for the monumental figure of Saint George in the *Legend*); the one drawing that may be connected, not with the portrait, but because of facial resemblances, with the man, is the *Study of a Male Profile* [Plate 34].[100] In the Vienna portrait, the emperor is shown in fullface, richly dressed, and he exhibits expressive qualities that go beyond the rigidity of drawing; in short, he is considered in an altogether different light. The precise link between the Vienna portrait and Pisanello's drawings consists in the graphic planning of the portrait[101] and the hair-fine strokes used in the upper part of the painting, especially in the beard and hair. On the other hand, the Louvre study may have been intended as a preliminary sketch for a medal of the Emperor Sigmund. This drawing, for all its naturalistic precision, is not one of Pisanello's most creative works. He seems to have seen his subject in a set pose, and portrayed only superficial appearance, without trying to penetrate the façade and express the sitter's true personality. The result is an impoverished form, while even the technique falls back on already well-tried procedures like the heavy strokes on the garments or the waviness of the hair.

A *Study for a Flagellation* [Plate 37], in which Pisanello's interest in nude figures is particularly manifest in the two scourgers, has formal resemblances to works of this period, but must be set at the beginning of a new wave of activity, the first Classical period. The flexion of the body of one flagellator effectively conveys the tension of his movement, while the various elements, pushed to the extreme limits of balance, anticipate some of El Greco's more daring constructions. The figure at the left, though, stands firm in a solid classicizing plasticity which forecasts Pollaiuolo's work. In this drawing the artist seems unusually interested in the anatomical details of the human body, and especially in the shading that models the flexed leg muscles. The Christ is similar to the seated figure in the preceding drawing; below, there is a lightly sketched male profile conceived along the same lines as other male portraits in the Vallardi Collection and the Boymans Museum. The graphic qualities of this drawing reappear on the other side of the sheet, which has a sketch of *Male Nudes, a Saint, and a Reclining Woman* [Plate 38]. It is interesting to note that in both these studies there is a recurrent combination of light strokes, indicating the faces, and heavier ones, forming the bodies.

The *Male Nudes and a Saint* [Plate 39] in the Berlin Museum, perhaps executed immediately before the studies for the *Legend*, is one of Pisanello's most representative works; the very

129 - STUDY OF HOOPOES - *Louvre* - Paris

130 - STUDY OF A DOG'S HEAD - *Louvre* - PARIS

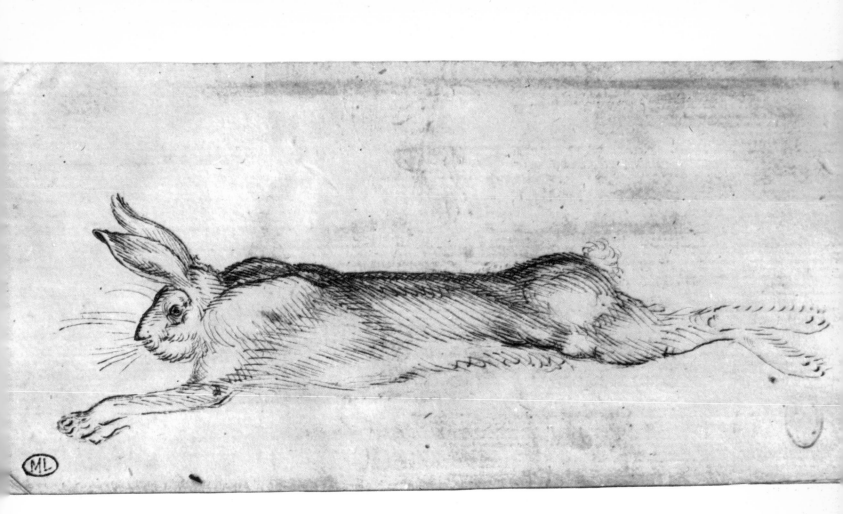

131 - STUDY OF A HARE - *Louvre* - Paris

132 - STUDY OF A RABBIT - *Louvre* - Paris

studied drawing is rendered even more precise by the almost invisible pen strokes on the parchment. And while the outlines of the nude on the left sometimes appear broken and imprecise even in the general elegance of the figure, and the subtle, unreal strokes that create the saint do not avoid a certain conventionality in his pose, stylization reaches its peak in the central nude. This is not only because the line is so fine and polished that it almost becomes imperceptible shading, but also because the form is determined by one line which flows continuously around the extravagantly supple body.

The classically inspired studies of this period must be compared with the probably earlier *Study of a Dancing Figure* [Plate 41] in the Ashmolean, Oxford, and a *Study from the Antique* [Plate 40] in the Ambrosiana, both derived from sarcophagi.[102] Pisanello employs an unusually compact form, probably dictated by his sculptured model, in the dancing figure with a tambourine; this is lightened by the scarf which swirls around the naked body and emphasizes its movement and rhythm. The grace expressed in this drawing is not surpassed by the artist's most delicate creations; the highly aesthetic and at the same time melancholy tilt of the head foreshadows the most mature phase of Pisanello's classicism. This is already anticipated in the Ambrosiana *Study from the Antique*, more in the absolute self-surrender of the painfully twisted figure than in the perfect rhythm pervading the other, more relaxed reclining woman.

In these drawings Pisanello, though considerably helped by Classical models, shows his mastery of all the graphic refinements necessary for outlining compositions and depicting movement, but most of all, for revealing even the slightest inner impulse. The line becomes finer and the strokes so imperceptible that they melt once more into gentle shading. These Classical experiments have considerable significance and importance when dealing with an artist like Pisanello, who is usually bracketed in the fixed category of International Gothic. They show how the artist adopted not only Late Gothic style, but also, and not by chance, another art very different in its formal structures. However, their greatest interest resides not so much in this juxtaposition, since Classical allusions were fashionable in the fifteenth century, as in the particular consequences it had for Pisanello. These consequences do not show simply in the material derivation of themes and elements from Classical sources, or in the three-dimensional plasticity so well suited to the requirements of a Renaissance man dedicated to the search for a more " concrete " means of expression. For Pisanello, Classical inspiration was only a fortunate opportunity of distilling the purest, inmost meaning of Classical art, of assimilating its most spiritual, and therefore most essential, concrete aspects, insofar as they could be recreated from first principles without the aid of outside elements.

In fact, through this new projection, almost a reliving, of Classicism, many of the movement's key elements received new life in Pisanello's Gothic world, where he succeeded in combining both currents and creating the unique poetic effects in which Gothic naturalistic feeling is intermingled with mysterious Classical strains. It was a daring blend, but once realized, more valid precisely because it was difficult to effect harmoniously. In fact, if we had to consider Pisanello's Classical studies solely as diligent, talented imitation (one might say, starting from the outside), we should find they had been of precious little use to him.

Among the many works inspired by antique art, *Emperor's Head* [Plate 42] is interesting for its line, which is realized in one continuous sweep in the lower part of the drawing, with a straightforward sharpness unusual for Pisanello. However, his characteristic touch reappears in the mass of the beard and in the hair softly surrounding the ear as if superimposed, while the lines of the face define the figure suddenly and spontaneously. The composition could be connected to the period of the medals, but the drawing must be placed in the preceding years because of its emphatic linearism and the lack of any hint of modeling.

The fine *Study of a Winged Bull* [Plate 43] can be set at the time of the Roman frescoes; it may have been a preliminary sketch for a Saint Luke. The figure of the reclining animal is apparently floating on air, as it was presumably destined for a vaulted ceiling. It is seen in foreshortening, resting its forefeet on an open book; the wing is suggested by a single line that follows the flow of air, while the minute dryness of the actual drawing transforms the subject and removes all feeling of naturalistic matter, so that it assumes its inevitable role of a symbol. This work is very different from the later *Study of a Reclining Bull* [Plate 44]. The subject is perhaps a wounded animal, as could be concluded from the painful tension that suffuses the whole body, from the incisive anatomical relief of the head, but most of all from the flaccidly slumped belly and the spasmodic stretching of the humped rear, rendered shapeless with pain. Here we have a clear example of Pisanello's ability to portray an emotion beyond the scope of literal naturalistic representation, this time using an animal as a point of departure. The figuration is all the more vivid because of the two-dimensional drawing, emphasized by the shading which fuses all planes into a single mass.

We can compare with this the *Study of a Horse* [Plate 45], seen in foreshortening, as if it were on a sloping plane. The minute broken strokes seem placed precipitously; shadow falls tenderly on the elongated hind legs, and, while the transition at the neck is rather forced, the tail spreads out in a long wavy band.

To this series of deformed creatures, seized at moments when outside forces strike them and change their normal state, we must add the *Study of a Wounded Lizard* [Plate 86], which conveys

133 - MEDAL OF SIGISMONDO PANDOLFO MALATESTA (reverse with standing warrior)
Museo Nazionale del Bargello - FLORENCE;
MEDAL OF SIGISMONDO PANDOLFO MALATESTA (reverse with warrior on horseback)
Bibliothèque Nationale - PARIS

134 - MEDAL
OF NOVELLO MALATESTA
Museo Nazionale del Bargello - FLORENCE

perfectly the animal's spasmodic contortions, once more through the contrasts created by shading.

The studies that we have just examined, with their rapid successions of strokes and lines, anticipate a new phase for Pisanello; we are on the threshold of his fully developed style, the poetic zenith, and already there are hints of the atmosphere of *The Legend of Saint George*. Atmosphere is changing, and with it form, rather than technical means, while there is a sort of severity in the air that promises drama to come.

A *Study of a Man's Head* [Plate 46, left], resembling Dante in the sharp, incisive lines of the profile, attracts one by the engrossed severity of its gaze, which is offset by the realistic lumps of the jaw; at the same time a motif of decorative elegance appears in the simple head-dress, and continues in the sinuous lines of the drapery. The pen strokes are thick and firm, as in other graphically analogous drawings, which must nevertheless be assigned to different periods. As we pointed out at the beginning of this chapter, it is not enough to rely on appearance as a guide to classification; one has also to refer to the various stages of the artist's spiritual development. In some cases knowledge of these stages allows us to extract more useful information from sifting technical data.

An original *Study of Male Profiles* [Plate 46, right] is stylistically akin to the last drawing, though the right-hand profile differs from it in its more pathetic expression and in the introversion which sharpens the strokes and seems to contract the face. The half-open lips, dilated like the nostrils, the wrinkled forehead, and the motionless eye are signs of a shaken state of mind. On the other hand, the lower profile is less interesting and belongs to the gallery of human types of which there is another example, not particularly typical of Pisanello, in the Boymans Museum [Fig. 38]. From a comparison with these we might also attribute the Capitoline Gallery portrait [Fig. 39] to Pisanello, uniquely on the grounds of facial resemblances.

A drawing of a *Warrior* [Plate 48] comes very close to the melancholy atmosphere of the *Legend*; it is sketched with heavy strokes clustered together in somber zones, and the facial expression shows dismay and sudden impotence, resignation to fate. All through this work the strong, dry, violent pen strokes bite into the paper.

Similar poetic results are achieved in the *Study of a Young Man Taking Off His Doublet* [Plate 47], which must be numbered among Pisanello's happiest inspirations because of the fantastic arrangement of the various parts of the composition, spread out rhythmically to form a broad circular frame around the thoughtful face.

A *Study of a Man's Head* [Plate 58] is directly related to the *Legend*, for it closely resembles the figure, presumably of a king, in the Sant'Anastasia fresco. The pen strokes, though still heavy and close, are here organized to give greater clarity of form. The few lines that barely suggest the coat on the man's back contrast with the careful, minutely detailed execution of the head, where the zones of light and shadow, extending into the sculptural hair to define an exact expressive form, indicate a more detached state of mind. In this the drawing differs from the painted figure, which can hardly avoid being caught up in the immediacy of the particular moment. An examination of the study reveals other striking characteristics: the development of the drawing as a work of art in its own right, with its own aims; and the elevated state following catharsis that pervades all these figures, though without loss of their naturalistic attributes. For further proof it is enough to look at the magnificent *Study of a Man in a Turban* [Plate 87], which belongs stylistically to the group of drawings just examined; its graphic procedures, however, are far more accomplished, reflecting a far more poetic purity in the dreaming face. The features are built up with tiny strokes, which themselves create the ascetic tension of the profile; the eye, its gaze fixed infinitely high, beyond all tensions and contretemps, shows that a transcendental experience has been undergone. This drawing, with its high poetic quality, combines several characteristics of Pisanello's graphic art: a wavy, free linearism, a strong, incisive sketching, and a dust-fine hatching.

The stylistic perfection, the artist's full participation in the poetic dream-play, can be well understood if this and similar drawings are considered in the period of their execution, that is, at the time of *The Legend of Saint George*.

Many studies can be related to the great fresco in Verona, either for stylistic reasons or because of figurative analogies. Two *Studies of Dogs* [Plate 72] have a corresponding figure in the fresco, standing at Saint George's right [Plate 52]. However, there are still important differences between the fresco detail and the drawings themselves. In the painting, or what little can still be seen of it, the figure is more static, as if paralyzed by the all-pervading tension; it is in a sense squared up by a sort of petrifying archaism, while in the drawing the conception does not settle on any particular note, so that the pen is free to transform the figures not just into models of animals but also into paragons of elegance. There are, however, stylistic differences even between the two sketches: in the dog with the muzzle and collar, the forms are stiff and cold, more naturalistic, while in the other, even in the faulty outlines of the two thighs, the chiseling is finer and culminates in a subtle elongation of lines and shading. Thus, here it appears clear that many naturalistic traits of Pisanello's art are resolved in as many formal symbols. While he expresses the most absolute respect for creatures of nature, he simultaneously exalts forms with a delicate transfiguration of style.

135 - STUDY OF A HORSE - *Louvre* - PARIS

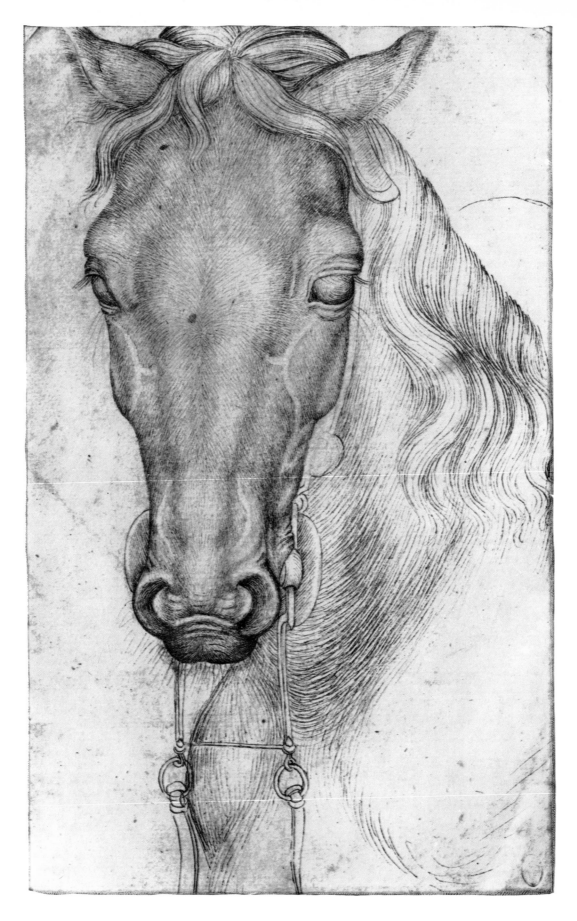

136 - STUDY OF A HORSE'S HEAD - *Louvre* - Paris

137 - PORTRAIT OF A LADY - *National Gallery of Art* - WASHINGTON, D. C.

Much closer to the *Legend* than the two drawings of dogs, the *Study of a Horse* [Plate 63] is vigorously drawn, and its mass is continued in foreshortening beyond the high undulating wall formed by the nearer part of the animal. This is one of Pisanello's most important drawings. The nearly symmetrical structure with the marked white spaces and rhomboidal bulges is composed almost entirely of separate parts linked together so as to produce a singularly new effect. The result is an astonishing shape, while the artist's naturalistic exaltation of his subject finds a corrective, even an advantage, in the graphic and compositional perfection of the work. The drawing can be considered a possible preparatory study for the large horse seen from the rear in the *Legend*. But in Sant'Anastasia the mass is less abstract, lighter, and more alive. The animal is standing still, yet at the same time it is warm and ready to spring into action; it, too, shares in the general waiting. Its rear hoofs, placed one behind the other, are ready to move, and the ovoidal arc above is split, whereas in the drawing these parts remain perfectly symmetrical. Finally, in the drawing, which is a piece of pure research, everything is governed by the need to transpose the subject into as unrealistic a key as possible.

Pisanello executed some studies for the hanged men in the *Legend*, who fulfill the important function of giving the scene a background of incumbent metaphysical atmosphere by linking the occult immediacy of the existential act with its most secret origins. Of these drawings, the *Study of Hanged Men, a Lady, and a Boy* [Plate 55], is a bold combination of expressionist strength and bitter, macabre irony. One is struck by the dryness of the medium, the absolute lack of shading, the absence of any sympathy for the real meaning of the subject, and, once more, the interest in the human figure as a pure representational fact, almost as a stage property. The general effect, though filled with the repugnance inspired by the subject, has something tragicomic, which, however, does nothing to eliminate the strong realism employed in drawing the fleshless skull of the hanged man on the left in the center row. The little boy below has a lively face worthy of Bronzino's finest works, while the subtly sketched lady with her stately elegance recalls certain feminine figures from contemporary French and Lombard art. It would therefore be easy to draw parallels between this figure and the *Lady* in the National Gallery, Washington, for the latter is stylistically attributed to Pisanello precisely because of the highly personal synthesis of French and Lombard traits.

Some motifs from this drawing appear in another *Study of Hanged Men* [Plate 56]; even closer to the figures in the fresco, the work is rich in dashing, elegant lines. Pisanello's acute penetration of the varied types and characters that passed before him is shown again in the *Study of Heads and an Archer* [Plate 57]. The faces, some of which are scarcely visible on the sheet under the light touch of the silverpoint, are grasped with profound realism in their highly charged strokes. They may be fanciful portraits of uncommon types, probably Oriental, over which the artist lingered, fascinated by their strange facial features and picturesque costumes. The sketch of the figure with the bow and arrow, a preparation for the Kalmuck in the *Legend*, is overpoweringly realistic, and all the more valid because of its incisive precision and the contrasts of tiny strokes which intensify the bony hardness of the face. The figure that stands behind the Kalmuck in the *Legend* is derived from the *Study of a Head* [Plate 61], which has not unreasonably been accounted for by Classical influence; indeed, it bears the marks of late Hellenistic art.

We have no drawings related to the figure of Saint George, but three *Studies of Women's Heads* [Plates 64, 67, and 68], which can be referred to the princess in the fresco, have come down to us. While they are similar in general composition and facial features, there are considerable differences of style between them. The head facing the right [Plate 64], with the large corded turban, is the most finished of the three; graphically impeccable, and the most elaborate, it is closest to the fresco in its icy structures of perfect lines, and it is also more painterly than the other two. Of these others, the girl facing left [Plate 67] is drawn with a particular elegance, which stems from the transparency of the few faint strokes that suggest the turban, the incisive and heavier roughness of the profile, and the assonances of lines running down from the short strokes on the forehead, cheeks, and jaws to set the expression in a frown of sad perplexity inside the brutal, thick outline of the face. This is the richest of the three in content, the most problematic, and the one most like a true sketch with its many potential solutions and its manifest freedom of execution in the quivering, frothy matter. The third study [Plate 68] contains a more perfect form, delicate and at the same time solemn. The diagonally placed turban dominates the figure, which seems crowned by waves turning round a vortex, while the pen strokes of the face seem on the point of being washed away. The profile and the shape of the figure stand out clear and pure, and the matter tends to disappear, leaving only the fantastic image.

A few watercolor drawings of costumed figures present some similarities to the princess in the *Legend*. However, it is probable that, instead of being executed at the same time as the fresco, they were done at other moments, perhaps before; even then it is more likely that these studies served just as guides for posing the princess, whose only graphic antecedents—and partial at that—are to be found in the three drawings of female heads just described. In the *Costume Study* [Plate 69] in the Musée Bonnat, Bayonne, the acute observation of courtly pomp reappears: the same richness of the garments, the same detailed descriptiveness show here as an abnormal structuring of elements. The decorative factor predominates in every figure, but always within the context of the artist's own amusement; he clothes the dummies (in fact, the human faces are barely traced) and creates a beautiful, tense, graphic and pictorial choreography. The head of the woman in the turban bears some resemblance to the princess, but the mantle forms an immense wing, its outline emphasized by superimposed and rather superfluous-looking, equally spaced bars of color over broad pen strokes that recall the manner of Stefano.

The other *Costume Study* [Plate 70] in the Musée Condé, Chantilly, is more stylized; the elongated lines are more vertical, and the decoration, especially in the figure on the left, more necessary to the drawing, and less pure decoration. The very continuity of line expresses the need to map out the mass more firmly, more abstractly, paying less attention to details. This same characteristic reappears in the male costume, in which decoration is limited to a part of the back, while the rest is brought to life by a few sudden splashes of watercolor. On the other hand, the faces in this sketch are drawn with greater care: the man's face has an expressivity of its own, while the woman's has linear qualities that recall Pollaiuolo. The characteristics observed in these two drawings are blended in another *Costume Study* [Plate 71], also heightened with watercolor, in the Ashmolean, Oxford. The extravagant decoration of the opulent clothes is more profuse than in the Bayonne drawing, yet in relation to the wearers it is not absolutely dominant. The two men, one on either side of the drawing, are no longer simply dummies, barely roughed-in figures, but are preliminary drawings for real portraits. The face of the right-hand man shows some similarity to the young man in the *Legend*, though this figure is probably closer to the *Study of a Young Man's Head* [Plate 62] in the Este Gallery, Modena. In this drawing there is a re-emergence of the strong, thick strokes that cannot, however, be placed in the *Legend* period, while the expressiveness of the face is accentuated by graphic contrasts and the emphatic relief of some features. Finally, in the center of the Oxford study there is the head of a woman with abundant hair elaborately dressed; she must be grouped in the typological series leading up to the Sant'Anastasia princess. The execution is delicate, covered with a network of imperceptible strokes; the hair is without heaviness, though composed of an infinity of tiny lines, while the face is perfectly portrayed with a few strokes. It is now very clear that Pisanello's technique is not enough in itself to date his drawings. Light sketching, short, dense strokes, slender lines or heavy strokes alternate even in the various studies which, for stylistic reasons, must be referred to a single creative moment. It follows from this, as we have said, that especially in the case of this artist, highly complex poetic considerations, and not the

71

simpler, more immediate observation of material technical structure, must dominate in establishing guiding criteria, if we are to arrive at discerning judgments.

Based on the pre-eminence of morphological or other immediately visible data, the method of material examination, which implies the attentive observing of external, and therefore superficial aspects of a work of art to give a skin-deep, "external vision," has indeed its own value and uses. However, on its own it can never be the determining factor of an effective critical judgment. To arrive at a more concrete understanding of a masterpiece as a cultural value of a period and an individual poetic achievement, one must not content oneself with studying the work's constructional syntax, establishing its relationships with other works, and disentangling the network of influences and technical experiments that went into its making; one must also look beyond the mere appearance of the expressive means—which may in themselves provide a fruitful field of investigation—toward an "internal vision" of the work, so as to grasp its true nature through the more direct language of its concrete form. Another typical example of the change in Pisanello's graphic style is the *Study of Cranes* [Plate 73], which recalls the analogous, half-hidden figures in the Sant'Anastasia fresco. It is a simple sketch formed with agitated, careless strokes, which contrast with the calmer observation of detail in other of Pisanello's works; here the strokes dash heedlessly over the individual parts and trace only their principal outlines with impressionistic speed.

Two *Studies of Young Men's Heads* [Plate 88] adhere to the theme of expressionist abandon which is abundantly represented in Pisanello's drawings. The deformation of the head on the left, emphasized by the rapid, agitated strokes, still records the subject's personality and his obvious state of enthrallment, from which the artist is trying to detach him by force. On the other hand, the pen strokes solidify on the petrified mask in the other study, and the face becomes inanimate, depersonalized, possessed by absolute surrender.

The *Study of a Young Man's Head* [Plate 89], whose backward-tilted profile is traced in black pencil with light shading, is one of the finest drawings in the Vallardi Collection. The tragic expression transcends the chance causes that determine it and is projected into a new dimension, while the artistic act perfectly underlines the two existential situations in force at the moment of catharsis. The forms are shown under extreme tension, from the band that clings to the head, the ear and the tuft of hair which seems almost unnecessary, sketched in like so much still life and then forgotten, to the half-open mouth, graven in black on the almost shapeless face, and the glazed eyes, expressively blinded by strong emotions and radiating anguish. The pencil strokes are soft and have lost their dry Gothic linearity; frothy, timid, breathless, they barely touch the feverishly alive subject.

138 - MEDAL OF LUDOVICO GONZAGA
Museo Civico - Brescia

139 - MEDAL OF CECILIA GONZAGA (obverse) - *Castello Sforzesco* - MILAN

140 - MEDAL OF CECILIA GONZAGA (reverse) - *Castello Sforzesco* - Milan

From the period of the Emperor John Palaeologus's visit to Italy we have the *Study for the Medal of John Palaeologus* [Plate 94]. Though the face sketched in charcoal hardly shows on the paper, its profile stands out, marked, not by dry, precise strokes, but by vaguely implied motifs, shaded as if through a veil of mist in a delicate contrast of lights and shadows. The angularity of the four Gothic points that surround the face, suggesting the two transversal axes, is offset by the serene vitality of the eye, set in the lean, haggard profile, thus remaining faithful to the intended transfiguring vision of the subject.

There is particular refinement in the fertile drawing *Study of Figures* [Plate 95], which portrays three characters, probably members of the emperor's entourage, to judge from the Eastern style of their costumes. These sketches are interesting for the way they show the development of a technique that becomes more familiar in what we might call Pisanello's last drawings. This technique depends principally on small, comma-like strokes which largely replace the habitual longer lines, and infuse the subjects with greater vitality. Moreover, naturalistic precision is virtually discarded, while the drawing takes on the character of a rough sketch.

At the lower right of the drawing there is the outline of Palaeologus on horseback, as he appears on the reverse of the corresponding medal. The same figure reappears in a contemporary *Study of Figures with a Cufic Inscription* [Plate 96], which is, however, graphically less satisfying than the preceding drawing because of the insufficient, weak penwork and the summary outlining of the figures.

A *Study of a Man in a Turban* [Plate 97] was probably inspired by the Oriental types Pisanello met at this time. This epically imposing drawing is remarkable for its graphic accuracy, its very refined style, and also for the facial expression, which is seen as if through an imaginary veil, projected into an aristocratically distant sphere.

Two *Studies for the Medal of Filippo Maria Visconti* [Plate 98], which correspond to the medal of the Duke of Milan, are facially similar but stylistically very different. In the ink drawing Pisanello's typical pen strokes show a lively freedom of expression and an insistence on minute details: the line thickens where wrinkles darken the face, and the shaven hair is indicated by tiny dots. The expression, rendered even more penetrating by the shadows, lays bare the inner sadness of the lord of Milan. But it is precisely this combination of naturalistic and individualizing emphasis that places the subject within its just limits, so that the ostentatious plasticity and the monumentality of the composition cannot outweigh the personal characteristics. An entirely different artistic conception is displayed in the parallel pencil drawing, whose lightness of touch makes it one of Pisanello's finest works. In it the pale, stony face is cast into the expressive heaviness, obtuse and cruel, of which the sitter becomes the archetype; light *sfumato* shadows depict the profile of this solid mass, but there is no lingering over details. There remain only a few elements which are fused into a sculptural block, and a moral tendency toward formlessness.

The *Study of a Procession and a Landscape* [Plate 105] may be placed at the beginning of Pisanello's most intense activity in the courts of northern Italy, that is, between 1425 and 1430. It was probably executed for the court of Mantua, either as a sketch from life or as a project for a fresco. The style is complicated, with noteworthy effects of synthesis. Much of the graphic work exploits the fruits of various experiments—solid, concise structures, extended contours thickly and darkly outlined as if in homage to Stefano—yet the trees on the left, freely sketched in with a few swirling strokes, give proof of a more mature graphic style, while the landscape which extends undulatingly, without perspective, represents a compromise between illusory perspective and the flat backcloth. On the right, beneath the curling strokes that form plants and helmet plumes, he outlines the massive rump of a horse, prefiguring the expansive manner of Leonardo and the early Baroque. This mixture of heterogeneous techniques produces a sense of impetuous, whirling movement, in which the plumed and armored figures, weighed down with their ornate trappings, find it hard to keep their dignity. The development of Pisanello's activity as a medalist is reflected in his drawings by the acquisition of a heightened plastic sense and a more calculated, refined pictorialism. Furthermore, his extensive Classical experience enabled the artist to continue perfecting his work in an endless pursuit of forms, at once more severe, more free, and more objective. The figures tend to be portrayed in terms of one particular "inner reality," one particular point in their spiritual life, and are thus conceived less naturalistically and, in a sense, more abstractly: more abstractly because of the immediate, though more complex, reaction they arouse. The pathos Pisanello had injected into some of the melancholy works dating from the fertile period of the *Legend* here gives way to a different, though equally elevated manifestation of his aesthetic sense. To trace this development is to relive a moment unique in Pisanello's artistic career, a moment that cannot be understood without relating certain of his works to a radical rethinking of his Classical experience. The aesthetically oriented plasticity of certain medals adapts itself well to some graphic works of a new tone, whose clearly outlined appearances seem suddenly enchanted, enveloped in a dazzling light that transforms them, freezing them into individual figurative blocks that have no further relation to time. The individual content (while not eliminated) is thus amalgamated into a mainly aesthetic vision of form which, here more than elsewhere, prevails over naturalistic interest.

A *Study of a Man's Head* [Plate 101] from the Vallardi Collection outlines the sitter with a few light, flowing strokes, wrapping him in a delicate, transparent light. The composition is similar to that of many fifteenth-century portraits, in particular to Pisanello's own of Lionello d'Este. The almost imperceptible consistency of the matter in this drawing gives the sitter a more exalted nature, without, however, sacrificing his individual personality. The profile has all the vivacity of a Gothic-Renaissance portrait, but at the same time, from the spare severity of its lines, one would say it was inspired by an archaic sculpture.

Another *Study of a Male Figure* [Plate 108], probably representing Niccolò Piccinino, is particularly interesting. The graphic result is much the same as that of the drawing, just described, but this work is covered by a veil of chiaroscuro which accentuates the drawing's pictorial qualities and lends the figure greater human warmth, while Pisanello's typical turn of the lips gives the face a mysterious and at the same time ironic expression. The influence of the Renaissance portrait technique pioneered by the Florentines has been traced in this drawing;[103] the mass is solid and dominates the surrounding space. While it is true that the placing of the profile confers a certain absent quality on the figure, it does not cut it off or exclude it from participation in the world of reality; on the contrary, the image seems connected to the more concrete, less idealized portrait manner that was current in northern Italian art and was to find one of its most significant exponents in Gentile Bellini. It is possible that this drawing should be considered a preliminary study for the effigy on the medal, but this is by no means certain in view of the difference that exists between the two works. The compositional softness of the drawing disappears in the medal, where the figure is portrayed in a more plastic manner, but with greater rigidity and expressive haughtiness.

Alongside the portraits produced in this fertile period, during which naturalistic inquiry is mingled with more rigorous organization of form, we can place a fantastic *Study of a Horse's Head* [Plate 99], probably prepared for the Francesco Sforza medal. The technique presents no great innovation, apart from a more pronounced contrast between the solidly shaded parts and the passages of rapid pen strokes; the extraordinary thing about the drawing is the sensation aroused by the dissolution expressed in this phantom, as majestic and demoniacal as his brother on the medal. One might be following an arduous, progressively more penetrating inquiry by Pisanello into the deeper reality that lies beneath appearances; here more than ever before, he seems to have settled for the barest form possible, where much of the mass is dissolved and only the essential outlines are retained, while the remaining, more solid parts wait to be eaten away in their turn.

And Pisanello digs still more deeply into matter, reducing it to its most concise extremes, in another *Study of a Horse's Head* [Plate 100] with the impressive, ghostly naturalism of the mummified, bony surfaces. The lively, erect ears, a pulsating naturalistic element, contrast with the nostrils, deformed by a stylizing line that deepens the cavities and lays them bare on the surface, while a secondary current erodes and impoverishes the material, reducing the whole to a surrealist whim.

This particular creative moment may also have produced "*Luxury*" [Plate 106], an allegorical vision in which the artist, though using penwork that still recalls Stefano, composes his drawing on very lively lines. The skeletal, naked figure, tautly expressed by strokes that replace the softness of flesh with dryness, stretches her angular, phallic, mannish form lasciviously. Her hair ends in a halo of flowers above the face, which shows only pleasure-loving apprehension as she wriggles her body on the caressing waves of her tresses. The tension of the body is magnificently well conveyed without stiffness so that it seems almost peacefully contorted in its provocative bareness. An analogous figure from the point of view of composition—which might point to a single antique source—appears on the Lionello d'Este medal whose reverse bears the reclining nude and vase [Plate 113].

This same period, when Classical forms appear, suffused with delicate expressionism, must include the vibrant *Study of Male Nudes* [Plate 107] in the Boymans Museum.[104] Graphically it is very similar to the preceding drawing; however, here the pen strokes, instead of flowing in a circular movement to stress the point of concentration of the subject, are arranged in transversal lines. These lines, like rain driven by wind, accentuate the tension of bodies held in an agonizing spasm. The face of the lifted figure is painfully prepared for surrender and his neck swells, certainly not through any formal defect, while his hands are placed without violence on the other's nape. The other figure stands solidly on the ground, his legs apart, perfectly balanced. He is no stronger than his opponent; if anything he is slimmer and more lightly built, and his muscles, shaded with tiny strokes, barely show. It is interesting to note how the physical assurance of this figure is proclaimed by the sober accentuation of the forms and the extreme tension generated through the entire pyramidal mass.

Pisanello's Classical experience shows even more clearly in the magnificent *Study of a Young Man's Head* [Plate 118], chastely outlined with its few bare forms faultlessly lit. The line is drowned in a generous application of "pointillist" strokes, creating shadows of varying intensity and a pictorial mellowness that is assimilated even where the line is dim or non-existent. The calmness of the figure contributes to the solidity of the pose, which is lightened by the easy way the figure fits into the surrounding space. The outline of the head is flawless, the facial profile agreeably gentle, with shadows indicating the details and giving the sustained expressivity that puts the young man's beauty beyond definition.

141 - STUDY OF A WOMAN'S HEAD - *Louvre* - Paris

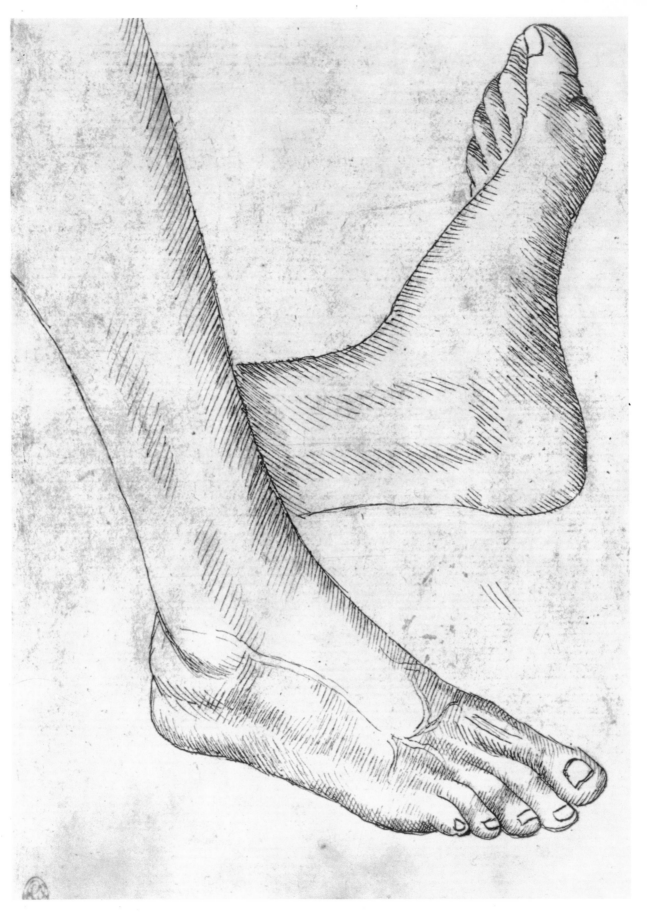

143 - STUDY OF A PEEWIT - *Louvre* - PARIS

This search for gestures, within the limits of controlled expressiveness, continues in the *Study of a Boy Reading* [Plate 119], in which the pen strokes, though hair-fine, are not quite pulverized. They are still continuous and form a graphic sequence resolved in spiral movements which, broad and generous at first in the hunched body, then faster and faster on the tilted face,[105] recompose themselves in the dome of thick hair. The concentration of the figure in the instant of transformation is well shown by the cramped fingers of one hand and the position of the right shoulder, which is raised and pulled forward.

Many drawings, especially of animals, can be related to the *Vision of Saint Eustace* [Plate 120] more because of their style, full of ardent naturalism, than because of their precise figurative dependency. These studies, which belong to the particular creative moment that fell in the most advanced and fertile period of Pisanello's courtly career, are visibly separate from the earlier naturalistic court drawings, and show a preference for finer definition of subjects through stylistic means that are at once more synthetic and more complete.

A colored *Study of a Stag* [Plate 125] was probably executed in preparation for a similar figure, barely visible in the painting and framed by the pointed summit of the second mountain from the left. Pisanello's technique here has none of the absolute stylized linearism, but rather a pictorial softness composed of warm tones in shaded gradations of colors without absolute contrasts. The lines of the drawing show through the most solid layers of color and, with their agile rhythms, help to give sinewy animation to the subject, which is defined in space by controlled dynamics harmoniously concluded by the little strokes clustered together in the tail and on the antlers which tower up from the animal's head in a tormented cadenza of discord. The *Study of a Duck* [Plate 126], also colored, may well be another preparatory study for the numerous and varied fauna that Pisanello used to populate the dark background of the *Vision* with lively shapes. The figure is swimming, but rendered motionless by the smooth, polished surface of the color, in accordance with Pisanello's recurrent intuition that fills even animals with anguish.

The colored figure in the *Study of Hoopoes* [Plate 129] recalls more directly the animal life in the *Vision*; in fact, it recalls precisely the hoopoe to the lower right in the painting, which is perched in the dark depths of a thicket depicted in the manner of the bush in Paolo Uccello's *Night Hunt*. The bird in color is alert and impatient, with elegantly slim, elongated lines, while the one in the background of the drawing is sketched in with few strokes, but by a rapid and gifted hand. The hare fleeing from the hound in the extreme lower right-hand corner of the painting is almost identical with one in the *Study of a Hare* [Plate 124] in the Vallardi Collection, and has been traced, because of its position, to a drawing by Giovannino de' Grassi [Fig. 11]. However, the stiff composition of the de' Grassi drawing sets it well apart from the Pisanello work, in which the subject's intense vitality is perfectly conveyed by the dynamic tension of the figure. This particular aspect, the irresistible impetus of the forms, establishes a connection between this drawing and another *Study of a Hare* [Plate 131] which, though figuratively different, is pervaded by the same enormous energy. Stylization is pushed to its utmost limits in the second work; the figure, scored with rapid strokes, is stretched out absolutely horizontally in midair, with all its energy massed in the bulging shoulder muscles.

An originally composed *Study of a Cockerel* [Plate 148, left] is also to be referred to this part of Pisanello's career. Only the head is naturalistically drawn, with a large crest and long wattles that are entwined around the throat like a knotted scarf; for the rest, Pisanello's naturalism, by which the forms of every individual part of a figure are usually stated, is here unleashed in a whirlwind of feathers that surround the imaginary bulk of the body, creating a sort of turbulence with a great void in the center.

In the fine *Study of a Rabbit* [Plate 132], our artist's hand is betrayed by the restlessness spread through the body by the clever arrangement of lines. The eye, brilliantly rendered with sharp contrasts between the light and dark parts, shines out hypnotically, while the rear mass of the body, graphically analogous to that in the drawing of the cockerel, is crystallized in the perfect oval traced in the mass of the haunches: a touch of stylization which demonstrates the real condition of a being by slightly deforming it. In fact, and examples are rare, Pisanello hardly ever conceived stylization of natural content as an end in itself; in other words, he did not stylize the natural form merely to increase its elegance by heightening his pictorial language, but depicted the object wholly or partially in a subtly idealized form in order to create new concrete motifs, facilitating a deeper understanding of its innermost nature. Harmonious structure is evident in a colored *Study of a Peewit* [Plate 143], in which the obvious naturalism of the most prominent parts is not divorced from the formal need to present the figure in a broad, firm composition.

Another drawing from the Vallardi Collection is the *Study of a Dog* [Plate 127], which is similar to the elegant animal preceding the Saint in the *Vision*; details are barely suggested and the whole, defined only by zones of delicate shading, is soaked in a particularly refined pictorialism. Another rare and precious example of this is to be found in the *Study of the Madonna Suckling the Child* that will be examined later. A watercolor drawing of a *Dog's Head* [Plate 130] must belong to the same period; again barely sketched, it illustrates the artist's excellence in breathing life into a stylistically perfect image.

A sheet of *Assorted Studies* [Plate 128] contains preparatory figures of a Crucifixion, presumably intended for the *Vision*. To the upper left there is a complete sketch of Christ on the Cross as He appears in the London painting, while below, a few strokes outline human bodies. In these figures the calligraphy is unusual, and the general figuration, far removed from fifteenth-century naturalism, could be compared to the expressionism of a Goya or a Daumier. Two arms, still inspired by the Crucifixion, rise in the center of the drawing; here we find one of Pisanello's traditional manners again, with its deliberate strokes and more intense pictorial contrasts.

The *Study of a Horse and Rider* [Plate 123], similar to the central group in the *Vision*, marks the boundary between the precise, careful manner and a more dashing style calculated mainly to express the subject's vitality. In this drawing, whose style might be said to be avant-garde for its new conception of graphic layout, the penwork, as in the preceding drawing, is not characterized by the usual long wavy lines and short bunched strokes, but moves freely in a new certainty of form which takes concrete shape in the generous space between the thinly scattered lines.

A combination of minutely detailed, naturalistic research and solidly plastic posing is realized in the *Study of a Horse* [Plate 135], perhaps a preparatory sketch for the reverse of the Novello Malatesta medal [Plate 134, bottom]. The actual drawing is particularly studied in the smooth connection of the various parts, which is managed by shading, almost pulverizing, the smallest possible strokes, and by crystallizing some forms into firmer blocks by the clear, white light. Through all this the dynamic potential of the figure is always openly stated, whether in the restless expression of the head or the twitching movements of the tail.

Pisanello's technical resources are exhibited in a finely graded scale in the *Study of a Horse's Head* [Plate 136], but he does not lose sight of the artistic aim in sheer enjoyment of the execution. An object seeming to derive from a very distant source inspired the realistically sculptured mass that stands out in the middle of this complex, elaborate interplay of graphic devices. The strokes radiate out in a fine network from the brow, forming oases of light, occasionally interrupted by clear rivulets, indicators rather than naturalistic details; the strokes turn into modeling at the extremities, even more in the livid ridges round the eyes than in the baroque elements of the lower parts. Accurately divided locks of the mane fall like ribbons on the forehead; the mane reaches down the neck, harmoniously cradled in the wavy movement of the lines. The animal's mask is greatly magnified and pushed forward to the nearest foreground; it springs out of a space whose depth is indicated by the receding neck but still left more or less undefined by the sudden accentuation of the foreground, so that the ghostly apparition appears all the more striking.

A *Study of a Woman's Head* [Plate 141], which may have been executed about the time of the Cecilia Gonzaga medal, shows Pisanello achieving a compassion reminiscent of Praxiteles.[106] Almost unbroken, continuous lines here make a fresh appearance, running in transparent skeins around the head, neck, and face, in a graphic fabric that gives body to the figure. The figure is slightly inclined in accordance with a compositional model that can be traced through the more rigid versions of Gentile and the Sienese and Byzantine schools, right back to Grecian statuary. However, the connection between Pisanello and his sculptural model is shown more directly by the almost imperceptible pathos that clouds the serene expression of the face.

In a *Study of Two Bare Feet* [Plate 142], a typical example of drawing as an end in itself, Pisanello combines stylistic elegance with an essential linear sense and a happy compositional invention. Using very fine lines and the gentlest of hatching, the artist conveys the lightness of the two motifs in his drawing. One of the feet is standing weightlessly on the ground, and is lightened by the descending, rhythmically curved lines of the upper outside profile. The other, even more lightly placed, is in fact suspended in thin air. It is composed with a new sense of synthesis and though the tracing of the veins, which seems to assume a purely decorative role, might be adduced as an instance of Pisanello's ever-present naturalism, the drawing obeys exclusively formal demands in the rigid definition of the ankle and the graceful leg. Thus the synthetic qualities of the drawing correspond to a real aesthetic need and so, to the elegance of the feet, here shown in a graceful dance step.

Spacious sketching, with floating strokes that disregard detailed definition of the subject, is to be found in the *Study of Shod Feet* [Plate 151], whose motifs are repeated in the bands that wrap the feet of the figure of Saint George in the *Apparition*. However, very few drawings can be related to the *Apparition* and no reference to the painting can be more than approximate. The figure of the Virgin in the round medallion seems connected to a *Study of the Madonna and Child* [Plate 152, right], which is similar in conception to the group in the painting, but characterized by a heavy touch that Pisanello seldom used, and most frequently when he was still under the influence of the Veronese and Lombard schools of Late Gothic.

Further links with Pisanello's first period can still be seen in a *Study of Two Saints* [Plate 152, left]. The seated figure is constructed with a Stefano-inspired calligraphy, while the saint on the right, who as a figure resembles Saint George in the *Apparition*, is distinguished by less uniform, more lively drawing. For this reason style and composition cannot provide decisive grounds for referring this drawing to the painting with any certainty; apart from anything else, the figure of the old saint is completely different from his painted counterpart.

144 - MEDAL OF VITTORINO DA FELTRE - *Museo Nazionale del Bargello* - FLORENCE;
MEDAL OF PIER CANDIDO DECEMBRIO - *British Museum* - LONDON

145 - MEDAL OF BELLOTO CUMANO
Castello Sforzesco - Milan

While in the drawing he is composed of a Gothically sophisticated mass, broken by draperies, very similar to certain contemporary northern sculptures, in the painting he is at once more solid and more essential, a symbolic embodiment of age, beyond concern for his person. This monastic elimination of the details of a human figure is easily observed in the *Study of a Seated Monk* [Plate 148, right], in which the figure is seen from the back, its expansive habit reducing bodily outlines to the minimum, so that one forgets the individual figure, wrapped up and neutralized in the cloak which dominates everything with the weight of its symbolic meaning. The drawing that can most surely be referred to the *Apparition* is the superb *Study of Horses' Heads* [Plate 149], typologically similar to the drawings of horses already examined, but differing from them in the tension of the forms, which are forced into an impatient immobility. In this work Pisanello's drawing is affected by a more abstract tendency to deform his subjects, particularly manifest in the upper head. This is entirely constructed of individual elements whose forms are modeled as unique pieces with surrealist care, and united by the elongated curves of the extremities. Nature sneers out through her own forms, become by chance different from themselves or, rather, differently expressed. The vitality of these forms, however, is less ghostly than it might be: in analogous studies the forms are more filtered by the embalmed surfaces, and the pen strokes, more organized and gentle, follow a well-defined course to meet at the most suitable points, while their vibrancy remains almost imperceptible. Here, on the other hand, these pen strokes, though graphically similar, are more disturbed and emphasize the impressive vitality of the forms. Even the tufts of the mane, which in another drawing [cf. Plate 136] are spread out with sculpturally calm modeling, here are fused into a single provocatively coquettish lock, a motif that contrasts with the fearful mask and detracts from its effect.

Though the aesthetically oriented procedures of a sophisticated naturalism progressively infiltrate the cycle of drawings for medals, the *Study for a Portrait of Alfonso of Aragon* [Plate 156] must be placed in this period. It is perhaps the most accurate definition of personal characteristics in the entire corpus of preparatory drawings for the Aragonese monarch's medal. The almost unbroken flow of strokes that run down the head to form the hair is most harmonious. The geometrically faceted structure of the face is unexpected, so that the profile is tormented and the sitter's basic melancholy is emphatically conveyed; the long, loose hatching strokes are widely spaced to shed the most light on surfaces, while the sharp, categorical line that cuts off the outer edge of the coat is of a more modern conception. The broad composition of this spatially monumental portrait is illustrated less well by the contemporary *Study for a Medal of Alfonso of Aragon* [Plate 155]—a medal which has not come down to us; the work exudes an intense Gothic quality, overloaded with excessively heavy drawing.

We now come to the last group of drawings. Though they contain certain precise characteristics, often already observed, of the artist's graphic procedures, they constitute a cycle apart, by virtue of the elevated style attained in them and their achievement in liberating this style from the seductive calls of naturalism, thus leaving it free to identify itself more closely with purity of form. So, in a *Study of Figures in Costume* [Plate 162], in the British Museum, the richness of former times is lessened by the softness of the furs, generously worked with "pointillist" strokes which froth up over the wide milky expanse. Graphically or otherwise motivated research is overshadowed by the formal accomplishment that crystallizes the figures, purged of any fortuitous, residual elements, transmuted into symbols of a definitive way of existing, while they freeze immobile in their particular situations.

Two *Studies of Legs* [Plate 164], though still reminiscent of a manner once dear to Pisanello's heart, must be placed among the artist's later productions, chiefly because of the exaltation of style as an end in itself, shown in the purity of line that becomes the imperative though extreme limit of form. This is most exquisitely expressed in the leg in the stirrup, where the naturalistic object is summarily indicated by the two indispensable outside outlines. In the leg in hose there is still a tendency to insist on the particular subject matter, though the slightly indicated slant presupposes an imaginary figure similar in many ways, but mainly in the upright, inclined balance of its pose, to the figure of Saint George in the *Legend*.

The *Study of a Wolf* and the *Study of a Wildcat* [Plate 163] must also be considered products of Pisanello's most advanced artistic phase. Both exploit a clever technique which is resolved in the wolf in the distinguishing of finely indicated details, while in the cat the rarefied mass of strokes becomes a stylized, symbolic "wild" costume. But a common element stands out in both, an unexpected factor of "psychological life" that pervades the animals, revealing the artist's rare ability to penetrate another world—the other dimension of the animal world—and thus to show the measure of his artistic maturity.

However, it is in the *Study of Lynxes* [Plate 165] that fusion of the figurative element and the formal act is most complete. The style here freely defines broad spaces, roughly sketching with splendid graphic elegance some parts of the bodies in accordance with a more global intuitive conception of the forms. On the other hand, the heads are masterpieces of polished realism, genuine fragments of life, isolated from the rest in all their expressive strength. But these apparently contrasting graphic intensities disappear in the *Study of Horses and a Page* [Plate 166], in which the generous spread of the strokes becomes spatially uniform;

146 - THE APPARITION OF THE VIRGIN TO SAINT GEORGE AND SAINT ANTHONY
National Gallery - LONDON

PISANELLO AND TUSCAN ART

It is now generally accepted that Pisanello's art is to be considered the splendid swan song of the last phase of Late Gothic culture.[107] The great painter from Verona uses his genius to portray the dramatic decline of a civilization slowly fading into the pallid horizon of the Middle Ages, whose fate it partly shared and with which it has often been equated, though not always exactly. At the same time some imperishable aspects of the painter's civilization are so exalted by his intuitive and creative strength that they appear to us as the essential springs of the vast historical process. Precisely at the moment when Gothic was moving into its declining phases, Pisanello, with his very great art, worked the miracle of reviving it and giving it new life as one of the most solid and real expressions of spiritual life.

Perhaps this last point has not been made clear, but it is nevertheless agreed that Pisanello is the most important figure in North Italian Gothic, just as it is acknowledged that the slow exhaustion of the movement did not lead to its sudden dissolution, but that on the contrary Renaissance art, at least in its relatively advanced phases, could hardly have avoided assimilating the most positive and durable aspects of Gothic art.

One particular side of Pisanello's art, however, has not been sufficiently examined: certain works of his have a pronounced Renaissance flavor. The general tendency has been to attribute them, without trying to penetrate their true nature, to a sudden change of direction caused by the inevitable decisive influence that the most immediate productions of the new, young art must have had on the artist's already well-formulated pictorial style.

When one passes from the purely Late Gothic paintings to the corpus of medals, those striking portraits of strong and violent or deeply spiritual men viewed in the penetrating light of humanism, it is not easy to reconcile these two opposed worlds in terms of such a conclusion, and a chasm that cannot have existed in reality opens up before us. In other words, one risks, if not actually distorting the picture of the artist's career, at least unaccountably doubling his personality. In fact, even when two distinct modes, two or more contrasting currents, can be detected in a truly creative production, there is always a deep-seated reason for this apparent dichotomy, and this reason makes it possible for such divergent modes to be related to the unique, if many-sided, personality of their creator.

Thus when attempts are made to reconcile the two seemingly different strains in Pisanello's art, it is not enough to limit oneself to graphological comparison of the sketches, drawings, and details of paintings or medals, and to jump to conclusions based on their apparently opposed natures, thereby devoting the greater part of the investigation to this useful but inconclusive visual philology. Instead, one must refer these two disconcerting facets of the various works to Pisanello's poetic sense, which was unique and indivisible; a poetic sense, furthermore, that viewed both worlds without animosity, excessive enthusiasms, or surrender. His poetic instinct remained faithful to its task of penetrating the artistic and cultural aspects of the moment of transition between two civilizations; it remained objective even though the artist was often carried away by melancholy northern atmospheres, refined drawing, and by Nordic colors that use space only for their pale withdrawal. However, this preference cannot be taken to mean, as might be supposed, that Pisanello was devoid of the knowledge necessary for creating spatial depth or relief in volumes. Yet it is strange that so talented and able an artist, capable of manipulating every technical resource, should have left no painting showing that he would use at least the three-dimensional nature of space: all the more strange as his medals show a new conception in spatial construction, and even more in the construction of the whole, if not in the scientific realization of these. Nonetheless, these conceptions vouch for the presence of a perfect rationality which establishes the relationships between individual elements that generate the breathtaking harmony of Pisanello's medals. As we have pointed out, one might then hold that the split in Pisanello's artistic production, if it is to be considered a split, was due to the artist's lack of contact with the new culture, but this could be disproved immediately, precisely by the medals. Thus it is by no means certain, and in fact highly improbable, that Tuscany remained *terra incognita* to Pisanello for long.

But where could he have found the matchless fifteenth-century models of his art, and why did he not incorporate them completely into his basic medieval Gothic formula? He certainly could not have taken them from the unsuitable works of Altichiero; these were steeped in Giotto's influence, to be sure, but even so they were far removed from the light, airy constructions of the Tuscan Renaissance. Definitely, Altichiero's style cannot have served as a source for Pisanello; if anything, it may have provided an opportunity for valuable academic study, apart from which it does not seem to have been assimilated in the least. The links between the painting of Altichiero (and Avanzo) and that of Tuscany (influenced by

147 - THE APPARITION OF THE
VIRGIN TO SAINT GEORGE AND
SAINT ANTHONY (*detail: Saint
George*) - *National Gallery* - LONDON

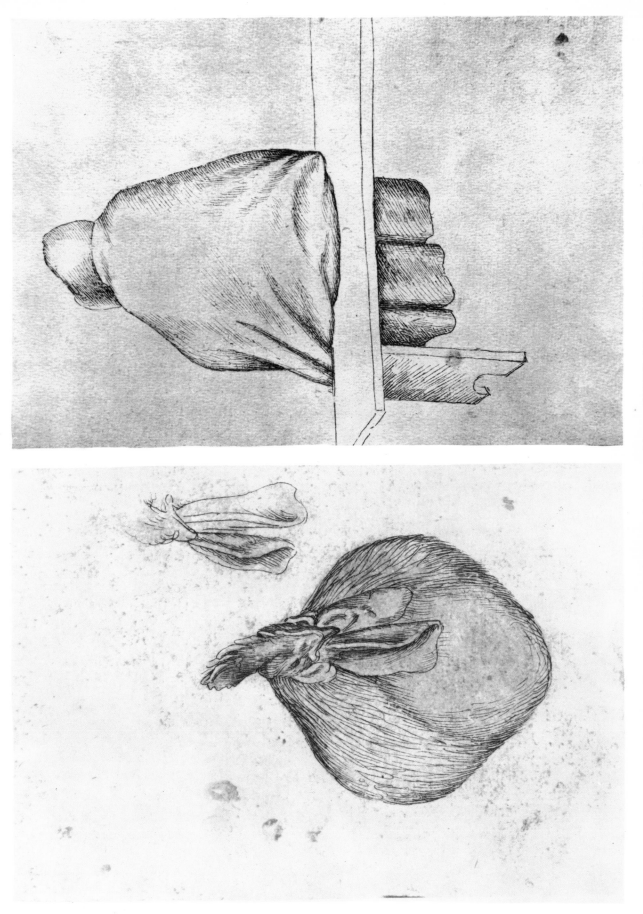

148 - STUDY OF A COCKEREL - *Biblioteca Ambrosiana* - MILAN; STUDY OF A SEATED MONK - *Louvre* - PARIS

149 - STUDY OF HORSES' HEADS - *Louvre* - PARIS

150 - THE APPARITION OF THE VIRGIN TO SAINT GEORGE AND SAINT ANTHONY
(*detail: Virgin and Child*) - *National Gallery* - LONDON

Giotto) could not have directed Pisanello's interest, nor could the painting of Giusto de' Menabuoi, though easily accessible in nearby Padua; Giusto was one of the so-called "dissident" Tuscans who were motivated by the need to shake off the Giotto tradition, but were no more Gothic for that.[108] Pisanello, as far as the past was concerned, was solidly anchored in the Gothic tradition, and indeed in its cosmopolitan variety, for more than a few of the motifs he adopted had come from beyond the Alps. It must have been directly from studying Tuscan culture and from frequenting Tuscan artists that he drew the inspiration for his "Renaissance forms"—those which stand out most of all, as we have shown, in his medals. And he cannot have lacked the opportunities for such experience, though all known documents are silent on this point.[109]

Documents attest to his presence in Rome in 1431 and 1432; it has even been supposed that he stayed there before 1428,[110] the date of the death of Gentile da Fabriano who was then working on the famous fresco cycle in San Giovanni in Laterano that Pisanello later completed. We also have proof of his presence in Naples at the court of Alfonso I of Aragon, where he was still mentioned in 1449. As we have already suggested, it is highly probable that he broke at least one of his journeys to or from Rome or Naples in Tuscany, more particularly in Florence.

When Pisanello met with Renaissance art during the first half of the fifteenth century, in Florence itself Gothic was still flowering luxuriantly and had many illustrious interpreters: Starnina, Lorenzo Monaco, Ghiberti, not to mention Masolino da Panicale. But most of all there was Gentile da Fabriano who, after bathing in the Gothic tides of northern Italy, produced in 1423 in Florence the celebrated altarpiece commissioned by Palla Strozzi showing the *Adoration of the Magi* [Fig. 8].

This work, though incorporating some Florentine plastic elements, remains a languid arabesque of decorative elegance which impresses one most of all by its rich colors and the harmonious arrangement of the figures; it is a sheet of brilliant external beauty, but devoid of any directing, creative, expressive force. It is, however, the most splendid specimen of the Late Gothic art then still very much alive in Florence, but precisely because it lacked a solid framework was incapable of standing on its own. This art, while it exercised a certain influence on the Florentine School, striving impatiently to renew itself along very different lines, had not the necessary means to contrast strongly enough with it. For this reason the guiding light of Masolino, who only a few years later was to give Florence his most creative work, in the Brancacci Chapel, was not one to fear the rival Gothic world expressed by Gentile and the other artists who gathered round him. Gentile may scarcely have noticed this, but he must have been more than a little troubled by the intimate refinement that persisted in running through Masolino's weak forms.

In Gentile's work one group of figures, the group on the right beyond the Magi, recalls an analogous group by Pisanello in *The Legend of Saint George*. Especially the central figure, who wears a beret with a horizontal curving brim, recalls the expressionless Kalmuck in the Verona fresco. But even in this example, one does not have to be an expert to see the substantial differences between the two painters. Whereas in Gentile's work everything pours out in a wandering, unpredictable stream, so that the *Adoration* is one of the few paintings that can be enjoyed immediately, without demanding an intense intellectual participation, in Pisanello's the emotional response required is very different, and the pleasant, decorative tone, though by no means absent, is outweighed by more real aesthetic content. Pisanello's poetry draws its content from a truer universal reality, while Gentile's remains tied to external observation of natural phenomena; this observation may be passionately involved, but in the end it is still largely superficial. Thus, Pisanello's interest does not seem to have been unduly aroused by the Gothic which flourished in Florence, just as, around 1418 or 1419, he was not greatly influenced by Gentile's work in the Ducal Palace. We may exclude Starnina and Lorenzo Monaco, Gothic provincials who, though agreeable enough, were too far removed from the spaciousness, the ardent creative richness of Pisanello's mentality. We may also exclude Ghiberti, who, although a sophisticated Gothic worker, was perhaps already captivated by Classical "coherency." (Pisanello's much discussed Renaissance-Classical side, as shown in his medals, is rather a problem and certainly only a superficial aspect of his remarkable work.) We are left, then, with only one artist who could plausibly have attracted Pisanello's attention: Paolo Uccello, the painter who really lived the problem of art conceived, not as the mannered exercise or the pressing need to excel to which Renaissance enthusiasms could easily have led, but as a problem far more complex in the vastness of its constituent elements, forcing the artist to relive dialectically and dramatically every value of the past, and to review them in the light of the latest innovations.

Even before Pisanello's journey to Rome, Paolo Uccello, this Tuscan artist fascinated by Gothic though he had spent his life in the middle of Tuscan disputations, crossed Italy to Venice, where traces of his visit can still be seen.[111]

He stayed in the North a good five years, so that we must not rule out the possibility of Pisanello's having met him then. In fact, despite the lack of documentation on his youthful career, we can conclude that Paolo Uccello must already have been quite well known for the Signoria of Florence to have sent him to the Most Serene Republic in answer to a request

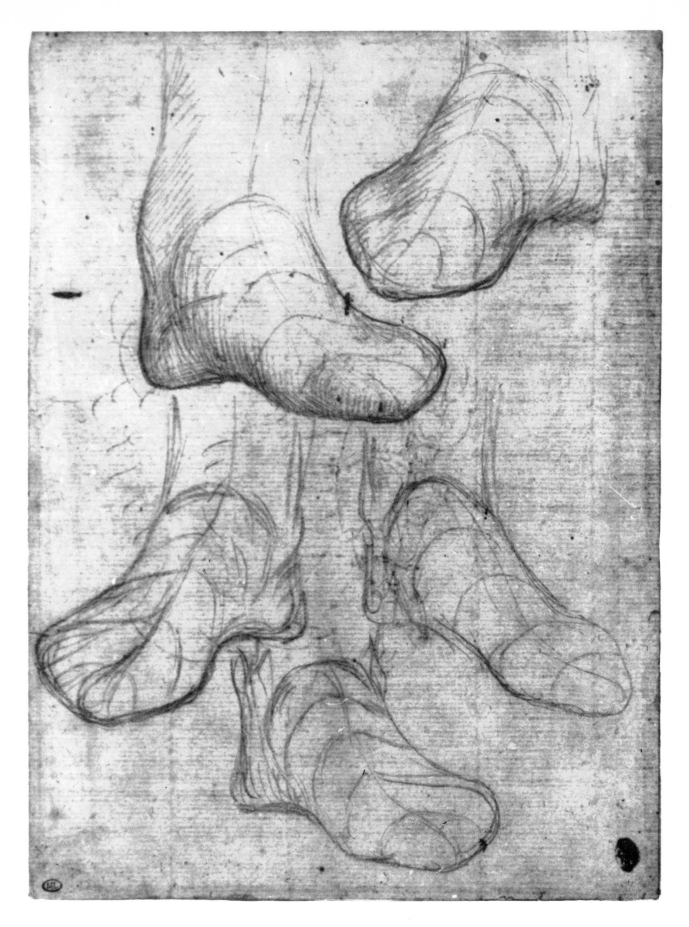

151 - STUDY OF SHOD FEET - *Louvre* - Paris

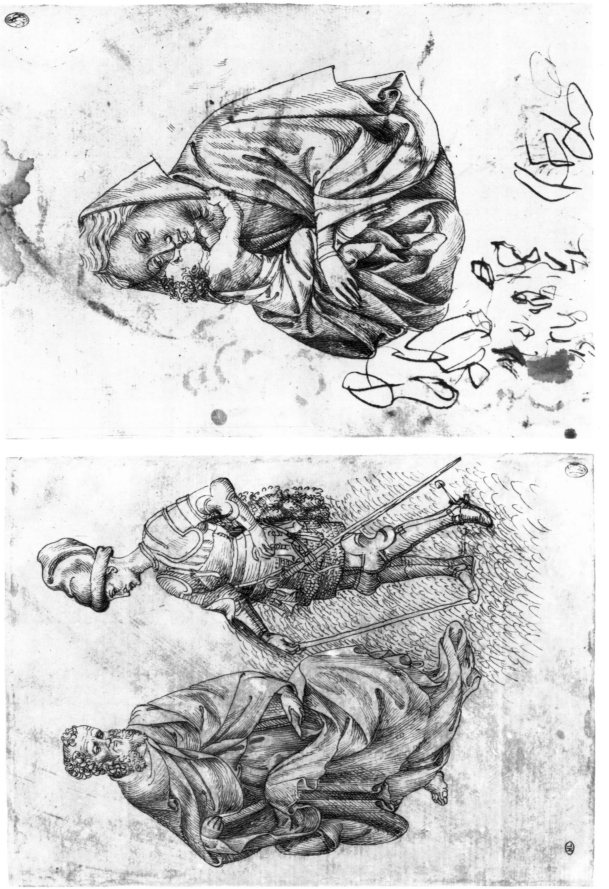

for a master mosaicist and restorer. Besides, Paolo arrived in Venice well informed about the controversy over technique and perspective which he had followed in Florence, keeping in touch with his master Ghiberti, and later with Brunelleschi; he must therefore have enjoyed considerable prestige in Venice. But during his first stay there his possible meetings with Pisanello could not have been sufficient to lead to his having any fundamental influence on the northerner: if anything, the reverse happened. Paolo Uccello, still thirsting for Gothic and medieval fantasy, certainly looked at Pisanello's works in the Ducal Palace, and admired their noble and chivalrous atmosphere, the ostentation of their courtly pomp, and also the pungent humor of some of the figures.[112]

So, when Paolo Uccello returned to Florence, if on his part he had left some contribution to the artistic world of Venice, he was himself variously enriched, above all by the completeness, perhaps stemming from confidence, that marked the art of North Italy in the early fifteenth century, in which realism and aristocratic finesse were blended with splendor of motifs, color, and daring, fantastic inventiveness.

Therefore there are several links between the two artists. These links were probably further developed and strengthened through later contacts; it is simply that in the unfolding of their respective arts the common factors are shown in inverse, but by no means opposed, ways. Both artists avoid plunging unconditionally into the Renaissance mainstream, but Paolo moves away from Gothic to oppose it dialectically to the massive four-square conceptions of the fifteenth century. He makes these conceptions more vibrant and splendid, without glorifying them, and thus achieves temporal, concrete, and critical reduction of timeless premises through the medium of a language—and, most remarkable—of a language which could range freely over a surging poetic world. Pisanello, on the other hand, fed entirely on the northern and Gothic worlds, assimilating and expressing their substance, the atavistic sentiments expressed with resignation, the mythical flashes of glory; but when there were signs of renewal, this clear-cut world still remained his own, his fundamental field of action, and the more obviously he adopted this position, the more he showed that he had lived through the new experience without letting it sweep him off his feet.

The humanistic breeze allowed him to classicize his creatures, to define them better by stressing and elevating formal beauty, choosing the moments when the essence of individual motive forces was crystallized. But finally he returned to his lifelong love and used every means to exalt it.

So, while Paolo fitted actively and "scientifically" into the new current of the fifteenth century, though always keeping his distance from it, Pisanello stayed on its edge. When, from time to time, he did make up his mind to explore it more deeply, it was only to give greater completeness to his own art and his over-all vision. It is a case of two similar but substantially different worlds, both participating in the decline of chivalrous life, and in its melancholy sunset. Each artist reacted in his own way, one as an acute but severe Tuscan, the other as a sad-hearted northerner. Pisanello turned the anguish of decline into drama, though he expressed it with severe rigor and without excessive expressionism. Paolo, though equally preoccupied by the consequences of this decisive moment in history, reacted differently, and his characters, instead of appearing stricken and pensive, take on an objective almost marionette-ish air, detached from their context and yet at the same time penetrating.

In short, for Pisanello the upheaval is complete, while for Paolo there is still a last resource, a means of escape. On the other hand, the two painters' attitudes are in opposition when they attack some aspects of religious subjects. Paolo Uccello portrays severely religious forms (he shares the world of Dante and Savonarola) except when he treats episodes in a Gothic anecdotal vein, but he always adheres to his unmistakable style whose unexpected results proclaim him the true son of a new culture, ready for the most impetuous enthusiasms. Pisanello, instead, sets his style the task of defining his religious figures in elegant lines and aristocratic forms; though their exuberant personalities are addicted to Gothic splendor, they are far removed from the call to metaphysical reality. They exist purely in terms of themselves, of their own traditions of beauty and greatness. Cut off from their fellow men, but mobile and actively participating in their own world, they turn their gaze to other spheres, where they virtually exist already. The angel in the San Fermo *Annunciation*, far from appearing with the usual celestial angelic beauty, is a powerful complex of curves and volumes, sometimes inflated; he is impatient to impose himself and thus he is foreign to any narrative or, one might add, to any religious situation.

It is of fundamental importance to examine these differences between Pisanello's pictorial style and the art of Paolo if one is to understand the nature of these two aspects of the International Gothic movement. Whereas in the Tuscan's work Gothic serves as a contrasting element and turns out to be merely a means of mitigating the excessive absoluteness of the new art, so that it cannot be considered an essential force, to Pisanello it is of basic importance. In the work of the painter from Verona, Gothic embodies the essential nature of the work and so cannot be reduced to the level of other contingent artistic and cultural experience, which can only circle around it. Pisanello's Gothic world fades away regretfully once stylization reaches an almost unhealthy summit, but it does not disappear. In fact,

Gothic aestheticism, and consequently the aesthetics of Antonio Pisano, may well have contributed to the value of some of the finest products of the Renaissance, rendering them less crude, while his motifs were to reappear from time to time through the history of art, whenever anyone in anguish and despair called on them for relief and release.

There are, then, points of contact between Pisanello and Paolo Uccello in particular, and so between the northern and Tuscan cultures in general. These are shown most clearly in Paolo's earliest and latest works and in Pisanello's medals. Furthermore, these relationships must have grown up naturally as the result of the convergence of two analogous cultural tendencies. The climate that could have gripped Pisanello in Tuscany must have been in reality fairly limited, conscious of the existence of a unifying historical and cultural reality, capable of sparing certain achievements of the past, the better to impose the exclusivity of the new art, magnificent, yet, despite the vast richness of its various features, one-sided and intolerant. Tuscan art seems to have grown and consolidated its advances in direct proportion to the rise to economic and political power of the new social élite, which showed unusual taste in surrounding itself with great artists subscribing to Renaissance humanism, while the old courtly expressive language survived only in superficialities such as decorative splendor, the phantasmagoric appearance of processions, and decoration intended to enhance prestige. These, however, were precisely the most deep-rooted, and so the more culturally attractive, elements of the closed, declining world, which the new "chosen people" wished to disown. But it was not so much the courtly vocabulary as such that came under fire, though the new turn of events might well have longed to refute it (while still imitating it occasionally). Rather, it was those other terms, universally and indissolubly linked to the feelings of the human soul: the secret, dignified sorrows of the heart, which were only rarely expressed by the most significant pre-Renaissance art, and then with feeble language and sugary languor, the continual pursuit of mastery of form, progressing in small, elegant steps, perhaps afraid of renewing the climate and space in which man was to be placed, for its aim was to exalt him slowly but profoundly, almost, it would seem, to the point of determining the leveling of every real form on the plane of aesthetics.

One may well marvel, in connection with this, that a courtly art, as it seems we must consider Late Gothic to be, should have succeeded simply by its formal strength, in smoothing out the disparities between being and being, between man and his natural setting; indeed, everything became merged in an atmosphere of general participation. The difference, substantial at first sight, between richly decorated and poorer figures or settings can be seen as no more than the outcome of a pure decorative game that does not encroach in the least on the unified artistic and formal conception. The all-pervasive atmosphere is one of natural, real vitality and tender, harmonious unity, not of predetermined "separateness."

Once again, an example can be found in Gentile's *Adoration,* in which every element—the Holy Family, the central group of kings and nobles, and the procession of followers—blends with the others in a natural setting of rejoicing, albeit vicarious rejoicing; everything merges, feebly perhaps from a formal standpoint, into the tone of joy that emanates from the golds and brilliant colors. And there is no distinction, but only unity, between the figures themselves and the outside world.[113] The same unity between diverse natures and disparate values can be seen in Pisanello's *Legend,* only here it is carried out on a higher level.

This unified relationship seems to break up in Renaissance art. The conception of metaphysical space, for all its formal glory, creates a gulf between man and his surroundings, between man and man. From being naturalistic, the harmony becomes metaphysical. While every work of art must have "metaphysical" elements, different from the normal retinal impression, in the fifteenth century metaphysical elements assume a directly antivisual character, linked to a dissociating and in some ways arbitrary construction of the human setting. With the accentuation of these elements, it becomes more and more difficult to reconcile the existences of the subordinate and the principal factors, imposed in a space that permits all dynamic (inherent in the composition) and visual (external to the composition—the onlooker's) interest to center on the principal factor of metaphysical space.

We have already affirmed and we repeat that, in the fifteenth century, art thinks of man "as having both feet firmly on the ground"—that is, as moving freely and spontaneously in an earthly world, without fixing his attention on transcendental problems. Nevertheless, this is true only in part. In fact, it is difficult to see how one could expect fifteenth-century art to represent fully this earthly exaltation of man, for though it does indeed exalt him, and with powerfully expressive means, where it should concentrate on an artistic transformation of his historical reality, it aims instead at a metaphysical glorification of him as a divine being, and so alienates him from the world. The convergence on one or more of the main figures of lines leading to infinity in space was intended to exalt one and only one element in the composition and this tendency increased as the laws of perspective became more precisely formulated.

Masaccio is more human in his expression of this point in the history of art. Andrea del Castagno feels its full drama. Fra Angelico welcomes it with open arms, for it makes his Madonnas more striking since, the more "separate" they are, the more divine they appear. Domenico da Venezia directly introduces crystal-clear, heavenly light. And Piero della

153 - MEDAL OF ALFONSO OF ARAGON
(reverse with eagle)
Museo Nazionale del Bargello - FLORENCE

154 - MEDAL OF ALFONSO OF ARAGON
(reverse with boar hunt)
British Museum - LONDON

Francesca, the supreme genius, transports man once more into a sphere of incommunicable substance. Originally pantheistic, as it had been in the Gothic and particularly the Late Gothic period, art now asserts its metaphysically monistic nature. The appearance of God as Man in early Renaissance art (cf. Cavallini's conception in this context) is now concluded in a concrete affirmation of Man as God (the prime mover).

This focusing of the artist's attention on one or more figures is a well-known, indisputable fact. Consequently, religious figures too are humanized; in other words, religion is rendered humanly, with its feet solidly on the ground, more in the image of man, so that it is possible through less hieratic forms to raise man to the level of the divine. It is precisely this new vision, with the new perspective and the three dimensions of unreal metaphysical space, "arbitrarily" constructed (in spite of the illusion of "reality" through depth), which in its turn places individual figures in an artificial visual setting. On the one hand it blows them up to gigantic size, while on the other it conceals their true humanity, which it has transfigured and transformed in terms of particular conceptions and aims, so that the myth of human reality in fifteenth-century art suffers considerable damage. The warm, humane Virgins, the plump little cherubs, the men, visibly strong and virile, are figures whose life is geared to exalt certain determined values in an aristocratic key, in a way which must have met with great approval from the new Tuscan society at the time of its rise to prominence.

But the difference between what is magnified and what is ignored is immense, not because there is no equality or, rather, no physical and visual harmony between the two parts, but because the harmonious, continuous relationship is broken up, and the single element, the dominating personality, prevails.

In short, this was an assertion, in a way, of a love for power which, evidently, had little in common with the devotion to learning that blossomed so luxuriantly at the same time. But art is not a pure expression of knowledge, an exclusively theoretical action: it must deal also with feelings and passions, and not only with cultural demands. So the wave of strength summoned up by a few individuals in the fifteenth century could not help affecting the arts whose means were deployed to express this new tidal force in a way adapted to the unprecedented reality, though still nobly transfiguring. However, it may be noted that in the medieval Gothic period, egoism and personal power dominated. Yet Gothic art itself often worked the miracle, as if in a supreme act of love, of reconciling all the potentially ill-assorted creatures in an attempt to elevate them in accordance with a pantheistic vision which did not divorce them from their surroundings.[114]

This process of pantheistic unity came to a halt with the Renaissance, just when it was beginning to show poetically interesting results, though using largely traditional methods. The artist was already alive to the demands of the new, different world in which he lived, and expressed them fittingly: he glorified man, but as an isolated phenomenon whose exaltation did not entail the exaltation of all reality. The new conditions made this unity impossible, for the pantheistic lyricism of Gothic art could not satisfy the fifteenth-century man's desire for individual supremacy. An artist who declared his love for all creatures, and in particular for all human beings, would have been considered an anachronism.

In fact, the naturalism that took shape in the fifteenth century was fundamentally different from Late Gothic naturalism. The latter shows its belief in man as a part of a cosmos in which the contrast between the composing parts is softened, if not actually eliminated, by a harmonic sense, in which a large part is played by so-called "illusory perspective." The naturalism which sprang from the Renaissance, however, has its roots in the difference between subject and object, between man and nature and, most important of all, between man and man. Though such naturalism drove the individual to scientific inquiry and the "possession" of the universe, the very way in which this inquiry was carried out betrayed its full adherence to a perilous formula based on idealism, whose chief proponents were to be found in Florence.[115] We then realize that mathematically exact space, as distinct from the usual "real" optical impression,[116] is shown as a mathematically ordered vision arranged along predetermined lines that enclose a preconceived reality whose poetics, even, are fixed in advance to conform completely to the conception—aristocratic rather than scientific— of the *homo novus*. Which is to say that art, with all its remarkable, aesthetically superb means, could not avoid supporting, though indirectly, a particular socio-political situation, in this case one perfectly embodied in Machiavelli and shrewdly assessed in more recent times by Bertrand Russell.[117]

Thus, the supremacy of man is exalted and, by analogy, attention in religious compositions is focused on one or a few figures. Space becomes stupendously unreal and, by the creation of an apparently real depth,[118] it determines a significant contrast between foreground and background. And while in one way man seems still to have his feet firmly planted on the ground, with the accentuation of his individual features and expressiveness, the inflation of one form at the expense of others alienates both, and human reality is once more distorted. At the same time, the spread of Platonic doctrines enabled artists to realize their best and most intensely creative resources, in forms that were as effective as ever but nevertheless somehow detached from reality—forms, in the Platonic sense of the word—that existed on a metaphysical plane. So, in spite of their avowed aim to bring man back to earth, they could not help causing a fresh alienation, a more urgent appeal for metaphysical existence. One cannot therefore speak of the detachment of man from the extrahuman sphere when dealing with earlier works of art (for example those of Late Gothic), and the theory of Renaissance man as foreign to the supernatural world is shown to be inaccurate.

The situation of art and culture in the fifteenth century cannot be seen as a civilized flowering destined to work miracles; many wonderful things were indeed produced, but they were not all purely original creations resulting from flashes of enlightenment. Various ancient and modern elements and qualities (classicism, perspective, Flemish coloring) came together at that time in Italy, above all, in Tuscany, so that men of intelligence could study them and elaborate them at the appropriate moment. They thus created noble forms of expression but often passed over works and compromises that were far from unimportant. Furthermore, how can one explain the fact that great artists—though disconcerted, and fascinated by the powerful protagonists of a new social reality which, while confused, was intimately related to the very nature of the Renaissance—managed to produce masterpieces of extraordinary formal perfection and serene eloquence? In view of the one meaning attached to the general concept of "Renaissance," this profound contrast between the situations of politics and art should not have existed.

Then, alongside the increasingly frequent manifestations of an egoistic individualism, there were many thoughtful and learned men who were miraculously able to preserve the idea of "humanity" on an elevated plane, certainly far higher than that of the rising tide that from one day to the next could cause the creation or the downfall of a prince, give opulent feasts, or light the faggots round a stake.

Basically, while on the one hand, artists were impelled more or less consciously by this very situation (and not by a sudden flash of guiding light) to create the precise terminology for expressing the new reality and the new feelings born of aristocratic exclusiveness, on the other hand, their role as essential factors, if not protagonists, of the fully developing humanist movement, led them to transfigure this same reality, including even those parts of it which did not suit their feelings. They sang the life of their times, idealizing their figures with such extreme rigor that they often reached the point of ghostly abstraction.[119] In this context the hypothesis advanced elsewhere,[120] that this particular "estrangement" of artists in the fifteenth century was planned to escape from the danger of falling completely under the yoke of the dominating class, seems sound. It was perhaps also this attitude, which spurred them to form a closed élite contrasting with the "practical men," that gave rise to so many Italian fifteenth-century masterpieces, outstanding for their "formal beauty," that is, for their exquisite abstraction of natural appearances. However, this abstraction itself harbored the seeds of the crisis in its dissociating duality. This same duality seemed in the process of being eliminated by Gothic linearism which, for all its abstract tendencies, took a "realistic," far from disparate, and so non-alienating view of things.

Fifteenth-century painting has always, and rightly, been considered a model of formal perfection, born at a moment in art history when the finest results of an aesthetic inquiry into essential values were gathered together. One cannot fail to realize that it could yet be penetrated by the consequences (antitheses and later crises) of the artist's extremist, almost inhuman efforts to make painting conform to a particular vision: these efforts were most pronounced when they turned their attention to the Classical art of the past or later to northern, and in particular Flemish, naturalism, with its rich, enveloping chromatic light.[121] How can one not notice that in the case under examination the values of Classical art, and so of classically inspired humanism and northern naturalism, which nonetheless had profound repercussions of their own, had to be adapted to fit the particular Renaissance conception of space in terms of the canons of linear perspective, and so had to lose some of their intrinsic characteristics? Thus naturalistic pantheism, excluded in Tuscany by certain premises of neo-Platonism,[122] finally expired in so many "formal caesurae" reinforced by geometrical techniques, while the color and light of the individual element that had formerly shone out in unison with its fellows[123] now seemed to retreat into carefully defined zones to lead its separate existence.[124] On the other hand, the resolution of the indefinable vastness of human feeling into particular, distinct individualities could, by virtue of the very nature of art, lead only to transposing the subject to a plane of isolating passivity. If art had not had recourse to these magnificent, heroically extreme means—the creation of an unreal, enclosed Platonic world—to exalt the individual subject, it would have degenerated into no more than a collection of character studies.

This supreme effort to achieve individualization and consequently abstraction, in a neo-Platonic, scientifically oriented vein, was without doubt one of the principal causes of the tension that later led to the loss of a sense of direction and the crisis of the end of the century.[125] This disorientation was due to the predominating neo-Platonic trend which, centered in the Tuscan élite, reached its summit at the court of Lorenzo de' Medici. Yet though this tendency had unparalleled merits, as indeed had all forms of Platonism, it could only lead to crisis. The lack of orientation was due at the same time to the fifteenth century's great discovery: perspective, figurative space. This space, with its "linear vision," created a harmony that was only apparent, enchanting onlookers by its metaphysical nature but re-

155 - STUDY FOR A MEDAL OF ALFONSO OF ARAGON - *Louvre* - Paris

156 - STUDY FOR A PORTRAIT OF ALFONSO OF ARAGON - *Louvre* - PARIS

maining the prisoner of its own laws, precisely because of its indissoluble links with the geometrical scientific approach that had determined it. These laws, aiming at the creation of absolute figurative harmony, basically achieved only "individual" harmony, which was all that was allowed by the tenets of perspective as a logical product of fifteenth-century culture. So the generalization and, in one sense, the imposition of these laws charged them with the expressive faculties of free artistic personalities.

The complex of reasons that illuminates the difference between the monist and individualist concepts of the fifteenth century and the naturalistic pantheism of Late Gothic and northern painting in general may explain the possibility of a meeting between the rational Paolo Uccello and the romantic Pisanello. Paolo was indeed a renowned exponent of perspective but at the same time he was an artist of broad vision, ready to assimilate any aspect of Gothic that fitted his growing Renaissance powers and so to enrich his world with a beauty beyond the pure joys of technical discovery. The other, the courtly painter steeped in Nordic poetry, had a rather detached view of the new forces that were appearing in the painting of his times, though he was not indifferent to their pulsating ferment.

However, the mere examination of a few individual figures, such as certain massive horses that appear in the works of both artists, will not give an exact idea of the similarity of their artistic conceptions. These facile comparisons, for all their usefulness, are never sufficiently valid in establishing points of contact, particularly in the case of Paolo Uccello and Pisanello, because their treatments of similar themes follow different lines. The Gothic element that both painters possess is used by each to create a different language. Yet they have a point in common: both understand, or feel, in spite of their different viewpoints, the singular delicacy of the "historico-cultural" moment, and both use their divergent languages to pin down the ephemeral as well as the durable values they encounter. One resolves the new means, in some cases, into an interplay of geometrical or stylized forms, set in not always coherent perspective; the other expresses forms, conceived in a world that combined chivalry and the Renaissance, in such a way that they are stripped of their real appearances, and reduced to vague ghosts of themselves. These forms, however, are rarely left wholly alone, for they are almost never shown in isolation, pressed as they are by other living creatures that never let their presence be forgotten.

But where the two artists really seem to agree is in the reticent attitude they adopt toward the new approach, when they have to penetrate the singular humanity of their time, when they have to exalt its character, its customs and manifold feats. Then both seem to lack enthusiasm and each in his own way shows himself cautious about totally accepting the new:

Uccello, with the famous irony that subtly allies itself with extravagant formal structures; Pisanello, with the chronic melancholy that pervades even his main subjects, grasping desperately at an undiscriminating, loving faith in all creatures.

These worlds, so different yet similar, must have overlapped at some point and left traces of their meeting. And precisely when one thinks of these contacts, one finds an explanation for the eclectic style of an artist who obviously assimilated aspects of the painting of both Uccello and Pisanello. This is the "Master of the Adoration," the author of the circular painting of the *Adoration of the Magi* in the Berlin Museum, which is usually attributed to Domenico Veneziano [Figs. 40-42].

It is easy to locate elements inspired by Uccello and Pisanello in this painting, and they have virtually always been noted.[126] However, apart from the courtly narration mixed with certain graceful poses and the unmistakable influences of Uccello, Pisanello, and northern and Flemish painting, it is essential to stress the particular atmosphere that fills the painting, the relationship between the parts and the whole, and finally the essential reasons that lead us to exclude this painting from the body of Domenico's works.

From a figurative point of view, the painting contains characteristics recalling Pisanello, which are balanced by others derived directly from Paolo Uccello and to a lesser degree from Domenico da Venezia. We shall see exactly what these characteristics are, to dispose of the figurative philology of these comparisons.

The main Uccello influences are to be noted in the group on the left, not so much in the two clumsily executed horses, which are a far cry from the calculated, abstract works of Paolo Uccello, as in the young man astride the first horse, with his arm outstretched rather stiffly, and in the other who stands facing us a little further to the right. The first figure's rather lifeless gesture is clearly derived from the *Hunting Scene* in the Ashmolean, Oxford, more precisely, from the group on the left, which is dashing toward an imaginary point in the night shadows. The second might find echoes in the faces on some shields in Prato Cathedral, that were executed either by Uccello himself or under his dominating influence,[127] especially in the face of a young man, tensely painted, with his curling hair sharply cut at the nape, which betrays its painter's efforts to equal the intellectual isolation of his master's style.[128] Other faces from these shields, not true works of Uccello, could also be compared with the face described but for a certain softness in their satisfied roundness; this last detail places them closer to the art of Domenico Veneziano.

We can already glimpse a reason for the stylistic disparity between Paolo Uccello, Domenico Veneziano, and the Master of the Adoration. The work of the first, essentially critical and fantastic in inspiration, is composed of diverse perspectives moved by dynamics that are an end in themselves; but as they are never fixed in advance, they never lead to a decisive effect transcending the normal logic of things, and their most extreme and subtle meanings are never sifted out. Domenico's art, despite the precious media he uses, betrays an unassertive personality and an indecisive creative power: his art is craftsmanly above all, the fruit of a highly accomplished technique that seems to rely exclusively on the means—on matter, light, and color—in combining the forms. The forms, therefore, still lack the fluidity along with the substance and the distinction that an elevated conception would have given them. When Domenico paints, he remains overawed by the discoveries of others (Brunelleschi, Fra Angelico, Andrea del Castagno, even Filippo Lippi), which, nonetheless, he elaborates on and in some ways even refines. Lastly, his pictorial style has not the indefinable spark that brings great creation to life. And while enormous poetic genius is revealed in the synthesis of light and color and form achieved by Piero della Francesca, in Domenico's work the relationship is limited to a simple light-color-space ratio, very skillful, but still not quite capable of determining outstandingly significant formal values. Domenico's pallid atmospheres, his washed-out crystalline transparencies, though leading back to the coveted Platonic sphere, have not the fiber necessary for pinning down the essence of the form, the concept reflected in the form (Piero, on the other hand, ranges over this field with absolute mastery). The Master of the Adoration, as can be observed, favors a more eclectic approach to painting. Less calm than Domenico, but also less acute than Paolo Uccello, he shows his preference for the latter painter. Nevertheless his work is at best that of an honest artisan, set off occasionally by the superficial appearance of devices gleaned from the work of others, though the general construction does have noteworthy elegance in a Nordic decorative idiom, often with Flemish overtones.

This art lacks the stupendous formal abstraction of Paolo Uccello or the luminous brightness and spatial determination of Domenico. Instead, the Berlin painting is rich in the Nordic decorative elements just mentioned, and especially in elements drawn from the work of Pisanello. This is particularly obvious in the central group, where the elegant, heavily embroidered cloak worn by the man seen from the back recalls several analogous Pisanello studies in the Ambrosiana and the British Museum, but most of all the famous drawing in the Louvre with which it has rightly been connected [Plates 24, 25, and 28]. Certainly, the mass of the garment, soft in the drawing, is stiffer in the painting, and the drawing shows more elegant lines in comparison with the predominantly decorative effect of the painted one, but this could be largely due to the difference in media, in addition, of

99

course, to the difference in quality between the two painters. Nevertheless, this figure and those that immediately surround it form by far the most interesting group in the *Adoration*. The young man on the left with the three-tiered hat seems to derive his absorbed expression from the celebrated portrait of Piccinino [Plate 109] modeled by Pisanello for one of his medals. And again, two faces at the right of the blond-haired figure in the cloak have the revealing quality that is fundamental for understanding their author's artistic personality. Though they stand close together, a strong contrast is established between them, comparable to the opposition that explodes in the group of courtiers in *The Legend of Saint George*. The elder, effectively portrayed with an outstanding sense of realism, and characterized by strong, penetrating strokes, is engrossed in thought, while the young man has an expressive perfection that it is difficult to refer to a real model. This contrast and the vague hint of expressionism clearly show Nordic influence, but the expressionism is different from the narrative expressiveness that sometimes appears in Domenico Veneziano's work, particularly in the *Miracle of Saint Zenobia*, in the Fitzwilliam Museum, which shows, if anything, affinities with the language of Vecchietta. In the barely suggested expressionism of the Berlin painting, and most of all in the face of the young man just mentioned, the strokes speak of a stylistic audacity revealed not in the emotion, but in the enchanted features of a face lightly overshadowed with worry. There are, however, links with Domenico Veneziano—to be more exact, with the group standing behind the Saint in his *Miracle of Saint Zenobia*—in a few of the figures closest to the three kings, and particularly in those that press forward to see the Infant Jesus, even though the faces are more fixed and colder than those in Domenico's predella.

The scene's culminating passage is composed of the three characteristic figures of Saint Joseph (derived from Uccello), the abstracted Virgin, and the old, kneeling king whose robe falls in folds of masterly elegance.

The Virgin's face does not seem to recall stylistically any woman's face by Domenico; we have come a long way from the satisfied but diaphanous expressions of his Madonnas. The Virgin in the Berlin painting is not fully defined and remains fixed in virginal demureness. The kneeling king repeats a motif that was then quite widespread. The entire group and the procession should be compared, not with Masaccio's *Adoration*, also in Berlin, but rather with Uccello's *Adoration*, now in the Seminario Maggiore, Cestello.

Behind the stable there is a young blackamoor, of a snaky elegance that Domenico would never have dared invent, sitting on a camel which immediately recalls an identical Pisanello drawing in the Louvre.[129] On the roof itself stands a peacock, treated in Pisanello's natural-

157 - PORTRAIT OF ALFONSO OF ARAGON (plaque) - *Metropolitan Museum of Art* - NEW YORK

158 - MEDAL OF ALFONSO OF ARAGON (reverse with the angel in a carriage) - signed copy (above)
National Gallery of Art - WASHINGTON, D. C.; unsigned copy (below) - *Bibliothèque Nationale* - PARIS

159 - MEDAL OF INIGO D'AVALOS (obverse) - *Museum* - BERLIN

160 - MEDAL OF INIGO D'AVALOS (reverse) - *Museum* - BERLIN

istic vein, but in coloring and in its petulant flaunting in the foreground very similar to its elegant brother in Stefano da Verona's *Adoration*. The entire scene is set in a meadow alive with animals and small flowering plants, luminous like flickering flames, conceived in a way dear to Paolo Uccello's fancy.[130] We are now in the most extraordinary and, in some ways, most significant part of the work: the landscape. This begins as a fertile countryside, embellished with houses and castles, peopled with varied creatures, and gradually fades in illusory perspective into a succession of hills, so that things seem to lose their direction, while the colors, paling toward the horizon, merge landscape and sky. There is an obvious relationship between this landscape and the very similar ones concocted by Pisanello in his famous late drawing of a *Fantastic Landscape* and on the reverse of the Inigo d'Avalos medal [Plates 161, 160]. The link is strengthened by the arrangement of the hills in all three works, set one behind the other in accordance with a distinctive formula of certain Flemish aerial perspectives, which creates depth by means of a succession of elements. This is a "naturalistic" landscape, to which all the scene remains attached, not the spatially intellectualized and metaphysical landscape that might have been imagined, for instance, by central Italian painters or artists still linked to the tradition of Giotto or Sienese Byzantine, or by the fifteenth-century Tuscan artists who followed the new rules of perspective, no less intellectualized and metaphysical. Here we have a vision of nature and things that unites and blends everything by means of the bands of light, identified with the innumerable colors, which are reflected in the atmosphere to give a naturalistic sense of communion between nature and people. The landscape itself leads us back, through its pantheist naturalistic inspiration, to those Flemish landscapes, often similarly conceived, by Jan van Eyck, the Master of Flémalle, Roger van der Weyden, Memling, and Bouts. The lake in particular, inserted like a sheet of mother-of-pearl between the alpine hills and the rocky outcrop on the right, is Nordic in conception, though it lacks the transforming polish of northern and Flemish painting. On its shore is a gallows with a hanged man, a motif particularly familiar to Pisanello (*The Legend of Saint George*) and to Uccello (*Nativity* of the San Martino alla Scala Hospital). The birds wheeling round above, though recalling Pisanello, lack his sensitive graphic execution.

These, then, are the main pointers given us by the pictorial language in the Berlin painting; they differ in every respect, so that they can hardly be referred to a single, well-determined artistic personality, even to one in a formative, or crystallizing phase. At various times they recall principally the influences of Paolo Uccello, Pisanello, Flemish artists, and Domenico Veneziano.

But the painting still contains one basic characteristic that convinces one that it must not be attributed to a Tuscan-trained artist and stil less to Domenico Veneziano. The most striking feature of the *Adoration* is not so much the number of details, alluding to as many different styles, as it is the absence of the geometrical and metaphysical conception proper to Tuscan painting, which arranges *a priori* the various elements of a painting according to "arbitrary" relationships understood in the context of a life, not of participation but of particularized absolutes.[131] The fact that formal values may be superior in this sphere should only concern us marginally, as it has so far.

The main advantage of an attribution to Domenico Veneziano is that it would resolve the stylistic contrasts, which would then be considered the result of the presence, in a Tuscan work, of details and a general conception that are pre-eminently Nordic. On these terms Domenico, who may really have come originally from Venice, could be the favored candidate for the authorship of the painting. Second, an attribution to Domenico Veneziano, in spite of all the doubts it would arouse, could reveal the unknown source of his artistic training. Apart from the *Madonna dei Carnesecchi*, the only work that is certainly due to his hand is the Santa Lucia de' Magnoli altarpiece, now in the Uffizi [Fig. 20], and this cannot in itself constitute a sufficient basis for all other suppositions. In any case, the *Adoration* could only be assigned acceptably to a youthful period of Veneziano's career. There could be no justification for referring this work to a mature phase of the artist's working life, since a "return" to forms supposedly familiar to him during his hypothetical youth would only have been possible if it resulted from a sudden, complete change in style, and this cannot be accepted because, among other reasons, no poetic motivations can be found to bear out the theory. In any case, the painting is definitely not qualitatively superior to the other works of Veneziano. But the presence of certain Uccello influences, which for stylistic reasons would have been impossible between 1430 and 1440 prevents its attribution to a youthful period. If, however, we do consider the Berlin painting as Domenico's work, we can reconstruct the biography of (the young, let us say) Domenico Veneziano. After a childhood spent in the limpid, changing atmosphere of the Lagoon, he became expert in Flemish-style coloring and was fired with enthusiasm for Pisanello's fabulous world. Then he suddenly appeared in central Italy, where he was influenced by a host of other painters: Paolo Uccello, Masaccio, Andrea del Castagno, Fra Angelico, Filippo Lippi—where, in short, he absorbed such an infinity of continuous and ever-present influences that it is impossible to see how a personality as concrete and well-defined as Domenico Veneziano's could have formed.

Every aspect of Domenico's work is contained in the Santa Lucia de' Magnoli altarpiece: it is marked by the transparency of coloring that lightens volumes and the motionless sweetness common to Fra Angelico and Piero della Francesca, but never by Andrea del Castagno's languishing suffering, which Domenico, even when he seems to emulate him, does not achieve or indeed try to achieve. There is, finally, the *a priori* conception of metaphysical space which renders the figures more than human, situating them among the rational architectures and the symmetrical porcelainlike frames that surround the protagonists in an atmosphere of subtle, peaceful musicality. This was a first, important step toward the realization of the elevated forms of Piero della Francesca, which were, however, to correspond to very different concepts. Domenico's figures stand fixed in a state of superlative abstraction, though bound up in an appearance of solidity that sets them distinctly apart from the Borgo San Sepolcro painter. And yet Domenico takes a fundamentally geometrical and metaphysical view of space, and combines it with the simultaneous dissolution and exaltation of color that need not be equated with the chromatic tints of the Lagoon.

Color becomes clearer in obedience to the dominating demands of space: it is less consistent and alive, it counts far less in defining figures and, becoming sublimated, it leaves space to absorb all individuality along its preconceived lines. Thus the definition of each form becomes dependent on this absorption of color in space.

All this is a long way from the Berlin painting with its palpable, rich chromaticism, its empirical conception of space, its naturalistic spirit, and its singularly individual sketches. Some elements in it that could not have occurred outside the second half of the fifteenth century might cause one to attribute the work to the mature period of Domenico's career. Yet its quality, not particularly high, and above all its distance from the style and the pictorial language of works definitely executed by Domenico cannot support the theory of a sudden regression and change of procedures on the artist's part.

Based on the Uccello-inspired elements in the painting, the attribution to a follower of Paolo Uccello was no means ill-considered, and even less so was its assignment to a painter from Verona. The spatial structure of the work reveals a Nordic conception that could only have been the result of a systematic assimilation of a Nordic culture over a considerable time. A northern painter, close to Pisanello for some years before moving to Tuscany, must then be the author of the *Adoration*. However, he remained foreign to the cultural activities of the humanist movement, which we have already outlined, and adopted only some of the external characteristics of Tuscan art.

On the other hand, though numerous traces of Pisanello have been pointed out, there can no longer be any justification for the old attribution to this master: not because signs of a new feeling for space show in the Berlin painting (as we have mentioned, this would correspond better to the Flemish Renaissance), nor because it contains Tuscan elements which were probably not unknown to Pisanello, but because the style, eclectic and rather diffuse, and the individual structures in the painting are inferior in quality to Pisanello's production and so, in spite of obvious parallels, cannot belong to it.

It is not the particular manner of constructing space that rules out Pisanello for the *Adoration*; for one thing, the empirical space realized in the painting leads to Flanders rather than to Tuscany and is probably closer to Pisanello than to the Florentine schools. Pisanello remained apart from the latter, not because he was incapable of comprehending and assimilating the diagrammatic procedures of the new art, but because they were associated with a grammar of feeling that was not his, that he could follow and understand but not make his own. While he assimilated Tuscan formal plasticity into his medals, even there Gothic pathos prevailed. The northern artist could not have avoided knowing—we maintain, by direct experience—the innovations that were fermenting in Tuscany and studying them, with a view to adopting their most original aspects. But Pisanello could not adopt these new technical means, for when they were used and further developed by an accomplished artist they came to constitute the basis and directing force for the elaboration of a particular new poetic repertory that could be called humanist-individualist, in spite of the fact that it did not by any means throw light on all aspects of fifteenth-century humanism. Though Pisanello wanted to work in terms of the widest possible human reality, he nonetheless used outside modes of expression simply to offset more effectively his personal poetic vision and the particular spiritual forces underlying his humanity. It may seem, then, that he preferred to stay locked up among the *schemata* of Late Gothic, which were by then becoming more stereotyped every day. On the contrary, however, he renewed their substance in his supreme struggle to charge them with the greatest possible meaning. His importance is in no way diminished by the fact that he was not fully understood and supported in his work and his creative vision. In fact, he gave Gothic art an impetus that deserved a better fate, but, by the same token, he was bound to remain an isolated figure, so that his personality, for all its greatness, could do nothing to halt the inexorable gravitation of art toward the clamorous advance of Tuscan innovations.

161 - STUDY OF A FANTASTIC LANDSCAPE - *Louvre* - PARIS

162 - STUDY OF FIGURES IN COSTUME - *British Museum* - London

163 - STUDY OF A WOLF; STUDY OF A WILDCAT - *Louvre* - PARIS

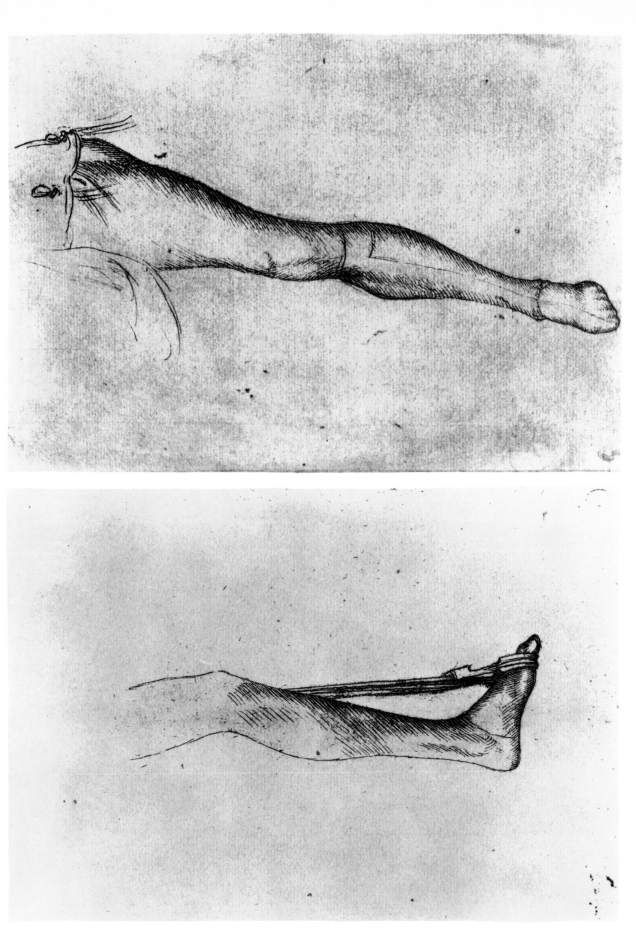

165 - STUDY OF LYNXES - *Louvre* - Paris

166 - STUDY OF HORSES AND A PAGE - *Louvre* - PARIS

167 - STUDY OF A FALCON - *Louvre* - Paris

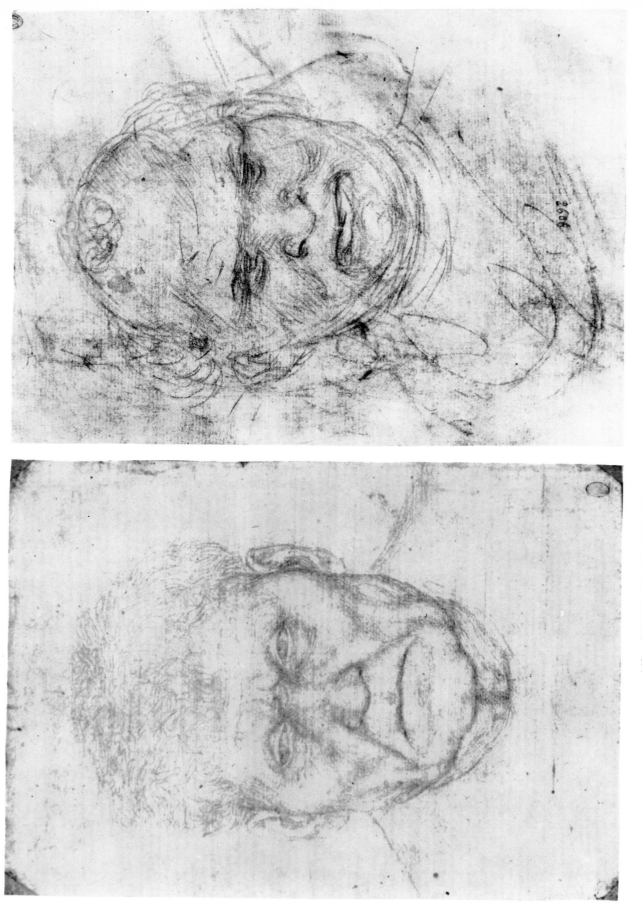

168 - STUDY OF AN OLD MAN; STUDY OF A FAT MAN - *Louvre* - PARIS

169 - STUDY OF TWO LANDSCAPES WITH FIGURES - *Louvre* - Paris

170 - STUDY OF A MAN'S HEAD - *Louvre* - Paris

171 - STUDY OF PEACOCKS - *Louvre* - PARIS

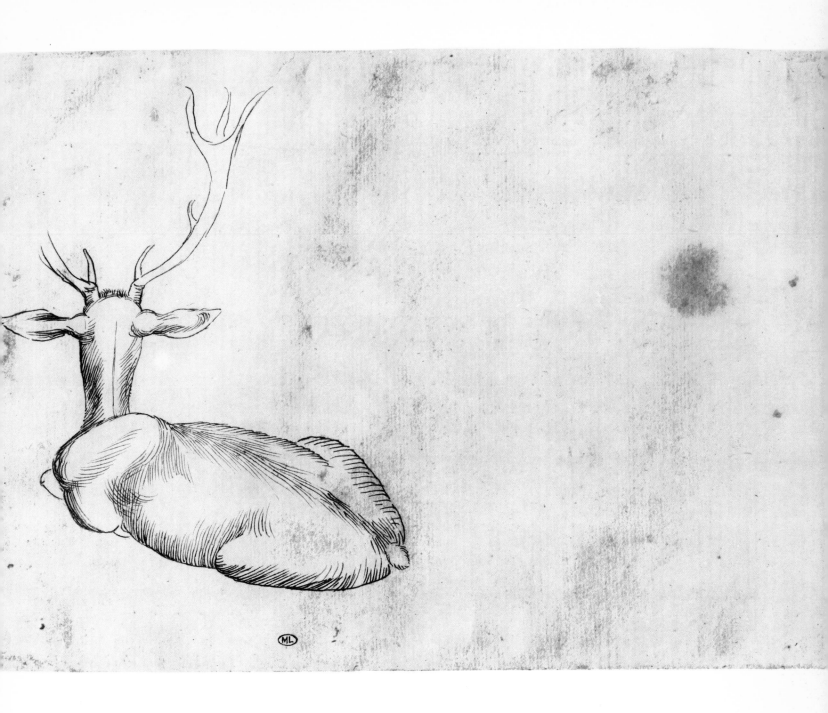

172 - STUDY OF A RECUMBENT DEER - *Louvre* - Paris

173 - STUDY OF THE MADONNA SUCKLING THE CHILD - *Louvre* - Paris

NOTES

1. As is more fully described in the catalogue of works, the fresco was removed and placed first in the Museo di Castelvecchio, and then in the Church of San Giorgetto in Verona.

2. "The image of the desert, that is, of horizontal representation, alternates with the image of the abyss, that is, of vertical representation." Translated from J. HUIZINGA, *The Waning of the Middle Ages.*

3. Evidently Pisanello transposed the fantastic version of the episode contained in the *Golden Legend* of Jacopo da Varagine into a more complex and symbolic key. Thus in the fresco the cruelty of the dragon appears closely linked to the condition of the figures: fatality is replaced by responsibility (shown in the cruel aspect of some of the faces). Moreover, in the painting the princess is completely separated from the knight, whereas in Jacopo's version the maiden, anxious about the saint's fate, pleads with him *"Bone miles mecum non pereas, sufficit enim si sola peream, nam me liberare non posses et mecum perires. Dum haec loqueretur ecce draco veniens caput de lacu levavit. Tunc puella irembacta dixit: Juge bone domine fuge velociter."* ("'O good soldier, do not die with me; for it is enough that I die alone, for you could not free me even if you were to perish with me.' While she was speaking, behold a dragon came and raised its head from the lake. Then the maiden, trembling, said 'Noble lord, flee quickly.'")

4. This separation of one figure from the rest of the composition (which is not without consequences) is one of the most characteristic features of Pisanello's art. Here, as in the *Apparition,* the painter was still composing without relating his figures "psychologically." As G. F. HILL (*Pisanello,* London, 1905, p. 154) suggests, he may have been passing through a transitional phase between the polyptych and the "composed" single canvas.

5. The lack of a precise solution, indeed the vague, general definition of "confused reality," only underlines the romantic nature of the work; it in no way limits its importance. For Pisanello this vague, undefined reality is not a mark of romanticism as an end in itself; this reality is only conditional, glimpsed in its most critical moment before the artist impresses on it the necessity of solution.

6. A very similar representation is to be found on one of the outer back walls of the transept of the Church of San Michele in Pavia (Fig. 7); Pisanello probably saw it during a visit to the Lombard city.

7. The figure of the princess and the massive bulk of the horses are indisputable proof of a more prominent, less traditional plastic sense; especially in the large horse in the center, so different from certain glossy Altichiero horses, matter expands with explosive vitality, imposing itself brutally on the surrounding space.

8. Pisanello's fame was widespread among his contemporaries; only this could explain the numerous poems, epigrams, and sonnets in Latin and Italian dedicated to him by such eminent poets of the time as Dati, Guarino, Basinio, Ulisse, Angiolo Galli, Tito Vespasiano Strozzi, and Porcellio. The relevant extracts are reprinted by A. Venturi in *Le Vite dei più eccellenti pittori, scultori e architetti scritte da Giorgio Vasari; Gentile da Fabriano e il Pisanello,* Florence, 1896, *passim.* (Hereinafter referred to as VASARI-VENTURI.)

9. In the register of Veronese citizens contained in the "Descriptio" (cf. note 40), one of the entries is "Bartolomeo de la Levada, brother-in-law of the rebellious painter Pisano."

10. The most important biographical studies are VASARI-VENTURI, *op.cit.,* G. BIADEGO, "Pisanus Pictor", in *Atti del Reale Istituto Veneto di Scienze, Lettere ed Arti,* Notes I-VI, 1908, 1909, 1910, 1913; and R. BRENZONI, *Pisanello,* Florence, 1952.

11. Cf. L. TESTI, "Vittore Pisanello o Pisanus Pictor," in *Rassegna d'Arte,* 1910. A. H. MARTINIE (*Pisanello,* Paris, 1930, pp. 6-12) throws no further light on the doubts advanced after Brenzoni's discoveries.

12. The traditional name of Vettore was thus removed from the crucial testimony, in spite of the fact that Vasari, who transmitted the name, had heard it from the Veronese friar Marco de' Medici who lived in the seventeenth century, in precisely that church of Sant'Anastasia where Pisanello had painted his masterpiece. The same name appears inexplicably in the works of the very erudite Giovio, who called Pisanello Vettore in 1551, one year after the publication of Vasari's *Lives.* Giovio had an extensive collection of Pisanello medals, and had been familiar with the information later published by Vasari. Cf. TESTI, *op.cit.* p. 132.

13. As early as 1909, Giuseppe Biadego pointed out, in his second note on "*Pisanus Pictor,*" that art criticism had become "conditioned." He meant by this that critics often showed complete indifference to even the most fruitful works, while foreign specialists hastened to attribute them to determined "schools." We must not forget the particularly fierce reservations made by TESTI (*op. cit.*) and by VENTURI himself in *L'Arte* (1908, pp. 467 et seq.; 1910, pp. 74-5) when appraising Biadego's valuable research. However, this hidebound mental attitude must not be held responsible for the fact that a most interesting piece of information passed unobserved six years earlier. In an article in *L'Arte* in 1902, ZIPPEL points out that in the oration "*pro nepote Galeotti Assassini*" (which is largely devoted to singing the praises of Galeotto degli Assassini, a favored member of the Este court), the man of letters Ludovico Carbone states: "*Plenum enim studiolum meum mille picturis, signis, tabulis, imaginibus. Nunquam illam Leonelli aspicio, quam Antonius Pisanus effinxit, quin lacrymae ad oculos veniant: ita illius*

humanissimos gestus imitatur." ("For my study is filled with a thousand pictures and paintings and medals and panels. I never look on the portrait of Lionello, which Antonius Pisanus executed, without the tears coming to my eyes, his gestures are so faithfully portrayed.") Thus before Biadego made his discoveries known, this document from the second half of the fifteenth century, mentioning the painter Antonius Pisanus who was working at the court of Lionello d'Este, had been published. Yet nobody noticed the contradiction between this "Antonius" and the traditional "Vettore," and even long after Biadego's contributions were published, some art critics continued to talk of "Vettore Pisanello" (perhaps just because of their hidebound mental attitude).

14. *"Opera di Vettor Pisanello del San Vi Veronese MCCCCXI"* is inscribed on the painting of the *Madonna and Child with Saint John the Baptist and Saint Catherine* in the Berlin Museum; this may have been taken as proof of the artist's name, but many years before Pisanello's real first name was discovered, this inscription was shown to be apocryphal by W. BODE and H. VON TSCHUDI, "Anbetung der Könige von Vittore Pisano und die Madonna mit Heiligen aus dem Besitz des Cav. Dal Pozzo," in *Jahrbuch der Königlich Preussischen Kunstsammlungen*, Vol. VI, (Berlin, 1885). DAL POZZO cites the painting as a work of Pisano da Bartolomeo in his *Le Vite dei Pittori, degli Scultori ed Architetti veronesi* (1718).

15. According to L. COLETTI (*Pisanello*, Milan, 1953, p. 29).

16. "Cum hoc sit quod ser PUCINUS CONDAM JOHANNIS DE CERETO CIVIS ET HABITATOR IN CIVITATE PISSARU IN CAMPO S. SILVESTRI IN DOMO HABITACIONIS IPSIUS TESTATORIS veniens ad mortem suum ultimum condiderit testamentum nuncupativum et in quo dominam Elisabeta, eius uxorem et filiam condam Nicolai Zuperii de S. Paulo Verone donam et dominam usufructuariam omnium bonorum suorum donec vidua vixerit reliquit et esse voluit et filios communes ipsius domine et testatoris ipsius custodire voluerit, SUUM AUTEM SIBI UNIVERSALEM HEREDEM INSTITUIT ANTHONIUM EIUS FILIUM LEGIPTIMUM ET NATURALEM ET DICTE DOMINE ELISABETE, de quo quindem testamento aparuit ibidem publicum instrumentum scriptum sub signo et nomine Fanucii notarii filii quondam Jacobi civis Pissani ANNO MILLESIMO TRECENTESIMO NONAGESIMO QUINTO indictione tertia DIE VIGESIMO SECUNDO NOVEMBRIS vissum et lectum per me Andream notarium infrascriptum in presentia suprascriptorum testium et coram infrascriptio domino Judice ad intelligentiam infrascriptarum partium; cumque sit quod ipsa domina Elisabeta administraverit et ad eius manus pervenerint tot de bonis mobillibus que fuere dicti condam ser Pucini que capiebant et ascendebant et capiunt et ascendunt ad summam sexcentorum ducatorum auri prout ipsa domina Elisabeta petente instante et requirente dicto magistro Anthonio eius fillio et herede predicto in presentia suprascriptorum testium et mei notarii infrascripti et coram dicto domino Judice et in eius presentia sic dixit et sponte et ex certa sua scientia et non alliquo errore iuris vel facti ducta confessa fuit; et exinde ipsa domina Elisabeta constituta coram egregio et sapiente iurisperito domino Jacobo de Ronerio de Tervixio Judice Communis Verone ad banchum Grifonis tempore regiminis magnifici viri domini Johannis Contareno de Venetiis pro Serenissima et excelsa ducali dominatione Venetiarum in Verona et suo districtu hon (*lacuna*) Potestatis sedente pro tribunali in dicta domo subtus lodiam penes ortum super

una catedra palearum quem lucum pro suo loco iuridico apto et honesto ad hunc actum celebrandum et pro honestate dicte domine ellegit et elligit, et volens agnoscere bonam fidem erga MAGISTRUM ANTHONIUM DICTUM PISANELUM EIUS FILLIUM ET HEREDEM PREDICTUM PICTOREM EGREGIUM per solemnem stipulacionem per se et suos heredes promisit dicto magistro Anthonio eius fillio ibidem presenti pro se et suis heredibus stipulanti et recipienti dare solvere et cum effectu numerare dicto magistro Antonio eius filio sexcentum ducatos auri pro valore dictarum bonorum, quot sic late valebant prout ipsa domina dixit et confessa fuit, hinc ad tres menses proxime futuros et ab inde in antea ad omnem ipsius magistri Anthonii sive sui legitimi nuntii voluntatem et requisicionem; et renunciavit dicta domina Elisabeta in predictis et circa predicta exceptioni dolli malli in factum actioni conditioni indebiti sine causa vel ex iniusta et non vera causa vis metusve fraudis deceptionis simulacionis contractus et non sic facte dicte promissionis et non sic actorum omnium et singulorum predictorum, nec non renunciavit statuto Communis Verone posito in volumine Statutorum in secundo libro capitulis CLXXXI sub rubrica de dotibus solvendis. Qui quindem magister Anthonius volens revereri et cum sincera caritate se genere erga matrem suam predictam, dictam primissionem et obligacionem acceptavit; hoc tamen adiecto quod ipse magister Anthonius nolebat compelere dictam suam matrem nec quod sui heredes compelant ad solvendum alliquid de dicta quantitate denariorum donec ipsa vixerit et steterit in humanis, sed post mortem suam volebat dictam obligacionem et promissionem esse salvam et omne suum ius contra bona et jura dicte sue matris usque ad integram satisfacionem omnium predictorum denariorum." Published in G. BIADEGO, *op. cit.* 1910, pp. 1052-53.

17. In his first note on *"Pisanus pictor,"* Biadego, basing himself on a document of 1422 which showed that Anthonius Pisanus was then 36 years old, maintained that the painter was born in 1397. However, he later (Note V) traced another document which not only revealed the true name of Pisanello's father, but also enabled Biadego to prove the birth date of 1397 inaccurate. The birth could not have happened later than 1395, since according to the new document, the painter was already born by that year.

18. Brenzoni has exhaustively covered this question. (R. BRENZONI, *op. cit.*, pp. 43-45).

19. It must be supposed that the marriage of Puccio and Isabetta took place in Verona, the bride's native town, rather than in Pisa, because it was the first marriage of Isabetta, who later remarried twice.

20. "There is no lack of other Pisanellos in the registers of Verona for the fifteenth century. For 1443 we find: *Andreas Pisanellus* merziarius ex. lbr. o.s. duodecim, lb. o.s. XII (1443. Estimum Communis Verone omnium Civium ecc. in campione De S. Johanne ad Forum c. 56)." In another for 1447 we read: *"D. Agnes ux. Pisanelli a Magatellis* est l.o.s. octo l.b o.s. VIII (Campionum Estimi Communis Verone anni MCCCCXLVII. De S. Johanne ad Forum)." Translated from TESTI, *op. cit.*, p. 135, note 28.

21. But most frequently he is referred to as Pisano de Verona. Cf. G. BIADEGO, *op. cit.* (1908), p. 839.

22. According to the most widespread opinion, Pisano was in Venice between 1415 and 1422, probably working first as a collaborator with Gentile. Biadego (Note II) fixes Pisanello's period of greatest activity in Venice between 1422 and 1427. Bartolomeo Facio and Francesco Sansovino mention the frescoes executed by Pisanello.

23. Cf. L. GRASSI, *Tutta la pittura di Gentile da Fabriano*, Milan 1953, pp. 24-25. But Destrée had already ruled out the possibility of any decisive influence of Pisanello on Gentile da Fabriano (J. DESTRÉE, *Notes sur les primitifs italiens. Sur quelques peintres de Toscane*, Brussels-Florence, 1899, p. 23).

24. Cf. Note 16.

25. Pisanello's stay in Rome is attested by various documents. Cf. E. MÜNTZ, *Les arts à la Cour des Papes pendant le XVe et le XVIe Siècle*, Ière partie, Paris, 1878, p. 47; VASARI-VENTURI, *op. cit.*, p. 33; R. BRENZONI, *op. cit.*, pp. 66-67.

26. Cf. B. DEGENHART, *Pisanello*, Turin, 1945, pp. 15-30.

27. Cf. G. VASARI, *Le Vite*, Milan, 1942 edition, p. 764.

28. According to Vasari, Pope Martin V met Pisanello in Florence and took him to Rome to paint frescoes in San Giovanni in Laterano. The meeting must therefore have taken place in 1419 or 1420. Apart from the improbability of such an encounter in Florence, it is possible that Vasari may have confused the issue by making Pisanello the recipient of the invitation sent by the Pope to Gentile da Fabriano at the same time; this invitation is vouched for by a letter written to Gentile, published by A. ZONGHI in *Repertorio dell'antico archivio comunale di Fano*, Fano, 1888.

29. In March 1420, Gentile da Fabriano was in Fabriano (Martin V left Florence on September 9, 1420); in 1422 he was in Florence, in 1425 in Siena and Orvieto, in Siena once more in 1426, and not until 1427 in Rome. Therefore we cannot conclude that Gentile went to Rome for a short while (from late 1420 till 1422) and then interrupted his work to stay away from the papal city for a good five years.

30. Cf. B. DEGENHART, *op. cit.*, p. 30; L. COLETTI, *op. cit.*, p. 29.

31. A document dated May, 1433, in the Lateran Archives, contains the following: "suppelectibus emptis tunc per capitulum Magistro Gentili q̄ postea remanserunt Magistro pisan̄ pictori venditis demum per dictum capitulum." ("... materials purchased for Master Gentile and then transmitted to Master Pisanus and sold on his behalf. ...")

32. Payments to Pisanello for his paintings in San Giovanni in Laterano are recorded in several documents (published by E. MÜNTZ, *op. cit.*, p. 47) covering the period from April, 1431 to February, 1432: "[April 18, 1431] ... Item die 18 dicti mensis. flor. auri de camera quadraginta solutos magistro Pisanello pictorj pro picturis per eum factis et fiendis in ecclesia sancti Johannis lateranensis proparte suae provisionis ..." (Mandates 1430-1434, sheet 14 v°). "[November 27, 1431] ... provido viro mag stro Pisano pictori in ecclesia lateranensi florenos auri de camera quinquaginta, in deductionem sui salarii et mercedes ratione pict[urae] dictae ecclesiae" (marked in the margin: *pro Pisanello*. Mandates 1430-1434, sheet 33). "[late February, 1432] ... Curcumspecto viro magistro Pisano pictori ecclesiae sancti Johannis lateranensis pro complemento provisionis et salarii sui ratione dictae picturae flor. aurj de camera septagintacinque" (marked in the margin: *pro magistro pisano picturj*. Mandates, sheet 42). (Published in VASARI-VENTURI, *op. cit.*, p. 33).
But the painter certainly stayed in Rome until July, 1432, when Eugene IV granted him the following safe-conduct pass to leave the city: "Littera passus pro Pisanello pictore.
"Eugenius etc. Universis et singulis ad quod presentes nostre littere pervenerint, salutem et apost. benedictionem, cum dilectus filius Pisanellus pictor familiaris

noster qui ad presens in Alma Urbe commoratur habeat aliquando pro diversis negociis ad diversas Ytalie partes se conferre. Nos cupientes eundem Pisanellum cum sociis et familiaribus usque ad numerum sex equestribus vel pedestribus equis rebus et bonis suis omnibus in eundo stando et redeundo plena ubique securitate atque immunitate gaudere Universitatem vestram et vestrum singulos requirimus et hortamur in domino Subditis nostris et gentium armigerum Capitaneis ubicunque ad nostra et ecclesie stipendia militantibus stricte precipiendo mandamus, quatinus ipsum Pisanellum cum sociis familiaribus equestribus vel pedestribus rebus et omnibus bonis suis predictis per nostram et vestram civitates castra villas territoria passus portus pontes flumina et loca qualiter tam per aquam tam per terram absque solucione alicuius passagii, dacii vel gabelle angarii pangarii etc. libere promittatis, nullamque sibi familiaribus et sociis predictis in personis rebus vel bonis eorum inferatis molestiam etc... quin ymo dictum Pisanellum benigne recommendatum habentes et gracia benivolerent pertractantes, sibi pro se et familiaribus predictis quociens requisiti fueritis ab eodem de sicuro transitu recepta et salvocunductu sic liberaliter providere curetis quod vestra exinde devocio apud nos et sedem predictam merito veniat commendanda etc ... "Dat. Rome apud Sanctum petrum. Anno Incarnacionis dominice MoCCCCmo ... VII kalendas Augusti, Pontif. nostri Anno secundo." As can be seen, this document (Archivio Segreto Vaticano, Registro. Eugenii IV n° 372 f. 53 r°.) published in VASARI-VENTURI (*op. cit.*, p. 36) demands safe conduct for Pisanello and "up to six companions on horse or on foot with all their horses, goods and belongings, on land or on water." The travelers are to be allowed to go to any part of Italy and are recommended to the grace and benevolence of "whom it may concern," while it is hinted that compliance with the request will be counted in favor of the respective authorities or rulers by the Vatican.

33. This is attested by a letter from Lionello to his brother Meliaduse, which says: "Pisanus omnium pictorum huiusce aetatis egregius cum ex roma ferrariam se contulisset tabulam quamdam sua manu pictam ultro mihi pollicitus est in qua Beatae Virginis imago erat. Et quoniam ipsa tabula romae apud quemdam ei familiarem erat; quamprimum veronam applicuisset, ad illum se litteras et in tuo dissessu nescio quid sim oblitus tibi, ut volui, dicere ... Quapropter si ut arbitror tibi tradita'est: eam tuto ad me mittas rogo. Illam enim mirum in modum videre cupio tum excellenti pictoris ingenio tum vero precipua Virginis devotione." Published in VASARI-VENTURI, *op. cit.*, p. 37. "Pisanus outstanding among all the painters of this age was to go from Rome to Verona with a picture painted by his hand, with the Blessed Virgin, intended for me. Yet in Rome the said painting was in the hands of some familiar of his; before he went to Verona, I do not know what I neglected to say ... it seems to me that you have made a mistake, and I ask you to send [the painting] to me, for I am eager to see this marvel, both for the skill of the excellent painter, and out of devotion to the Virgin."

34. "The Castle or Palace (which would be a more fitting name for it) was, as we have said, one of the finest buildings to be seen, but the Gallic fury ruined with its artillery its finest parts, on the park side. This room was large enough to house the entire court of any King or Emperor, and it is square in shape and has in the middle a great space well suited for jousts, tourneys and other princely amusements, with its archways that surround it above and below (as can still be seen) all with marble columns, and the stairs fashioned so that a man could ride his horse up them. The halls and chambers on the upper and lower floors are all vaulted and painted with various histories in diverse manners; the skies were coloured with finest azure, wherein were

placed all manner of beasts done in gold, like Lions, Leopards, Tigers, Greyhounds, Beagles, Stags, Boars, and others. Especially on the side overlooking the Park (which as I have said was ruined by the artillery of the French army on the 4th day of September in the year of Our Lord 1527) in which (as it was when I saw it whole) there was to be seen a great Saloon seventy feet long and twenty wide, all painted with most beautiful figures that represented hunting and fishing and jousts and other amusements of the Dukes and Duchesses of this State." Translated from S. BREVENTANO, *Istoria della Antichità, nobiltà et delle cose notabili della città di Pavia*, Pavia, 1570, Vol. I, p. 7.

35. "(Archivio di Stato in Modena Registro di Mandati 1434-36, a.c. 80 v.°) LEONELLUS; Mandato Illustris domini Leonelli Estensis etc. Vos factores generales domini dari et solvi faciatis .... famulo Pictoris Veronensis clarissimi ducatos duos auri, quos Idem dominus Leonellus sibi donari vult: quando ad ipsum dominum Leonellum famulus idem pisani nomine Divi Julji Cesaris effigiem detuit et presentavit." "AUGUSTINUS de VILLA *scripsit primo februarji 1435*" published in VASARI-VENTURI, *op. cit.*, p. 38. Thus we have a record of a gift of two gold ducats made to the painter, and of his presentation to Lionello of "the effigy of the divine Julius Caesar." Salmi (1957) traced direct derivations from Pisanello's lost painting of 1435, in a miniature (Fig. 15) in the copy of Plutarch's *Vitae Virorum illustrium* in the Biblioteca Malatestiana, Cesena (Ms. S. XVII, F. 29).

36. In a letter written in Rome on June 28, 1431, signed "Pisanus P." described by MÜNTZ (*op. cit.*, Vol. 1, p. 47), and belonging to the Fillon Collection in the nineteenth century, Pisanello appeals to Filippo Maria Visconti, asking him to wait till the end of October for the work he was to carry out for him, as he was very busy in a church (San Giovanni in Laterano). However, it is fairly unlikely that the work referred to was the medal Pisanello struck for the Milanese prince; it is highly improbable that the artist executed it without having his subject before his eyes. Therefore it must have been a painting and not the medal, which Pisanello struck later, probably in Milan in 1440.

37. Cf. R. BRENZONI, *op. cit.*, pp. 52-53.

38. (Archivio di Stato di Verona - Arch. Rettori Veneti N. 8 - Fasc. "Pro Simone Judeo" sheets 439-40v° and 441, dated October 17, 1441) "Stephanus quondam Bonacursi sartor de Clavica testis etc.... et vidit in domo dicti judei aliquos stipendiarios [... *lacuna*] et dum ipse testis et *Anthonius pictor vicinus* rogarent ipsos stipendiarios ne ita facerent quia pinera non erant judeorum sed civium, illi voluerunt verberare ipsum testem et dictum *Anthonius pictorum* etc. ... M. Johannes marangonus de Tridento de contrata Ponte Petre [... *lacuna*] interrogatus quibus presentibus et quo tempore respondit quod multi erant presentes de quorum nominibus non recordatur nisi de *Antonio pictore*, de tempore quo supra." Published in R. BRENZONI, *op. cit.*, pp. 52-53.

39. Bartolomeo della Levata, son of the lawyer Andrea, married Pisanello's stepsister Bona.

40. The "Descriptio" was sent to the Council of Ten in July, 1441. Among its contents is the register of "Citizens of Verona who came with the Marquis of Mantua when he entered Verona and thus did solicit his favors against the Signoria and retreated with him when he was routed." In this register we find "Pisano the painter plotting evil in the house of Andrea della Levada." (Archivio di Stato di Venezia, sheet 182 v° of register 12, Misti, Consiglio dei Dieci.)

41. Shortly before the hall was destroyed, Filippo Andreasi and Luca Fancelli sent the following letters to the Marquis of Mantua (translated from the texts published by ROSSI in *Archivio Storico dell'Arte*, 1888, p. 455): "Most illustrious Lord—last evening toward the first hour of the night a keystone and part of the roof of the Pisanello room did fall. The ribs that remain standing, as saith Job, are but set into the walls and are insecure. Early this morning I went with Luca to have him do all necessary that the rest might not fall into ruin: he will not fail to preserve and restore it. I recommend myself to the graces of your Lordship. Mantua, 15th December, 1480. My illustrious Lordship, your faithful servant Philippus de Andreasis."
"My most illustrious Lordship: This day spent in anguish lest the roof fall in the white room. We did relieve it of a great weight of tiles and as I believe you are informed, a rib of the vault in the Pisanello room did fall with a part of the ceiling because the said ribs were added in the past and were not set directly into the walls, with no support whatever. I am having the ceiling propped up and raised so that no more may fall, then your Lordship will please to instruct me what is to be done and I will inform you what other steps are necessary, I recommend myself to your graces. Mantua, 15th December, 1480, your humble servant Luca of Florence."

42. Evidence of this is found in the decision of the Council of Ten, dated October 17, 1442, which confined Antonio Pisano to Venice "for foul dishonest words spoken in Mantua with lord Ludovico Gonzaga, proved by the writings read before this council."

43. The relevant document was published by G. BISCARO in *Archivio Storico Lombardo*, 1911, p. 171.
"1440, die Mercurii, XI mensis madii [... *lacuna* ...] Actum Mediolani, in aula prefati Illustrissimi principis et excellentissimi d.d. duci M.sita in platea arenghi, presentibus—Pisano de Verona fg. Puzii habitatore dicte civitatis Mantue omnibus testibus etc." (Arch. Not. di Milano, Imbreviature del notaio Dionisio de Cermenate).

44. In the Este Library Codex, "*Rime di Petrarca e di altri*" there is a sonnet by Ulisse mentioning the contest between Pisanello and Bellini, which ended in the latter's favor:
"ULIXIS. PRO INSIGNI CERTAMINE"
"Quando il Pisan fra le famose imprese
sargumento cuntender cum natura
e convertir limmagine in pictura
dil nuovo Illustre lionel marchese
Già consumato havea il sexto mese
per dare propria forma ala figura
alor fortuna sdegnosa che fura
lumane gloria cum diverse onfexe
Strinse che da la degna e salsa riva
Se movesse il Belin summo pictore
novelo fidia al nostro ziecho mondo
Che la sua vera effigie feze viva
ala sentenzia del paterno amore
onde lui primo e poi il Pisano secondo"
published in VASARI-VENTURI, *op. cit.*, p. 46.

45. "E adi XVJ de Agosto L. tre S/di quindice marchesine contate a Jacopo Marazo nochiero per suo nolo de condure a tre rimi da farrara a Mantoa el pisano depintore, come sue valixe e bixaze" (Archivio di Stato di Modena, Registro Camerale 1441, sheet 212). ("This day XVI of August the sum of fifteen pieces of gold paid to Jacopo Marazo helmsman for his pains in carrying in a trireme from Ferrara to Mantua the painter Pisano with his bags and baggage.")

46. Cf. Note 50.

47. According to BIADEGO (*op. cit.*, Note I, p. 849): "... he seems to have remained unmarried, although the register of 1433 mentions an infant daughter, Camilla, then four years old, of whom there is no further

trace." Further information about Camilla, but with no reference to her mother, is provided by the act of dowry of 1448, rediscovered and published by Brenzoni (*op. cit.*, p. 34), part of which is reproduced below: (Archivio di Stato di Verona—Antico Ufficio del Registro—Anno 1448—sheet 276 v°)
"Dos Domine Camilla uxoris Jacobu Turtois de Martinengo.
"In Christi nomine amen, Anno nativitatis ejusdem 1448 indic. XI die sabbati 8 mensis Junij Verona in contrata San Vitalis in domo habitationis infrascripte D. Camille presentibus, etc. [... *lacuna*] Egregius Vir Bartolomeus quondam D. Andree a Levata de S. Maria in Clavica Ver. procurator et procuratorio nomine infrascripti Antonij Pisano ad infrascr. constit. e instrumento ipsius procure rogato per Nicolaum notarium quondam ser Patri a Tabula de Feraria die 26 mensis januarij 1447 ind. X et registrato per Antonium notarium de Avento de Feraria predicta et comendato per litteras legalitatis ipsius comunitatis Ferarie scriptas die 2 aprilis prox. scriptis ibidem viso et producto et per me notarium infr. lecto titulo et nomine dotis domine Camille filie providi viri magistri Antonij Pisani pictoris quondam putij de pisis, et habitatoris de presenti Ferarie in contrata S. Marie de Vodo et sponse infrascripti Jacobi dicti Jacomini jure conditio salvo jure pensionis et renovationis debitis temporibus de bendarum Ecl.S. Marie in Organis Verone dedit tradidit et doptavit nomine et vice Domine Camille Jacobo dicto Jacomino quondam Tonini de Turtoijs de Martinengo districtus Pergami et habitateri Brixie in contrata S. Marie ad Carminum sponso suprascriptie domine Camille ibidem presenti pro sé et suis heredibus recipienti aquirenti et acceptanti unam petiam terre casalivam cum duabus domibus moratis coppatis et solaratis cum uno orto et uno revoltello jacentem Verone in contrata S. Pauli a duabus partibus via communis de ante et de retro, de ante usque ad Athesim, ab alia parte Antonius a Clodis in parte et in parte Guillelmus de Montagna, et ab alia parte Jacobus a Clodis frater suprascripti Antonij, etc."

48. "To Pisano of Verona in Ferrara.
"Distinguished friend—We have heard in a letter from you of your deliberations etc. And we reply that we have always the greatest pleasure in hearing news from you. As for the subsidy you ask for, the Lord be my witness that we have not the means to send it to you as we should like to. But as soon as possible we shall send you your due, for such is our intention.—Burgifortis, XI September, 1443." (Mantua, Gonzaga Archive, Correspondence of the Marquis).

49. "Pisano de Verona,
"We are satisfied to have received your letter regarding which we should like to know which rooms you used to occupy here at the court. At present you write requesting money etcetera. At the present moment know that we can give you nothing. But when you delay your departure to go to His Majesty, as you have decided, we shall see if it is possible to make provision for you, and if so we shall do it gladly, for it has always been our nature to satisfy those who are due anything from us—Mantue, XI March, 1444." (Mantua, Gonzaga Archive, Correspondence of the Marquis).

50. "Pro Pisano pictore de Verona. De consensu nostro. Mandato etc.—Rector generalis introitum prefacti domini faciat debitorem Pisanum de Verona pictorem de ducatis centum octuaginta in rationem soldorum octuaginta sex parcorum pro ducato erga creditores nonnulos quibus ipse Pisanus obligatus est, qui quindem ducati retinebuntur ad pagas suas et hoc absque fidejussione.
"Antonius Zeno prefati Illu. Domini scripsit XXVIJ martii 1441, ad eius mandatum." (Mantua, Gonzaga Archive, Register of Decrees).

51. Cf. Note 47.

52. This is shown in the documents reproduced below; the proposal to start proceedings against Antonio Pisano were approved by 10 votes to 4, 3 being declared null (so that the real margin was 3 votes). The proposal that his tongue be cut out was unanimously rejected (17 out of 17), but an equally unanimous vote decided his exile.
"1442, 17 octobris. Capita et advocatus comunis. Si videtur vobis per ea que dicta et lecta sunt, quod procedatur contra Antonium dictum Pisanum pictorem de Verona pro verbis turpibus et inonestis quibus usus fuit in Manthua cum domino Ludovico de Gonzaga sicut constat per scripturas lectas in isto consilio.
de precedendo ——————————————10
non   4 non sinceri 3.
Dominus dux consiliarij omnes et capita.
Volunt quod iste Antonius Pisanus pictor remaneat confinatus his Venetijs. Et non possit eidem dari licentia nisi per quatuor partes istius consilij, non possendo vendere bona sua sine licentia huius concilij, sed bene gaudeat bonis suis. Et si contrafecerit frangendo confinem tractetur pro rebelle et eius bona intelligantur confiscata in nostrum comune.
de parte ——————————————17
Advocatus comunis.
Vult quod iste Antonius die Veneris proximi XVIII presentis post nonam ducatur in mediam duarum colonarum in platea sancti marci et ibi amputetur eius lingua, Et postea baniatur perpetuo de Venetijs et de omnibus terris et locis nostris tam a parte terre quam maris ....
De parte ——————————————0, non sinceri ————————————0."
(Cons° X Misti R° 12, sheet 118.) Published in W. Bode, G. Gronau, D. F. v. Hadeln, *Archivalische Beiträge zur Geschichte der venezianischen Kunst aus dem Nachlass Gustav Ludwig*, Berlin, 1911, pp. 120-21.

53. This is vouched for in a letter the Marquis Ludovico sent to Gugliemo Gonzaga:
"Dearest cousin, as we hear that the painter Pisano is with you and says that he can no longer come to us, because he is under such orders and if he came all his goods would be seized, we should like you to intervene in his favor, if this be the case, and give us news soon in your next letter. Dat. Mantuae, February 27, 1443." Translated from A. Luzio and R. Renier, "Fidelfo e l'Umanesimo alla corte dei Gonzaga," in *Giornale Storico della Letteratura Italiana*, Vol. XVI, 1890, p. 131, Note 1.

54. "To Pisano of Verona in Ferrara.
"As we have heard that you took with you a painting of ours, of canvas on which is portrayed Our Lord, we send this horseman to take it, you should give it to him so wrapped that it may not be damaged, that he may bring it back to us.—Mantua, X November 1443" (Mantua, Gonzaga Archive, Correspondence of the Marquis).

55. In that year he is inscribed in the register of the San Paolo district of Verona; this is shown in a document published by Biadego (*op. cit.*, Note I, p. 805)

56. In 1449, Pisanello was at the Aragonese court, where honors and privileges were granted him, as is shown in a document of February 19, edited by Venturi (Vasari-Venturi, *op. cit.*, pp. 59-61) in which we read: "Cum itaque preclara multa eximia ac pene divina de singulari et picture et sculpture enee pisani arte ex multorum sermonibus accepissemus admirabamur prius singulare illius ingenium atque artem ubi vero illa perspecta sunt nobis et cognita studio in eum et amore incensi sumus quippe cum arbitremur hanc nostram suo etati, singulari artificio cedet Quapropter instituimus eum graciis et beneficiis prosequi ipsum itaque in

familiarem nostrum recipimus ceterorumque familiarum nostrorum numero ex certa scientia agregamus ita ut decetero illis honoribus favoribus muneribus dignitatibus et inmunitatibus pociatur et gaudeat quibus alii familiares nostri potiuntur et gaudent cui pisano ut in nostris serviciis honorifice commorari possit provisionem annuam ducatorum quatricentorum de carlenis argenti decem pro ducato quolibet computato ad nostrum beneplacitum tenore presencium de dicta nostra scientia motu proprio benignissime concedimus ac liberaliter elargimur exolvendam sibi aut legitimo eius procuratori pro eo a die data presencium in antea in consuetis tribus solucionibus in super quibuscumque pecuniis procenturis ex iuribus dirictibus salis interra francaville deprovincia Aprucii nobis et nostre curie debitis et spectantibus super quibus pecuniis provenientibus ex iuribus salis predicte terre eidem pisano dictam annuam provisionem ducatorum quatricentorum modo supradicto per presentes assignamus."

Also in 1449, Porcellio, poet and secretary of King Alfonso, composed the following elegy in honor of Pisanello.

"PORCELLUS VATES ROMANUS IN LAUDEM PISANI PICTORIS"

Si qua per ingenium et dignitos divina putamus
ingenii si nunc pictor et artis habet;
Ille es qui miras pingis, Pisano, figuras,
Perpetuaque viros vivere laude facis.
Naturam in rebus variis imitaris et artem,
Unde dicam Phidiae, Praxitelisque manus.
Humanis similes vultus atque ora loquentum
Effingit, videas pascere saepe feras;
Ac similes quondam natitare et acquora pisces,
Tendere iter celeres saepe videbis aves.
Vidi egomet sylvas, currentia flumina, montes,
surgere latrantes per cava tecta canes.
Quid loquar? effigies humanas aere refuso
Non hic mortales morte carere facit?
Aspice quam nitide Leonelli principis ora
Finxit, et anguigeri lamina vera Ducis.
Mille alias finxit mira novitate figuras.
Quas inter vivet Porcelli effigies.
Pace loquar veterum pictorum, et pace novorum.
Aequiperat veteres, vincit et ille novos.
Vive decus pictorum et gloria, et alter Apelles,
Cujus ob ingenium tempora prisca virent."
(Published in VASARI-VENTURI, op. cit., p. 62)
(The painter is here compared with Phidias and Praxiteles; various works are mentioned by name and praised, including a portrait of the poet. Pisanello is extolled for the faithful naturalism of his portraits, which rates him the appellation of "a second Apelles." He is said to equal the triumph of Classical art; indeed, the poet concludes: "Without wishing to give offense to ancient and modern painters, I can say that he is as good as the ancients and better than the moderns. Live, honor and glory of painters! Second Apelles!!! through whose genius ancient times flower anew!")

57) One of the most difficult obstacles facing Pisanello's biographers has been the establishment of the date of his death. The fact that from 1450 on complete silence falls around the painter led certain students, A. Venturi in particular, to conclude that he died about 1451. However, lack of news as the sole indicative evidence cannot suffice for fixing the date of Pisanello's death, nor is it enough that after 1449 no new work of the great painter and medalist is mentioned. (Venturi observed that it was strange that—as far as we know—no medals were executed by Pisanello after that date; precisely when his medals were most sought after, we might add.) Moreover, some documents seem to indicate a much later date for the painter's death—more exactly, 1455. BARTOLOMEO FACIO in his De viris illustribus of 1456, writes, "Pisanus Veronensis in pingendis rerum formis, sensibusque exprimendis ingenio prope poetico putatus est"; which

implies that Pisanello was already dead in 1456. However, it is impossible to say just how long he had been dead then. The will of Bartolomeo della Levata, Pisanello's brother-in-law (published by BIADEGO, op. cit., p. 858), is much more helpful: we learn from it that Pisanello and his mother, Isabetta, owed Bartolomeo considerable sums of money, lent over the period from November 16, 1434 "usque ad presentem diem,"—that is, July 14, 1455, the date on which the will was drawn up. Therefore Pisanello was, presumably, still alive in July, 1455 (we know that Isabetta was dead by 1452, so only Pisanello himself could have borrowed money between then and July, 1455). But are we to interpret this "usque ad presentem diem" as meaning that Antonio (as has been shown, only Antonio could have borrowed latterly; so the references are to the "combine" as Biadego rightly calls it, of "Antonio Pisano and Donna Isabetta") continued borrowing until July 14, 1455; or is it simply that, on the contrary, the past debts contracted by the "combine" remained outstanding? Since Isabetta, who was certainly dead, is referred to as though she were alive, there is no reason not to suppose that Antonio, though referred to as a living person, was also dead, even very recently. What remained was the "combine," perpetuated by its debts which were still unpaid when the will was signed. While this document offers precious little real information, it gives some grounds for supposing that Pisanello was still alive toward 1455, if not actually in July of that year, especially because the document refers to "Antonio Pisano and Isabetta" as if the "combine" were not altogether extinct, and there still remained a field in which to work, legally valid because Bartolomeo della Levata insisted on his rights (for example, Pisanello's goods, which had only recently passed into the hands of others). So for this reason alone we propose to place the artist's death approximately in 1455.

It is even more difficult to accept without reservations the testimony in the note sent by Carlo de' Medici to his brother Giovanni (published by G. GAYE in Carteggio inedito di Artisti dei secoli XIV, XV, XVI, Florence, 1839, I, p. 163), which contains the sentence: ". . . on that day I had bought about 30 bronze medals, very fine ones, from an apprentice of Pisanello's, who died that day." Thanks to VITTORIO ROSSI's detailed examination "L'indole e gli studi di Giovanni di Cosimo de' Medici," in Rendiconti della R. Accademia dei Lincei, 1893) it is possible to date the letter in October, 1455. But the meaning of the sentence is not clear and the doubts expressed by A. Venturi (VASARI-VENTURI, op. cit., pp. 63-64) are still valid; indeed, it is impossible to decide if the phrase "who died that day" refers to the apprentice or to Pisanello himself. It is probable that Pisanello had been dead for some time before, probably in Rome where his apprentice could have begun to sell whatever medals he possessed. Besides, HEISS (Les médailleurs de la Renaissance: Vittore Pisano, Paris, 1881, p. 7, note 2) pointed out that "in an account of 1455 kept in the Archives of the State of Modena, we find that on August 17th of that year Pisanello is debited 50 gold ducats." F. MALAGUZZI-VALERI (Pittori Lombardi del Quattrocento, Milan, 1902, pp. 88-89) draws attention to a document showing that the employees of the Ducal Chamber of Milan in 1456 included Antonello da Sicilia, Piero di Burges, and "il Pisanello," who was commissioned to buy horses (Missive register of payments, 1452-58, no.11, 15th March, 1456), but this is obviously a mere coincidence of names.

58. Y. BONNEFOY, "Le temps et l'intemporel dans la Peinture du Quattrocento," in Mercure de France, February 1959, p. 209.

59. Cf. P. TOESCA, La pittura e la miniatura della Lombardia dai più antichi monumenti alla metà del Quattrocento, Milan, 1912, p. 439.

60. For more detailed information about this fresco cycle, see GIAN LORENZO MELLINI, "La 'Sala grande' di Altichiero e Jacopo d'Avanzo e i Palazzi Scaligeri di Verona," in *Critica d'Arte*, 1959, no. 35.

61. The *Madonna Enthroned* in the Poldi-Pezzoli Museum, Milan, shows the fundamental differences between Moretti's Virgins and those of Pisanello; the unimpeded flow of Pisanello's pictorial dialogue is substantially different, from the colder, more rigid structure of the Moretti work, though there may be figurative resemblances on the more material level. Influences of the School of Verona were detected in the Moretti *Madonna* by MALAGUZZI VALERI (*op. cit.*, p. 88). BABELON postulated contacts between Moretti and Pisanello (*Pisanello*, Paris, 1931, p. 22); he contended that Moretti was a pupil of Pisanello's and responsible for the frescoes in the Torriani Chapel in San Eustorgio, Milan.

62. The hypothesis of collaboration by Pisanello on Gentile's *Adoration* was advanced by DEGENHART (*op. cit.*, p. 25) and later accepted by COLETTI (*op. cit.*, p. 29).

63. Cf. G. F. HILL, *op. cit.*, p. 91.

64. The doubts expressed by Calabi and Cornaggia about the authenticity of the majority of the medals (A. CALABI and G. CORNAGGIA, *Pisanello. L'opera medaglistica paragonata a quella pittorica, distinta dalla produzione di seguaci e falsificatori dei sec. XV e XVI*, Milan, 1928) were rightly dismissed by critics.

65. Cf. DEGENHART, *op. cit.*, p. 81, and "Das Wiener Bildnis Kaiser Sigismund ein Work Pisanellos" in *Jahrbuch der kunsthistorisches Sammlungen in Wien*, 1944; N. RASMO, "Il Pisanello e il ritratto dell'imperatore Sigismondo a Vienna," in *Cultura Atesina*, 1955.

66. The design of the garment was definitely drawn from life and cannot therefore be compared with other works of Pisanello to show identity of style. Such decorative elements can be found more or less everywhere: for example, in the Giambono *Madonna* in the Galleria Barberini, in the *Portrait of Louis II of Anjou* (Fig. 12), in the *Portrait of a Young Man* in the Palazzo Rosso, Genoa (Fig. 36), and even in some figures in the frescoes of the Palazzo Trinci, Foligno. If typological parallels must be established, there is a certain resemblance between the *Head of Herod* in the Bolognini Chapel in San Petronio, Bologna (Fig. 14) and the *Apostle* in the Prague National Gallery (Fig. 13).

67. Cf. N. RASMO, *op. cit.*, pp. 14-16.

68. This element of realism is not found in other portraits attributed to Pisanello, which were executed in a more conventional and stylized manner.

69. The fullface position may have been dictated by the two large lobes of the headdress.

70. Cf. A. H. MARTINIE, *op. cit.*, p. 58.

71. "The costume in the latter painting is visibly French (or Burgundian), but the relief work of the jewelry was at that time known only in northern Italy, in the works of painters such as Michelino da Besozzo and, later, Pisanello. This may therefore be the portrait of a French lady, painted in Italy by a northern painter who borrowed some techniques from local work. However, mention of *orfaverie* (goldsmith's work) as well as gold, supplied to Malouel in 1413, for the portrait of Jean Sans Peur, could refer to relief ornaments similar to those on the Washington *Lady*." Translated from CHARLES STERLING, "La peinture de portrait à la Cour de Bourgogne au début du XVe siècle," in *Critica d'Arte*, 1959, p. 312.

72. Cf. F. H. TAYLOR, *The Taste of Angels*, Boston, 1948, pp. 85-90.

73. "We also know that Pisano was the first to rediscover the art of the medalist, lost and forgotten by the Middle Ages; subsequently, with no apparent effort and inexplicable mastery, he equaled the finest works of Greece and Rome, combining study of character with breadth of style and achieving with his very first attempts a perfection that has not been surpassed since." Translated from J. DESTREE, *op. cit.*, 1899, p. 24.

74. Cf. A. VENTURI, *Pisanello*, Rome, 1939, p. 35 and B. DEGENHART *op. cit.*, 1945, p. 43.

75. The critical catalogue of all Pisanello's medals was compiled by G. F. HILL in his fundamental work *A Corpus of Medals of the Renaissance*, 2 vols., London, 1930. The motifs and persons figuring on Pisanello's medals were well described by A. VENTURI (*op. cit.*, 1939). On the reverse of his medals Pisanello always depicted allegorical subjects connected with the lives of the people to whom the medals were dedicated. Furthermore, the reverses of some of the Lionello d'Este medals have been correlated with the hermetic occult sciences of which Lionello is alleged to have been a devotee.

76. G. A. BAZZETTA, "Milano a Vittore Pisano," in *La Perseveranza* (9-16-1908).

77. In his *De viris illustribus*, FACIO notes in particular that: "Pisanus Veronensis in pingendis rerum formis, sensibusque exprimendis ingenio prope poetico putatus est. Sed in pingendis equis, ceterisque animalibus peritorum judicio ceteros antecessit. Mantuae aediculam pinxit, et tabulas valde laudatas. Pinxit Venetiis in Palatio Fredericum Barbarussam Romanorum Imperatorem, et eiusdem filium supplicem: Magnum quoque ibidem Comitum coetum germanico corporis cultu, orisque habitu: sacerdotem digitis os ditorquantem, et ob id ridentes pueros tanta suavitate, ut aspicientes ad hilaritatem excirent."
("Pisanello was considered to be of almost poetic genius in painting the forms of things and in expressing feeling. But in painting horses and other animals he excels the rest, in the opinion of connoisseurs. He painted the shrine in Mantua and very highly praised paintings; in Venice he painted Frederick Barbarossa the Roman Emperor, in the Palace, and his suppliant son... [he painted] a priest twisting his mouth with his fingers and boys laughing at this, with such charm that those who saw it burst out laughing...")

78. Nevertheless, this splendid motif was considered by A. VENTURI (*op. cit.*, 1939, p. 39) as "among the least significant of Pisanello's genius as a medalist."

79. Cf. A. VENTURI, *op. cit.*, 1939, p. 40.

80. In another medal (Fig. 18), dedicated to Lionello and sometimes attributed to Pisanello, only a vase, similar to the one shown in the medal described, is depicted.

81. The motif of the pelican feeding its young was exactly reproduced by Andrea Guazzalotti (1435) on the reverse of the Pius II medal executed between 1458 and 1464 (cf. Fig. 19).

82. Cf. A. VENTURI, *op. cit.*, 1939, p. 52.

83. The Berensonian attitude, which sees in the severe "noneloquent" painting of a Piero della Francesca or a Cézanne the most satisfying manifestation of artistic creation, cannot stop us from finding "noneloquence" even in expressionist works; "noneloquence" in this case is taken as meaning all that a true work of art never fails to suggest, but does not reveal openly, even through a more "eloquent" language.

84. "By drawing we mean the profiles and contours contained in the subject." Translated from P. DELLA FRANCESCA, *De prospectiva pingendi*, Florence, 1942 edition, p. 63.

85. It might be objected that the magnificent preliminary drawings, many examples of which have been admired for their spontaneity of execution when they became visible during the removal of wall paintings, represent typical examples of sketches, that is, drawings incomplete in terms of the subject they treat, but still rich—richer than the subject, in fact—in complex spiritual meaning. But while it is difficult to decide where the working drawing, a simple linear tracing, ends and the esthetically valid sketch begins, it is clear that the Tuscan preliminary drawings are only "linear tracings," geometrical simplifications that serve as a guide during the execution of the fresco; they are merely *schemata* for composition (construction) and so a "composition sketch" can be no more than this. It does not mean that a Tuscan preliminary drawing cannot be a splendid specimen of graphic art, superior in this sense to the actual painting (which was often completed with the aid of assistants); but except in exceptional cases, such a drawing contains nothing of the original idea that motivated the work. It is therefore purely functional, not an end in itself but merely a point of departure, unlike the sketch proper.

86. Cf. L. GRASSI, *Storia del disegno*, Rome, 1947, pp. 13-22.

87. Cennini foreshadows this concept of duality when in addition to the purely technical drawing—the so-called external drawing—he considers the artist's capacity for drawing "in his head." Cennini met with opposition from Alberti's geometrical conception, according to which drawing is no more than "that tracing of lines all round the areas" (a conception whose roots may lie in Giotto's work); while Ghiberti, who remains very Florentine even at his most Gothic, credits the drawing with a more active role, one that is more basic to the elaboration of the work of art than a mere outline plan. The two Tuscan tendencies converged in the diverse work of Leonardo, in which the dualism is obvious, as Grassi has already pointed out. While Leonardo considers the line,—that is, linear graphism— as not having "in itself any matter or substance" and, therefore, as no more than a pure working plan to guide the artistic search, at the same time he endows drawing with a new function of fulfillment by his exaltation of the sketch as an essential moment of creation. This new function leads, as can be seen, to the theory of *sfumato*, where the "end of one color is the beginning of another"; furthermore, this theory implies a choice between two different ways of considering reality. The first, abstract, mathematically predetermined, is linked to the scientific theories of the early Renaissance; the second, more concrete, closer to feeling and reality, pervades the Late Gothic current and makes its influence felt as far as the revolutionary discoveries of Leonardo.

88. Drawing, for example, as a purely anatomical delineation of the human face.

89. It is easy to understand the importance the Florentines attached to drawing, when one remembers that for them the drawing-plan defined the composition *more abstractly*.

90. This has been pointed out by GRASSI (*op. cit.*, p.16).

91. To justify the pre-eminence of the sketch as pure artistic expression, it must be noted that whereas the finished work may have to fulfill certain decorative requirements, in the sketch (not in the simple graphic plan) only the artist himself is expressed, without any outside influence coming into play.

92. Among the museums which now possess the finest Pisanello drawings are: the British Museum, London; the Ashmolean, Oxford; the Albertina, Vienna; the Berlin Museum; the Boymans Museum, Rotterdam;

the Stockholm Museum; and the Museums of Narbonne and Chantilly; but the most important is the Louvre, Paris, which houses the magnificent Vallardi Collection of several hundred drawings. This last collection's history is worthy of note. It takes its name from Giuseppe Vallardi, who acquired it in 1829 from an Emilian family and published it in 1855 under the title "*Disegni di Leonardo da Vinci, posseduti da Giuseppe Vallardi*," the drawings being at that time attributed to Leonardo. In 1856 the collection was bought by the Louvre. The drawings reproduced in this volume have been chosen from among the most significant of Pisanello's works, to offer as broad and complete a vision as possible of the many aspects of the artist's graphic production. It should be noted that some Pisanello drawings carry inscriptions with the names of other more or less famous artists. For example, the *Study of Male Nudes* (Plate 107) is marked at the lower left with the name Andrea Orcagna. These names must have been added later, probably by the collectors who owned the individual pieces.

93. Magagnato is not wholly without grounds when he attributes this drawing to Stefano (L. MAGAGNATO, *Da Altichiero a Pisanello*, Venice, 1958, p. 50). Two drawings (Figs. 2 and 3) which have also been attributed to Pisanello must be placed among the works of Stefano.

94. References to the art of the neighboring region led experts to assign certain Pisanello drawings to the Lombard school and vice versa. In this way the Lombard school was credited with the Pisanello colored drawing already described, along with the *Study of Dogs Hunting Game* (Plate 18), while Pisanello was claimed as author of the *Study of a Woman with a Helmet* (Fig. 4), which is better attributed to the Lombard school of the first half of the fifteenth century.

95. DEGENHART (*op. cit.*, 1945, p. 21) relates the face of the woman who is putting up her hair (lower right) with the archangel (Plate 11) in the San Fermo *Annunciation*.

96. There are obvious figurative parallels between this drawing and the fresco of the *Annunciation* painted about 1436 above the tomb of Beato Pacifico in the Church of the Frari in Venice (Figs. 5 and 6). The fresco, whose current bad state of preservation calls for careful restoration, was attributed to Pisanello by Bode (in P. PAOLETTI, *L'Architettura e la Scultura del Rinascimento a Venezia*, Venice, 1893, p. 78). Indeed, it is possible to discover elements in it, particularly in the angel, that recall Pisanello; but nevertheless it is easy to recognize the work of a different hand, resembling that of Gentile da Fabriano rather than Pisanello. Even so, an attribution to Giambono would be more convincing.

97. Cf. DEGENHART, *op. cit.* 1945, p. 37.

98. Cf. R. VAN MARLE, *The Development of the Italian Schools of Painting*, VIII, The Hague, 1927, p. 63.

99. DEGENHART (*op. cit.*, 1945, pp. 49-52) maintains that this group of drawings was executed for the triumphal arch of Castel Nuovo in Naples.

100. Another drawing (Louvre 2479), though rather different graphically from the one examined here, has been identified as the Emperor Sigmund (DEGENHART, *op. cit.*, 1945, p. 32).

101. This point has already been raised by DEGENHART (*op. cit.*, 1945, p. 81).

102. Recently B. DEGENHART and A. SCHMITT ("Gentile da Fabriano in Rom und die Anfänge des Antiken-

studiums," in *Münchner Jahrbuch der bildenden Kunst*, 1960) assembled numerous drawings from the antique belonging to the Late Gothic movement of the first half of the fifteenth century and showed them to be derived from Classical sarcophagi. But at the same time that they were carrying out these valuable comparisons, the two German specialists tried to separate from their corpus an outstanding group of drawings traditionally regarded as the work of Pisanello, and to attribute them to Gentile da Fabriano. Now while Gentile cannot be ruled out for some of these drawings, we feel it is impossibile to credit him with certain others, among the most brilliant of these studies, which could have been executed only by Pisanello. We also disagree completely with their attributing to Gentile a part far more important than he could have played, which would give him the credit for having discovered the elements of Classical art and for having revealed them to the Renaissance. As we tried to show in the third chapter of this volume, Gentile's painting, even including the *Adoration of the Magi*, contains no decisively revolutionary elements and does not possess the pulsating aesthetic language found in Pisanello's work and, above all, in his unmistakable drawings.

103. Cf. A. Venturi, *op. cit.*, 1939, p. 40.

104. Probably a study for Hercules and Antaeus.

105. A similarly foreshortened figure appears in Gentile's *Adoration*, at the feet of the youngest of the Magi (Fig. 8).

106. This figure seems more closely linked to Grecian art (cf. Fig. 21) than to the work of Gentile da Fabriano (cf. Fig. 8, the female figure behind the Virgin).

107. This last chapter, expanded to include more detail and further illustrative material, originally appeared in *Fede e Arte*, 1960, No. 2, pp. 172-195, under the title "Gotico e Rinascimento—Pisanello, Paolo Uccello e il Pittore dell'Adorazione," by E. Sindona.

108. For the characteristic features of this antitraditional movement in Tuscany, see especially S. Bettini, *Giusto de' Menabuoi*, Padua, 1944, pp. 26-28.

109. None of the known documents relating to Pisanello points to his having stayed in Tuscany. In his *Lives*, Vasari, following his usual procedure of Tuscanizing famous artists, has Pisanello spend a long time in Florence. However, while Vasari's exaggerations are not to be accepted we cannot rule out the possibility that Pisanello made frequent visits to Tuscany. We must not forget what Giovio said in his well-known letter to Cosimo de' Medici, speaking of the John Palaeologus medal (a version of the one cast in Verona): "... I have also a very fine medal of John Palaeologus, Emperor of Constantinople, with his odd Greek hat such as emperors used to wear: it was made by that Pisanello man in Florence, at the time of the Council of Eugenio, when the said Emperor was there..." It is held as very probable that Pisanello went to Tuscany by Martinie (*op. cit.*); A. Venturi (*op. cit.*, 1939); Degenhart (*op. cit.*, 1945); Coletti (*op. cit.*, 1953); Grassi (*op. cit.*).

110. Cf. Note 26.

111. Cf. E. Sindona, *Paolo Uccello*, Milan, 1957, pp. 24-26 and Plates 13-16.

112. Cf. Note 77.

113. Cf. also F. Antal, *La pittura fiorentina e il suo ambiente sociale nel Trecento e nel primo Quattrocento*, Turin, 1960, pp. 442-443.

114. Cf. E. Sindona, *op. cit.*, 1957, pp. 10-11. Gothic naturalism, then, fulfilled the function of maintaining in the artistic sphere the breath of liberty and social progress, which had sprung from communal institutions and which, in spite of the reaction that took place at the end of the twelfth century, was proving impossible in other spheres. The arts, which in such cases always have the opportunity of indicating suppressed demands by avoiding specific historical examples, found their most adequate answer in Gothic naturalism. The particular role which thus fell to Gothic art had without doubt a decisive influence—much greater than is generally imagined—on the new world-vision which was open to every possible way of studying the whole of reality in depth. However, this vision met with considerable obstacles after the aristocratic turn taken by art and thought during the Renaissance period.

115. "Placing the idea conceived by the artist in his innermost self at the center of artistic creation and giving it so absolute a metaphysical value signifies that art is from now on to be considered only in the function of the pure ideal paradigms it can produce, and in its capacity to translate a purely intellectual content in terms of the senses. Just as the mind of God created the Idea within itself, but must 'overflowing outside itself' place its stamp on the sensorial world, so the artist, fashioning the material into ideal images, accomplishes a similar act, analogous to the one which inspires all divine creation." Translated from C. Vasoli *L'Estetica dell'Umanesimo e del Rinascimento*, Milan, 1959, p. 358.

116. "Only since the Renaissance has painting been based on the assumption that the space in which things exist is an infinite, continuous, and homogeneous element, and that we usually see things uniformly, that is to say, with a single and motionless eye. But what we actually perceive is a limited, discontinuous, and heterogeneously compacted space. Our impression of space is distorted and blurred at the edges in reality, its content is divided into more or less independent groups and pieces and, since our physiologically conditioned field of vision is spheroid, we see, to some extent, curves instead of straight lines. The picture of space based on planimetric perspective such as Renaissance art presents us with, characterized by the equal clarity and consistent shaping of all parts, the common vanishing point of the parallels and the uniform module of distance measurement, the picture which L. B. Alberti defined as the transverse section of the optical pyramid, is a daring abstraction. Central perspective produces a mathematically accurate but psycho-physically impossible representation of space." A. Hauser, *The Social History of Art*, Vol. I, London, 1951, p. 334.

117. "Few rulers were legitimate; even the popes, in many cases, secured election by corrupt means. The rules for achieving success were not quite the same as they became when times grew more settled, for no one was shocked by cruelties and treacheries which would have disqualified a man in the eighteenth or the nineteenth century. Perhaps our age, again, can better understand Machiavelli, for some of the most notable successes of our time have been achieved by methods as base as any employed in Renaissance Italy. He would have applauded, as an artistic connoisseur in statecraft, Hitler's Reichstag fire, his purge of the party in 1934, and his breach of faith after Munich." Bertrand Russell, *History of Western Philosophy*, London, 1946, p. 526.

118. The conception of space in the works of early Renaissance artists is based on "cubic space," which has close affinities with scenographic space.

119. A parallel, which may help us to understand the contrast between the "historico-social" reality of the Quattrocento and the artists who tried to escape from it through aesthetics, can be drawn with the "historico-social" situation which faced twentieth-century artists in Italy during the decades after the First World War.

120. "The latent conflict between the intellectual and the economic upper class is nowhere openly engaged as yet, least of all by the artists, who, with their less developed social consciousness, react more slowly than their humanistic masters. But the problem, even if it is unadmitted and unexpressed, is present all the time and in all places, and the whole intelligentsia, both literary and artistic, is threatened by the danger of developing either into an uprooted, 'unbourgeois' and envious class of bohemians or into a conservative, passive, cringing class of academics. The humanists escape from this alternative into their ivory tower, and finally succumb to both the dangers which they had intended to avoid." A. HAUSER, *op. cit.*, p. 339.

121. The relations between Flanders and Italy in the fifteenth century are well known. Flemish influence penetrated not only by means of illuminated books, but also with paintings by Jan van Eyck and Hugo van der Goes, and with the presence in Italy of Roger van der Weyden and Joos van Ghent.

122. We must not forget a fundamental characteristic of the cultural climate in which Pisanello was brought up and lived, that is, a climate conditioned by the teachings of Averroes which were then popular in Venice, though in some ways opposed to the Platonism which was making a fresh appearance in Florence. The interest in natural sciences shown by the Averroists of Padua and Venice, their attempt to reconcile every difference in a pantheistic view, is very important for the understanding of certain tendencies in north Italian art, and its particular role in elaborating the new vision of the world.
Some of my ideas about various aspects of Renaissance humanism, expressed in this chapter and in the issue *Fede e Arte* (1960) mentioned in Note 107, have been valuably supported in GEORGE WEISE's interesting book, *L'ideale eroico del Rinascimento e le sue premesse umanistiche*, Naples, 1961, particularly in his chapter on the "*duplice concetto di Rinascimento.*"

123. It is enough to think of the all-enveloping, life-giving light in Jan van Eyck's *Adoration of the Mystic Lamb.*

124. One cannot fail to be struck, for example in Domenico Veneziano's altarpiece in Santa Maria de' Magnoli, by the two zones of red, completely isolated from the chromaticism of the rest of the painting—the vivid red of John the Baptist's tunic and Santa Lucia's shoes.

125. At that time, however, the lyrical, "loving" pantheism of a Leonardo or a Giorgione seems to establish a balance with the shattered humanity of the Quattrocento.

126. The circular painting (diameter $33^1/_{16}$"), formerly in the Palazzo Guicciardini and ascribed to Dello Delli, reached London in 1874 as part of the Barker Collection, where it was attributed to Filippo Lippi. MÜNTZ (*Les Collections de Médicis au Quinzième Siècle*, Paris 1888, p. 64) points out that in 1498 the canvas was listed in Venice as a work of Pesello. CROWE-CAVALCASELLE (*A New History of Painting in Italy*, London, 1864) also held that it was a Pesello, while Bode (W. BODE and H. VON TSCHUDI, *op. cit.*, pp. 10-12) attributed it to Pisanello, as did MÜNTZ (*L'arte italiana del Rinascimento*, Milan, 1894), LUDWIG and MOLMENTI (*Vittore Carpaccio*, Milan, 1906), and TESTI (*Storia della pittura veneziana*, Bergamo, 1915). MORELLI (in I. LEMORLIEFF, *Kunstkritische Studien uber Italianische Malerei, Die Galerie zu Berlin*, Leipzig, 1893) claims it is by a Veronese painter influenced by Pisanello but excludes any contact with Tuscany. BERENSON (*The Golden Urn*, Fiesole, 1897, p. 197) assigned it for the first time to Domenico Veneziano, and

RANKIN ("Cassone Fronts in American Collections," in *The Burlington Magazine*, 1907, p. 63) to a follower of Domenico's. A. VENTURI (*Storia dell'arte italiana*, Vol. VII, Milan, 1911, p. 340) holds out for a follower of Paolo Uccello, and LAYARD (*The Italian Schools of Painting*, I, London, 1907, p. 262) for a Florentine painter, probably Dello Delli; A. COLASANTI (*Gentile da Fabriano*, Bergamo, 1909, p. 88) proposes the Veronese school, and HILL (*op. cit.*, p. 215) an imitator of Pisanello. Later critics generally favor the attribution to Domenico Veneziano; R. LONGHI ("*Un frammento della Pala di Domenico Veneziano per Santa Lucia de' Magnoli*," in *L'Arte*, 1925) considers it a work of Domenico's youth, as do VAN MARLE (*op. cit.*, X); BOECK ("Domenico Veneziano" in *Pantheon*, 1934, pp. 79-85); TOESCA ("Domenico Veneziano," in Enciclopedia Italiana, XIII, p. 117); PUDELKO ("*Studien über Domenico Veneziano*," in *Mitteilungen Kunsthist. Inst. in Florenz*, 1934); POPE-HENNESSY ("The Early Style of Domenico Veneziano," in *The Burlington Magazine*, 1951, p. 223); PACCAGNINI ("*Una proposta per Domenico Veneziano*," in *Bollettino d'Arte*, 1952, pp. 115-126); COLETTI (*Pittura veneta del Quattrocento*, Novara, 1953, p. LXXX); and PALLUCCHINI (*La pittura veneta del Quattrocento*, Bologna, 1956, p. 200). SALMI sees it as a work of maturity (*Paolo Uccello, Andrea del Castagno, Domenico Veneziano*, Milan, 1938, p. 90), and BERENSON claims it is later than 1450 ("*Fra Angelico, Fra Filippo e la cronologia*," in *Bollettino d'Arte*, 1932, p. 12). BRENZONI (*op. cit.*, p. 188) places it among the works that can be cautiously attributed to Pisanello. For certain Flemish features in the roundel, see R. LONGHI ("*Il Maestro di Pratovecchio*," in *Paragone*, 1952, p. 13) and M. SALMI ("*Fuochi d'artificio o della pseudo critica*," in *Commentari*, 1954, p. 68). Gothic inscriptions can be seen in some parts of the painting. Beside the two heads on the right: "*grace fai die (u)*"; on the coat of the young man to the left: "*ansi—va—le—Ȯ (monde)*"; on the horse's harness: "*Honia Bôa In Tenpor*"; on the hat of one of the boys carrying baggage: "*tenpo.*"

127. For the attributions of the frescoes in the Chapel of the Assumption in the cathedral of Prato, cf. E. SINDONA, *op. cit.*, p. 59.

128. The ghostly leanness of this figure recalls Flemish painting. Cf. E. SINDONA, *op. cit.*, Fig. 12.

129. Comparisons between drawings of costumes and of a camel and the costume and the camel in the circular painting were made by A. Venturi in the work quoted on the lives of Gentile da Fabriano and Pisanello. (VASARI-VENTURI, *op. cit.*).

130. See especially the ground in the Oxford *Hunting Scene*, and that in the Karlsruhe *Adoration of the Child*.

131. "Italian art founds the value of form on the *idea* in the Platonic sense of the term; it formulates the *a priori* concept of space in which it inserts and by which it justifies all experience. Flemish art, on the contrary, founds form on experience, and while seeming to attribute importance exclusively to things as things, it elaborates its own concept of space, but *a posteriori*. However, while Italian art is not, and could never be, pure geometry, Flemish art is not and could not be a faithful copy of sensory data. It is best to say, then, that the Italians define form through the concept, and the Flemish through experience; form is for them both the supreme aim to be attained. Form—that is to say, the conscious representation of the world, the objective translation of spiritual structures and content, the recognition of the spatial and temporal conditions into which human existence is inserted and in which the value and autonomy of the individual are affirmed." Translated from J. LASSAIGNE and G.C. ARGAN, *De van Eyck à Botticelli*, Geneva-Paris, 1955, p. 7.

SUPPLEMENTARY ILLUSTRATIONS

Fig. 1) STEFANO DA VERONA - *Madonna and Child* - Galleria Colonna, Rome (p. 29). – Fig. 2) STEFANO DA VERONA - *Study for a Saint* - Albertina, Vienna (Note 93). – Fig. 3) STEFANO DA VERONA - *Study of the Virgin* - Bacri Collection, Paris (Note 93). – Fig. 4) LOMBARD SCHOOL, FIRST HALF OF 15TH CENTURY - *Study of Woman with Helmet* - Boymans Museum, Rotterdam (Note 94). – Figs. 5 and 6) MICHELE GIAMBONO (?) - *The Annunciation* - Church of the Frari, Venice (Note 96). – Fig. 7) LOMBARD ROMANESQUE ART - *Dragon* - Church of San Michele, Pavia (Note 6). – Fig. 8)

GENTILE DA FABRIANO - *The Adoration of the Magi* - Uffizi, Florence (pp. 31, 87, 88). – Fig. 9) CRISTOFORO MORETTI -
The Virgin Enthroned - Museo Poldi Pezzoli, Milan (p. 29; Note 61). – Fig. 10) GIOVANNINO DE' GRASSI - *Study of Dog and Stag* - Biblioteca Civica, Bergamo (p. 60). – Fig. 11) GIOVANNINO DE' GRASSI *Study of Animals* - Biblioteca Civica, Bergamo (p. 60).

Fig. 12) FRENCH SCHOOL, FIRST HALF OF 15TH CENTURY - *Portrait of Louis II d'Anjou* - Bibliothèque Nationale, Paris (Note 66). – Fig. 13) BOHEMIAN SCHOOL, FIRST HALF OF 15TH CENTURY - *Head of an Apostle* - National Gallery, Prague (p. 36). – Fig. 14) EMILIAN SCHOOL, FIRST HALF OF 15TH CENTURY - *Head of Herod* - Church of San Petronio, Bologna (Note 66). – Fig. 15) 15TH-CENTURY MINIATURE - *Portrait of Julius Caesar* - Biblioteca Malatestiana, Cesena (Note 35). – Fig. 16) *Medallion of Gordiano Antonino* - Loggia of Can Signorio, Verona (p. 42). – Fig. 17) *Medal of the Emperor Heraclius I* - Kunsthistorisches Museum, Vienna (p. 42). – Fig. 18) *Medal of Lionello d'Este* - Bibliothèque Na-

15

16

17

21

22

CLARVS INSIGNI VEHITVR TRIVMPHO·
QVEM PAREM SVMMIS DVCIBVS PERHENNIS·
FAMA VIRTVTVM CELEBRAT DECENTER·
SCEPTRA TENENTEM

23

tionale, Paris (p. 123; Note 80). – Fig. 19) ANDREA GUAZZALOTTI - *Medal of Pius II* - Galleria Nazionale di Capo-
dimonte, Naples (Note 81). – Fig. 20) DOMENICO VENEZIANO - *The Madonna Enthroned with Saints* - Uffizi, Florence
(p. 119). – Fig. 21) *Head of Eirene* (Roman copy of the original by Cephisodotus) - Glyptotek, Munich (Note 106). –
Fig. 22) PIERO DELLA FRANCESCA - *Triumph of Federico da Montefeltro* - Uffizi, Florence (p. 51). – Fig. 23) ATTRIBUTED
TO PISANELLO - *Saint Jerome* - National Gallery, London (p. 118).

Fig. 24) ATTRIBUTED TO PISANELLO - *The Story of Saint Aloysius* - Church of Santa Caterina, Treviso (p. 119). – Fig. 25) ATTRIBUTED TO PISANELLO - *Hermit Saint* - Museo Poldi Pezzoli, Milan (p. 119). – Figs. 26, 27, and 28) ATTRIBUTED TO PISANELLO - *Three Scenes from the Life of Saint Benedict* - Uffizi, Florence (p. 119). – Fig. 29) ATTRIBUTED TO PISANELLO - *Saint Francis, Saint James, and Saint Anthony Abbot* - Massari Collection, Ferrara (p. 119). – Fig. 30) ATTRIBUTED TO PISANELLO - *The Rape of Dejanira* - Agnew Collection, London (p. 119). – Fig. 31) ATTRIBUTED TO PISANELLO -

27   28   29

33   34   35

Saint Jerome - Clark Collection, London (p. 119). – Fig. 32) ATTRIBUTED TO PISANELLO - *Saint* - Museum, Pisa (p. 119). – Fig. 33) ATTRIBUTED TO PISANELLO - *Saint Peter and Saint Paul* - Berenson Collection, Settignano (p. 119). – Fig. 34) ATTRIBUTED TO PISANELLO - *The Resurrection* - Church of Sant'Apollinare, Ferrara (p. 118). – Fig. 35) ATTRIBUTED TO PISANELLO - *Portrait of a Member of the Strozzi Household* (lost) (p. 119).

Fig. 36) Attributed to Pisanello - *Portrait of a Young Man* - Palazzo Rosso, Genoa (p. 119). – Fig. 37) Attributed to Pisanello - *Portrait of a Young Man* - Private collection (p. 119). – Fig. 38) Artist of the First Half of the 15th Century - *Study of a Man's Head* - Boymans Museum, Rotterdam (p. 118). – Fig. 39) Attributed to Pisanello - *Portrait of a Man* - Galleria Capitolina, Rome (p. 118).

Fig. 40) MASTER OF THE ADORATION - *The Adoration of the Magi* - Museum, Berlin (pp. 98-100).

Figs. 41 and 42) Details of Fig. 40.

CATALOGUE OF PISANELLO'S WORKS *

PAINTINGS

The Madonna Enthroned
(Plate 1)
Rome, Palazzo Venezia Museum
Painted on wood $37^3/_4 \times 19^1/_4''$

Attributed by most critics to Stefano da Verona; see, in particular, Berenson (1907); Hermanin (1923); Sandberg-Vavalà (1926). Longhi (1928) found links between this painting and the work of Cristoforo Moretti. Morassi (1930) and Degenhart (1945) assigned it to a Lombard painter. The attribution to Pisanello was suggested by Coletti (1947) and accepted by Magagnato (1958). We confirm the attribution to Pisanello's youth.
(Page 29)

Madonna of the Quail
(Plate 6)
Verona, Museo di Castelvecchio
Painted on wood $19^3/_4 \times 13''$

Provenance: Galleria Bernasconi. Formerly attributed to Stefano by Frizzoni (1904), Berenson (1907), and Sandberg-Vavalà (1926). Attributed to Pisanello by A. Venturi (1908); Martinie (1930); Thiis (1941); Degenhart (1945); Pallucchini (1946); Avena (1947); Brenzoni (1952); Coletti (1953); Chiarelli (1958); Magagnato (1958). Longhi (1928) saw a connection between it, too, and the work of Cristoforo Moretti. We do not find links with the art of Gentile, as did Degenhart (1945) and Magagnato (1958); such links would be rather tenuous in view of the poetic freshness and the lively rhythm of this delightful little painting. Nor are there any resemblances between the light, elegant angels here and the heavier, archaically expressed, though still beautiful ones in Gentile's *Coronation* in the Brera. We uphold the attribution to Pisanello and place the work in his youthful period.
(Page 29)

The Annunciation
(Plates 7-12)
Verona, Church of San Fermo (Brenzoni Tomb)
Fresco. Damaged; signed lower right: PISANUS PINSIT.

Executed by Pisanello toward 1425. The tomb, built on the orders of Nicolò Brenzoni (died 1422) by the Florentine, Nanni di Bartolo, was completed in 1426, as is attested by an inscription published by Biadego (1913, Note VI). Since Pisanello was absent from Verona from 1420 till 1424, the fresco must have been executed between 1424 and 1426. It is unlikely that the frescoes were painted long after the completion of the tomb. Biadego dates the work between 1435 and 1440 (Cf. BIADEGO, 1913, and BRENZONI, 1952, pp. 141-143).
(Pages 30-32)

The Legend of Saint George
(Plates 49-54, 59, 60, 65, 66, 74-85)
Verona, Church of San Giorgetto (formerly in the Church of Sant'Anastasia, Pellegrini Chapel)
Fresco $88 \times 169^1/_4''$. Damaged, removed, restored, and mounted on canvas

This is the main section of the painted decorations of the Pellegrini Chapel, of which Vasari speaks admiringly in his *Lives;* it is also the only part to have survived except the Arms of the Pellegrini Family (Plates 90 and 91). Authorities are by no means unanimous on the date of the work; some place it in the period immediately before the painter's journey to Rome, that is, about 1429 (when Andrea Pellegrini, who died shortly after, left money for the construction and decoration of the chapel) or 1430 (Brenzoni, 1952). Others claim that it was executed between 1433 and 1438 (Hill, 1905, who specifies 1438; A. Venturi, 1939, who fixes it at 1436; Degenhart, 1945); Arslan (1948) places it in 1445-46. Though a Late Gothic vision dominates the work, there are obvious signs that Classical and Renaissance experience has been assimilated, and it should be dated between 1435 and 1438.
(Pages 7-14)

Arms of the Pellegrini Family
(Plates 90, 91)
Verona, Museo di Castelvecchio (formerly in the Church of Sant'Anastasia, Pellegrini Chapel)
Fresco $74^3/_4 \times 43^1/_2''$. Removed, restored, and mounted on canvas

Hill (1905) detected the hand of a helper (Bono da Ferrara). Indeed, in view of the quality of this part of the decorations, we must not rule out the possibility that Pisanello may have given a pupil a more or less free hand on this section.
(Page 32)

* The page numbers appearing at the end of each description indicate parts of the text where the work is treated more extensively.

The Vision of Saint Eustace
(Plates 120-122)
London, National Gallery
Painted on wood 25³/₄ × 21″

Provenance: Ashburnham Collection. Attributed to Dürer and Jean Fouquet. Bode (1885) assigned it to Pisanello. Bode's attribution was generally accepted from then on, except by Manteuffel (1912-17) who gave it, not to Pisanello, but to one of his followers, and by Richter (1929), who expressed doubts. Van Marle (1927) and A. Venturi (1939) place the work in the painter's youth, as does Coletti (1945); Hill (1905) dates it 1430, while Degenhart (1945) and Brenzoni (1952) consider it a work of the artist's maturity. The stylistic quality of the work seems to indicate a late dating. (Pages 32, 33)

The Apparition of the Virgin to Saint George and Saint Anthony
(Plates 146, 147, and 150)
London, National Gallery
Painted on wood: 18¹/₂ × 11¹/₂″. Restored, signed lower center in Gothic characters: PISANUS PI.

Formerly in the Costabili di Ferra Collection, and then acquired by the National Gallery in 1867. It is rightly held to be a late work, except by Van Marle (1927) who considers it earlier than the Sant'Anastasia frescoes.
(Pages 34, 35)

Portrait of the Emperor Sigmund
(Plate 36)
Vienna, Kunsthistorisches Museum
Parchment mounted on canvas: 24 × 16¹/₄″

Many scholars detected direct reference to Pisanello in this portrait, with its extraordinary convergence of courtly Gothic modes and those featured in some of the typical figure representations of Bohemian art (cf. DEGENHART, 1946, p. 181 and 1949, p. 11; BRENZONI, 1952, p. 179). However, the first attribution to the Veronese painter by Degenhart was not published until 1944. The portrait, which hung in the castle of Ambras near Innsbrück before passing into the Vienna Museum, was attributed to Konrad Laib by Wilde (1930), and to Pfenning by Baldass (1934), who dated the work around 1457. After Degenhart's Pisanello attribution, the critics who did not accept this thesis generally turned toward a Bohemian master, following Rasmo's study (1955). On the other hand, Degenhart's attribution was accepted by Brenzoni (1952), Coletti (1953), Marcenaro (1959), and, with reservations, by Middeldorf (1947). Furthermore Degenhart claimed in his works of 1946 and 1949 that his findings were upheld by Toesca, Baldass, and Mauro Pelliccioli. We are dealing with a work that presents serious problems for definitive attribution because of the complex

figurative culture assimilated in it. But if one considers that "Pisanello" elements are the only ones able to coexist with Bohemian traits, and that the latter are incapable of expressing the complex spiritual life that gives form to many Late Gothic works and dominates decisively in this portrait, it is impossible to avoid proposing Pisanello rather than a Bohemian painter as the author of this particular portrait. Still, the doubts left unresolved advise against too categorical a pronouncement. Besides, the Bohemian elements in the painting cannot be thought of as foreign to Pisanello's style; we know that Pisanello did not hesitate to adopt features of other artistic currents: French, Lombard, and Tuscan, for example. Therefore it is not in the least surprising that the artist should have felt sympathy for Bohemian modes at the precise moment when the Emperor arrived in Italy on his way from eastern Europe. The portrait was executed between 1432 and 1433, probably on the occasion of the discussions between the Emperor and Giovanni Francesco Gonzaga prior to the naming of the latter Marquis of Mantua.
(Pages 35-37)

Portrait of a Lady
(Plate 104)
Paris, Louvre
Painted on wood: 17 × 11³/₄″

In 1860 in Paris, the diplomat Felix Bamberg acquired this painting as a work of Piero della Francesca; the work became a part of the Louvre collection in 1893. A. Venturi (1899) first attributed it to Pisanello, and this assignment was generally accepted. The emblem of the Este family is embroidered on the left side of the gown, which would appear to prove that the lady was a member of the house of Este. There are, however, various opinions on her identity. In 1889 Venturi wrote that there were no valid reasons for deciding if "we are in the presence of Verde, Lucia, or another daughter of Nicolò III." Later Ravaisson (1893) advanced the hypothesis that the lady might be Cecilia Gonzaga, because of her resemblance to the portrait on Cecilia's medal. Then Gruyer (1893-94) proposed Margherita Gonzaga, Cecilia's sister, who married Lionello d'Este. Finally Hill (1905) suggested Ginevra d'Este, the wife of Sigismondo Pandolfo Malatesta. Recently, critics, with perhaps excessive zeal, have turned their attention to identifying the person portrayed by Pisanello in this magnificent painting. So, while Venturi in 1939 avoided committing himself and insisted that the theories mentioned all lack a sure foundation, other scholars advanced further arguments in favor of Margherita Gonzaga (Degenhart, 1945) or Ginevra d'Este (Brenzoni, 1952; Coletti, 1953). Nor is there agreement over the date of the painting. Coletti places it in 1433, Hill (1905) in the period immediately after Pisanello's return from Rome; Degenhart, Brenzoni, and Magagnato (1958) prefer 1438-1440. For stylistic reasons this last dating seems the most acceptable. (Pages 37, 38)

Portrait of Lionello d'Este
(Plate 117)
Bergamo, Galleria dell'Accademia Carrara
Painted on wood: 11 × 7¹/₂″

This is probably the portrait of Lionello executed by Pisanello in the notorious contest with Jacopo Bellini, described by the poet Ulisse in his famous sonnet (see note 44). The work can be dated 1441. (Pages 38, 39)

Portrait of a Lady
(Plate 137)
Washington, D. C., National Gallery of Art
Painted on wood: 21 × 12¹/₄″

Attributed to Pisanello by A. Venturi (1925), then by L. Venturi (1931), who identified the subject as Isotta degli Atti; also by Martinie (1930), Berenson (1932) and D'Ancona (1953). Brenzoni (1952) attributes it to Pisanello, but with reservations. Richter (1931), Thiis (1941), Degenhart (1945), and Coletti (1953) assign the work to the French school. We agree with the Pisanello attribution, and date the work 1442-1445. (Page 39)

LOST PAINTINGS

Meeting Between the Emperor Frederick Barbarossa and His Son Ottone
Venice, Ducal Palace
Frescoes. Destroyed in the fire of 1557. Cf. Facio (1456) and Lorenzi (1868).

Miracle of Saint James
Florence, Church of the Tempio
Frescoes. Cf. Vasari.

Scenes from the Life of John the Baptist
Rome, San Giovanni in Laterano

Frescoes. Cf. Vasari; Facio. Destroyed during alterations carried out in the basilica by Borromini in the 17th century. In the Staatliche Kunstbibliothek in Berlin there is a drawing made by order of Borromini, from which we can glean a very vague idea of one part of the Lateran frescoes executed by Gentile da Fabriano and Pisanello. Even attempts to refer some fifteenth-century drawings to the fresco cycle are frustrated by the fact that we know virtually none of the Pisanello work sacrificed by Borromini. (Cf. Degenhart, 1945; Brenzoni, 1952). A fragment of a fresco conserved in the Vatican Museum, probably showing Charle-

magne, which was originally taken from San Giovanni in Laterano (Cf. Grassi, 1953) cannot defensibly be related with Pisanello's output; it might, however, be part of the paintings executed by Gentile.

Scenes of Courtly Life
Pavia, Castello
Frescoes. Cf. Michiel (1520-40) and note 34.

Saint Eustace Caressing a Dog and Saint George Replacing His Sword in Its Sheath
Verona, Church of Sant'Anastasia
Frescoes. Cf. Vasari.

Scenes with Various Subjects
Mantua, Ducal Palace and a Chapel
Frescoes. Cf. Facio (1456) and note 41.

Portrait of Julius Caesar
Cf. Salmi (1947), note 35, and Fig. 15.

God the Father
Painting on wood. Cf. note 54.

Saint Jerome
Painting on wood. Cf. Facio (1456).

PAINTINGS ATTRIBUTED TO PISANELLO

Saint Jerome
(Fig. 23)
Signed: BONUS · FERARIENSIS · PISANI · DI-SIPVLVS.
London, National Gallery

Cf. Richter (1929); A. Venturi (1922 and 1939); Degenhart (1945); Longhi (1934). The signature was held to be apocryphal because it shows signs of retouching, especially in some letters of the second word; however, in the light of recent examination

it must be recognized as authentic (cf. Davies, 1951).

Portrait of a Man
(Fig. 39)
Rome, Galleria Capitolina

Cf. A. Venturi (1918), who, however, later advanced doubts (1939). Coletti (1953) does not rule out the possibility of the work's being Pisanello's. A drawing (Fig. 38) in the Boymans Museum has some points in common with this portrait. Creighton (1961) attributes it, not without cause, to Bellini.

The Resurrection
(Fig. 34)
Ferrara, Church of Sant'Apollinare
Cf. A. Venturi (1933 and 1939).

Saint Francis, Saint James, and Saint Anthony Abbot
(Fig. 29)
Ferrara, Massari Collection
Cf. A. Venturi (1933).

Saint Peter and Saint Paul
(Fig. 33)
Settignano, Berenson Collection

Cf. Degenhart (1953). Volpe (1958) attributes the two saints, formerly attributed by Berenson to Stefano da Verona, to Gentile da Fabriano as part of the Valle Romita polyptych.

Saint
(Fig. 32)
Pisa, Museum
Cf. Degenhart (1953).

The Story of Saint Aloysius
(Fig. 24)
Treviso, Church of Santa Caterina

Attributed to Pisanello by Coletti (1947 and 1953), who also attributes a fresco fragment of a Madonna (Treviso Museum) to the young Pisanello. Coletti refers to Pisanello's circle two figures (perhaps Adam and Eve) painted in fresco in the cathedral of Pordenone. The attribution was accepted by Degenhart (1949).

The Adoration of the Magi
(Figs. 40-42)
Berlin, Museum
Cf. Bode-Tschudi (1885); also pp. 98-100 and note 126.

Hermit Saint
(Fig. 25)
Milan, Museo Poldi Pezzoli

Three Scenes from the Life of Saint Benedict
(Figs. 26-28)
Florence, Uffizi

The hermit saint, usually identified with Saint Benedict, was connected with the three scenes in the Uffizi (previously in the Cannon Collection) by Richter (1931) and Degenhart (1942 and 1949). Richter attributed the hermit saint to Pisanello; the work had been referred to the school of Jacopo Bellini by Sandberg-Vavalà (1926) and, more defensibly, to Gentile da Fabriano by Berenson (1907), followed by Morassi (1936) and Wittgens (1937) after the name of Stefano da Ve-

rona had been established (Frizzoni, Morelli and Van Marle). The Pisanello attribution was accepted, with reservations, by Coletti (1947 and 1953), by Degenhart, who assigned all four paintings to Pisanello, and by Longhi (1958) who, in 1946, assigned the three Cannon panels to Niccolò di Pietro, a painter favored by Ferrari (1953) and Grassi (1953). Fiocco (1952) proposed the Bohemian painter Wazlaw Pehm (Master Wenceslas). Rasmo (1955) pointed out that "these paintings do not really deserve the discussions they have aroused."

Saint Jerome
(Fig. 31)
London, Clark Collection
Cf. Richter (1929).

The Rape of Dejanira
(Fig. 30)
London, Agnew Collection
Cf. Richter (1929).

Portrait of a Young Man
(Fig. 36)
Genoa, Palazzo Rosso

Formerly attributed to Giovanni Bellini, D. Morone, and J. Fouquet, it was placed among the works of Niccolò Giolfino by Berenson (1936); Suida (1906) considered it to be executed in Pisanello's manner, and Marcenaro (1959) assigned it to this artist. (Cf. also O. Grosso, *Le Gallerie d'arte del Comune di Genova*, Genoa, 1932). Cuppini (1962) recently attributed it to Michele Giambono. The portrait might better be referred to a painter influenced by Fouquet's Italian essays.

Portrait of a Young Man
(Fig. 37)
Private collection

The fine reproduction given by Zeri (1958), who published the work, shows none of the formal strength always found in Pisanello's portraits.

Portrait of a Member of the Strozzi Household
(Fig. 35)
Lost

Attributed by L. Venturi (1954) to Pisanello on the grounds of elements discovered in the catalogue of the Bardini Collection Sale (London, 1902).

Madonna of the Pergola
Lost; formerly Rome, Paolini Collection. Signed: ANTONIUS PISANUS.

Cf. Richter (1929); Coletti (1947); Brenzoni (1952). Even from the reproductions available it is not difficult to note the mediocre execution of this work.

MEDALS

Medal of John Palaeologus
(Plate 92)
Paris, Bibliothèque Nationale, Cabinet des Médailles
Diameter: $3^5/_{16}''$

Obverse: The Emperor is shown in profile facing right, surrounded by the inscription: ΙΩΑΝΝΗС· ΒΑΣΙΛΕΥΣ·ΚΑΪ·ΑΥΤΟΚΡΑΤΩΡ·ΡΩΜΑΙΩΝ ·Ο·ΠΑΛΑΙΟΛΟΓΟС.

Reverse: The Emperor is shown on horseback in a rocky landscape, facing a cross supported by an obelisk. Behind there is a page on a horse, seen from the rear as in the Novello Malatesta medal. The inscription reads above: OPVS · PISANI · PICTORIS; below: ΕΡΓΟΝ·ΤΟΥ·ΠΙСΑΝΟΥ· ΖΩΓΡΑΘΥ.

Can be dated 1438.
(Page 43)

Medal of Filippo Maria Visconti
(Plate 93)
Milan, Castello Sforzesco, Medagliere
Diameter: 4''

Obverse: Profile facing right within the inscription: PHILIPPVSMARIA · ANGLVS · DVX · MEDIOLANI·ETCETERA·PAPIE·ANGLERIE· QVE · COMES · AC · GENVE · DOMINVS ·

Reverse: Mountains, behind which appear the towers of a city and a large statue carrying a scepter; in the foreground, the Duke in warrior's armor; his helmet is surmounted with the Visconti serpent; he is followed by a shield-bearer and a page. Below: OPVS · PISANI · PICTORIS.
Datable 1440.
(Pages 43, 44)

Medal of Gianfrancesco Gonzaga
(Plate 102)
Brescia, Museo Civico
Diameter: $3^5/_{16}''$

Obverse: Profile facing left. Center inscription: IOHANES FRANCISCVS · DE · GONZAGA · Below: PRIMVS · MARCHIO · MANTVE. Above: CAPIT · MAXI · ARMIGERORUM.

Reverse: Gianfrancesco Gonzaga, armed and on horseback, is shown with his commander's baton. In the middle ground a page on horseback. Above: OPVS · PISANI · PICTORIS.
Datable 1440.
(Page 44)

Medal of Niccolò Piccinino
(Plate 109)
Brescia, Museo Civico
Diameter: $3^1/_2''$

Obverse: Profile facing left surrounded by the inscription: NICOLAVS · PICININVS · VICE-

COMES · MARCHIO · CAPITANEVS · MAX AC · MARS · ALTER ·

Reverse: Griffin suckling two infants, Braccio da Montone and Niccolò Piccinino (grandson of Braccio); the beast wears a collar inscribed: PERVSIA. To the right: N. PICININVS. To the left: BRACCIVS: Below: PISANI · P · OPVS.
Datable 1440.
(Pages 44, 45)

Medal of Francesco Sforza
(Plate 103)
Milan, Castello Sforzesco, Medagliere
Diameter: $3^3/_8''$

Obverse: Profile facing left, surrounded by the inscription: FRANCISCVS · SFORTIA · VICECOMES · MARCHIO · ET · COMES · AC · CREMONE · D ·

Reverse: Symbols of Sforza's activities: horse, sword, and three books. Surrounding them: OPVS · PISANI · PICTORIS.
Datable circa 1442.
(Page 45)

Medal of Lionello d'Este (reverse with three-faced head)
(Plate 109)
London, British Museum
Diameter: $2^{11}/_{16}''$

Obverse: Profile facing right. Surrounding it, among olive branches: LEONELLVS · MARCHIO · ESTENSIS.

Reverse: Three-faced head of a cherub flanked by olive branches and military trophies. Upper and lower center: OPVS · PISANI · PICTORIS.
Datable 1441-43.
(Pages 45, 46)

Medal of Lionello d'Este (with sail)
(Plate 114)
London, British Museum
Diameter: $2^5/_8''$

Obverse: Profile facing left. Surrounding it, among olive branches: LIONELLVS · MARCHIO · ESTENSIS.

Reverse: A ship's mast with an unfurled sail, with two seated male nudes, one young and the other old. Above: OPVS · PISANI · PICTORIS.
Datable 1441-44.
(Pages 45, 46)

Medal of Lionello d'Este (with canephori)
(Plates 110,111)
Paris, Bibliothèque Nationale, Cabinet des Médailles
Diameter: $2^3/_4''$

Obverse: Profile facing left. Surrounding it, among olive branches: LEONELLVS · MARCHIO · ESTENSIS.

Reverse: Two male nudes, one young, the other old, carry two baskets filled with olive branches. Further back are two closed vases on which it is raining heavily. Beside the two vases: OPVS · PISANI · PICTORIS.

Datable 1441-44.
(Pages 45, 46)

Medal of Lionello d'Este (with nude and vase)
(Plates 112, 113)
Paris, Bibliothèque Nationale, Cabinet des Médailles
Diameter: 2 $^{11}/_{16}$″

Obverse: Profile facing left. Surrounding it, between two concentric rings: LEONELLVS · MARCHIO · ESTENSIS · D · FERRARIE · REGI · 7 · MVTINE.

Reverse: A male nude, reclining on the ground; further up, a vase attached to two anchors, one of which is broken. Above: PISANI · PICTORIS · OPVS.

Datable 1441-44.
(Pages 45, 46)

Medal of Lionello d'Este (with lynx)
(Plate 115)
Brescia, Museo Civico
Diameter: 2 $^{11}/_{16}$″

Obverse: Profile facing left. Surrounding it, between two concentric rings: LEONELLVS · MARCHIO · ESTENSIS · D · FERRARIE · REGII · 7 · MVTINE.

Reverse: A fettered lynx on a cushion. Below, between two concentric rings: PISANVS · PICTOR · FECIT.

Datable 1441-44.
(Pages 45, 47)

Medal of Lionello d'Este (with lion and winged cherub)
(Plate 116)
Milan, Castello Sforzesco, Medagliere
Diameter: 3 $^{15}/_{16}$″

Obverse: Profile facing left, surrounded by the inscription: LEONELLVS · MARCHIO · ESTENSIS. Below: D · FERRARIE · REGII · ET · MVTINE. Above: GE · R · AR.

Reverse: A winged cherub (symbolizing Love) unrolls a scroll of music in front of a lion to calm it. Behind, an eagle and a column on which a mast and sail are shown. Upper center: · M · CCCCX-LIIII; to the right: OPVS · PISANI · PICTORIS. The medal, dated 1444, was executed by Pisanello on the occasion of the marriage of Lionello to

Maria of Aragon, which explains the references above: GE(ner) R(egis) AR(agonum).
(Pages 45, 47)

Medal of Sigismondo Pandolfo Malatesta (with standing warrior)
(Plate 133)
Florence, Museo Nazionale del Bargello
Diameter: 3 $^{9}/_{16}$″

Obverse: Profile facing right, surrounded by the inscription: SIGISMVNDVS · PANDVLFVS · DE · MALATESTIS · ARMINI · FANI · D.

Reverse: The figure appears, completely encased in armor. On either side, two plants support the helmet crowned with the elephant's head and the shield with the initials of Sigismondo and Isotta. Below: OPVS · PISANI · PICTORIS.

Datable circa 1444.
(Page 47)

Medal of Sigismondo Pandolfo Malatesta (with warrior on horseback)
(Plate 133)
Paris, Bibliothèque Nationale, Cabinet des Médailles
Diameter: 3 $^{7}/_{8}$″

Obverse: Profile facing right, surrounded by the inscription: SIGISMVNDVS · DE · MALATES-TIS · ARMINI · 7C · E · ROMANE · ECLLESIE · CAPITANEVS · GENERALIS.

Reverse: Sigismondo clad in armor, on horseback, holds a scepter in his hand and turns toward a castle bearing the date · M · CCCC · XLV. The adjacent tower bears the monogram of Sigismondo and Isotta. Below: OPVS · PISANI · PICTORIS.
(Page 47)

Medal of Novello Malatesta
(Plate 134)
Florence, Museo Nazionale del Bargello
Diameter: 3 $^{5}/_{16}$″

Obverse: Profile facing left. In the center: MALA-TESTA · NOVELLVS · CESENAE · DOMINVS. Above: DVX · EQVITVM · PRAESTANS.

Reverse: Novello Malatesta clad in armor, kneeling at the foot of a crucifix in a rocky landscape. Behind, his horse seen from the rear. Below: OPVS · PISANI · PICTORIS.

Datable 1445.
(Page 48)

Medal of Ludovico Gonzaga
(Plate 138)
Brescia, Museo Civico
Diameter: 4″

Obverse: Profile facing left. In the center: LVDO-VICVS · DE · GONZAGA. Below: MARCHIO · MANTVE · ET · CET. Above: CAPITANEVS · ARMIGERORVM.

Reverse: Ludovico Gonzaga on horseback, entirely clad in armor, holding his commander's baton. In the background there is the sun and in front, a sunflower. To the left: OPVS · PISANI · PICTORIS. Datable circa 1447.
(Page 48)

Medal of Cecilia Gonzaga

(Plates 139-140)
Milan, Castello Sforzesco, Medagliere
Diameter: 3 7/16''

Obverse: Profile facing left, surrounded by the inscription: CICILIA · VIRGO · FILIA · IOHANNIS · FRANCISCI · PRIMI · MARCHIONIS · MANTVE.

Reverse: A seated girl with a unicorn in a barren landscape; a crescent moon in the sky. On the right, on a stone tablet: OPVS · PISANI · PICTORIS, and the date: · M · CCCCXLVII.
(Pages 48, 49)

Medal of Vittorino da Feltre

(Plate 144)
Florence, Museo Nazionale del Bargello
Diameter: 2 5/8''

Obverse: Profile facing left, surrounded by the inscription: VICTORINVS · FELTRENSIS · SVMMVS.

Reverse: A pelican feeding its young, surrounded by the inscription: MATHEMATICVS · ET · OMNIS · HVMANITATIS · PATER · OPVS · PISANI · PICTORIS.
Datable 1446-47.
(Page 49)

Medal of Belloto Cumano

(Plate 145)
Milan, Castello Sforzesco, Medagliere
Diameter: 2 5/16''

Obverse: Profile facing left, surrounded by the inscription: BELLOTVS · CVMANVS.

Reverse: An ermine among bare trees; surrounding this, separated by four-petaled flower motifs, the words: OPVS · PISANI · PICTORIS. Upper center: the date · M · CCCCXLVII.
(Page 49)

Medal of Pier Candido Decembrio

(Plate 144)
London, British Museum
Diameter: 3 3/16''

Obverse: Profile facing right, surrounded by the inscription, some of whose words are separated by four-petaled flower motifs: · P · CANDIDVS · STVDIORVM · HVMANITATIS · DECVS.

Reverse: An open book resting on a rock, surrounded above by the inscription: OPVS · PISANI · PICTORIS.
Datable 1447-48.
(Pages 49, 50)

Medal of Alfonso of Aragon (with eagle)

(Plate 153)
Florence, Museo Nazionale del Bargello
Diameter: 4 1/4''

Obverse: Profile facing right between a crown and a helmet engraved with an open book. Above: DIVVS · ALPHONSVS · REX . Below: TRIVMPHATOR · ET · PACIFICVS. To the right, the date: M · C · C · C · C · XLVIIII.

Reverse: An eagle on a branch surrounded by vultures; at its feet, a dead fawn. Above: LIBERALITATIS · AVGVSTA. Below: PISANI · PICTORIS · OPVS.
(Pages 50, 51)

Medal of Alfonso of Aragon (with boar hunt)

(Plate 154)
London, British Museum
Diameter: 4 1/4''

Obverse: Profile facing right, above a crown, surrounded by the inscription: DIVVS · ALPHONSVS · ARAGO[niae] · SI[ciliae] · SI[ciliae] · VA[lentiae] · HIE[rosolimae] · HVN[gariae] · MA[ioricarum] · SAR[diniae] · COR[sicae] · REX · CO[mes] · BA[rcironae] · DV[x] · AT[henarum] · ET · N[eopatriae] · C[omes] · R[osciglionsis] · C[eritaniae].

Reverse: A nude huntsman in the act of stabbing a boar held by one ear by a dog. Above: VENATOR · INTREPIDVS. Below: OPVS · PISANI · PICTORIS.

Datable 1448-49.
(Pages 50, 51)

Medal of Alfonso of Aragon (with the angel in a carriage)

(Plate 158)
Above: Washington, D.C., National Gallery of Art (signed copy)
Diameter: 4 5/16''
Below: Paris, Bibliothèque Nationale, Cabinet des Médailles (unsigned copy)
Diameter: 4 1/4''

Obverse: Profile facing right, above a crown, flanked by the inscription, which continues round the edge: DIVVS · ALPHONSVS · ARAGONIAE · VTRIVSQVE · SICILIAE · VALENCIAE · HIE · HVN · MAIO · SAR · COR · REX · CO · BA · DV · AT · ET · NEO · AC · CO · RO · E · C.

Reverse: A carriage drawn by four horses, driven by a winged spirit. Above: FORTITVDO · MEA · ET · LAVS · MEA · DOMINVS · ET · FACTVS · EST · MICHI · IN · SALVTEM. Below (in the signed copy): OPVS · PISANI · PICTORIS.
Datable 1448-49.
(Pages 50, 51)

Portrait of Alfonso of Aragon (plaque)
(Plate 157)
New York, Metropolitan Museum of Art
$3\,^9/_{16} \times 1\,^{15}/_{16}''$
Profile facing right, above a crown, flanked by
the inscription: ALFOS REX.
Datable 1448-49.
(Page 50)

Medal of Inigo d'Avalos
(Plates 159, 160)
Berlin Museum
Diameter: 3''

Obverse: Profile facing right, surrounded by the
inscription: DON · INIGO · DE · DAVALOS.

Reverse: Fantastic landscape. Below: PER · VVI ·
SE · FA. Around: OPVS · PISANI · PICTORIS.
Datable 1448-49.
(Page 51)

LOST MEDALS

For a list of medals by Pisanello mentioned in old
sources (Vasari; Giovio; Basinio; Porcellio) and
no longer traceable, see HILL, 1930, p. 13. Follow-
ing is a list of some of them. *Medal of Alfonso
V;* reverse with helmet (Giovio). *Medal of Giovanni Aurispa* (Basinio). *Medal of Basinio da Parma*
(Basinio). *Medal of Braccio da Montone* (Vasari).
Medal of Giovanni Caracciolo (Vasari). *Medal of
Girolamo Castelli* (Basinio). *Medal of Borso d'Este*
(Vasari). *Medal of Ercole d'Este* (Vasari). *Medal of
Carlo Gonzaga* (Basinio). *Medal of Guarino Veronese*
(Basinio). *Medal of John Palaeologus;* with a cross
held by two hands on the reverse (Giovio). *Medal
of Carlo Malatesta* (Vasari; Hill supposes the latter
was confused with the Novello Malatesta medal).
Medal of Sigismondo Malatesta and Isotta (Giovio).
Medal of Martin V (Giovio). *Medal of Filippo de'
Medici* (Vasari). *Medal of Mahomet II* (Giovio).
Medal of Giannantonio Pandoni (Porcellio and Ba-
sinio). *Medal of Niccolò Piccinino;* with an armed
horse on the reverse (Giovio). *Medal of Giovanni
(?) Toscanella* (Basinio). *Medal of Giangaleazzo Vis-
conti* (Vasari). *Medal of Tito Vespasiano Strozzi* (Cf.
VENTURI, 1939, p. 91).

MEDALS ATTRIBUTED TO PISANELLO

Medal of Pisanello

I. *Obverse:* profile facing left and the inscription:
PISANVS · PICTOR. (See unnumbered plate
preceding page 15)

Reverse: F.S.K.I.P.F.T. (i.e. *Fides, Spes, Karitas,
Iustitia, Prudentia, Fortitudo, Temperantia*).

II. *Obverse:* Profile facing left, surrounded by the
inscription: PISANVS · PICTOR.

Reverse: The letters F.S.K.I.P.F.T. above olive
branches.
Cf. Rossi (1888); A. Venturi (1896), who, however,
in 1939 places it among the doubtful medals;
Nocq (1914); Martinie (1930).

Medal of Lionello d'Este

Obverse: Profile facing left surrounded by the inscription: LEONELLVS · MARCHIO · ESTEN-
SIS.

Reverse: A vase of flowers and two broken anchors
surrounded by the inscription: D[ominus] · FE-
RAR[ie] · REG[u] · ET · MVT[ine]. Below:
PISANVS · P[ictor].
Cf. Venturi (1896); Nocq (1914); and also Fig. 18.

Medal of Sigismondo Pandolfo Malatesta

Obverse: Profile facing left surrounded by the in-
scription: SIGISMONDVS · PANDVLFVS · DE ·
MALATESTIS · RO · ECLESIE · C · GENERAL-
IS.

Reverse: A large castle surrounded by the inscrip-
tion: CASTELLVM · SIGISMONDVM · ARI-
MENSE · M · CCCCXLVI.
Cf. Martinie (1930); Brenzoni (1952).

Medal of Niccolò III d'Este

I. *Obverse:* Profile, facing right, of the Marquis
wearing a beret, and the inscription: NICOLAI ·
MARCHIO · ESTENSIS · FER.

Reverse: The Este coat of arms surrounded by
the initials N and M.
Cf. Bernasconi (1862); Friedländer (1882); Rossi
(1888).

II. *Obverse:* Profile facing right with the inscription: NICOLAI · MARCHIO · ESTENSIS.

Reverse: The Este coat of arms in a wreath of
laurel surrounded by the initials N and M.
Cf. Bernasconi (1862); Friedländer (1882); Rossi
(1888); Gruyer (1897).

Medal of Leon Battista Alberti (ellipse-shaped)

I. Profile facing left and the inscription: L · BAP.
No reverse.

II. *Obverse:* Profile facing right.

Reverse: the inscription: LEO · BAPT · ISTA · AL ·
surrounded by a laurel wreath.

III. Profile facing left. No reverse.
Cf. Venturi (1896).

LIST OF DRAWINGS REPRODUCED

Studies of the Madonna, Animals, and Demons
(Plate 2)
Pen on parchment, $7^1/_8 \times 9^1/_8''$
Paris, Louvre (no. 2398)
(Pages 57, 58)

Study of Figures and the Madonna Suckling the Infant Jesus
(Plate 3)
Pencil and pen on parchment, $6^3/_4 \times 9^1/_4''$
Paris, Louvre (no. 2542)
(Page 57)

Study of Female Figures and Animals
(Plate 4)
Pen on parchment $10^1/_8 \times 7^1/_4''$
Vienna, Albertina (no. 16)
(Page 58)

Study of a Young Man's Head
(Plate 5)
Pencil on paper, $8^1/_4 \times 7^1/_4''$
Paris, Louvre (no. 2330)
(Page 58)

Study of Nudes and an Annunciation
(Plate 13)
Pen on parchment, $8^3/_4 \times 6^1/_2''$
Rotterdam, Boymans Museum (no. 520)
(Page 58)

Study of a Leg, Flowers, and Squid
(Plate 14)
Pen on paper, $9^5/_8 \times 7^3/_8''$
Paris, Louvre (no. 2262)
(Page 58)

Study of Figures
(Plate 15)
Pen and pencil on parchment, $8^1/_4 \times 6^1/_4''$
Vienna, Albertina (no. 44640)
(Page 59)

Study of Faces (male profile and female face)
(Plate 16)
Charcoal on parchment, $6^1/_2 \times 9^1/_4''$
London, British Museum (no. 11 v.)
(Page 59)

Study of a Deer and Goat
(Plate 17)
Watercolor on parchment, $8 \times 5^3/_8''$
Paris, Louvre (no. 2550)
(Page 60)

Study of Dogs Hunting Game
(Plate 18)
Watercolor on parchment, $10 \times 6^3/_4''$
Paris, Louvre (no. 2568)
(Page 60)

Study of Dogs Hunting Game
(Plate 19)
Pen on paper, $8^5/_8 \times 7^5/_8''$
Paris, Louvre (no. 2547)
(Page 60)

Study of a Seated Man, Deer, and Rabbits
(Plate 20)
Silverpoint and watercolor on parchment, $9^1/_8 \times 6^7/_8''$
Paris, Louvre (no. 2436)
(Page 59)

Study of Warriors
(Plate 21)
Pen on paper, $11 \times 7^7/_8''$
Paris, Lugt Collection (no. 4876)
(Pages 60, 61)

Study of a Young Man with a Sword
(Plate 22)
Pen and pencil on reddish paper, $9^7/_8 \times 7^1/_8''$
Paris, Louvre (no. 2509)
(Page 61)

Study of Figures in a Vaulted Room
(Plate 23)
Pen on reddish paper, $9^7/_8 \times 6^7/_8''$
Paris, Louvre (no. 2520)
(Page 61)

Costume Study
(Plate 24)
Pen on parchment, $10^7/_8 \times 7^5/_8''$
Milan, Biblioteca Ambrosiana (F 214, no. 6)
(Page 61)

Costume Study
(Plate 25)
Pen on parchment, $10^7/_8 \times 7^3/_8''$
Milan, Biblioteca Ambrosiana (F. 214, no. 61)
(Page 61)

Study of Jesus Addressing a Pilgrim
(Plate 26)
Pen on parchment, $10^3/_4 \times 7^5/_8''$
Paris, Louvre (no. 2541)
(Pages 61, 62)

Study of a Leopard and Columns
(Plate 27)
Pen and watercolor on parchment, $6^1/_2 \times 5^5/_8''$
Paris, Louvre (no. 2425)
(Page 63)

Study of a Mantle
(Plate 28)
Pen on gray paper. The mantle reproduced is a detail of a page measuring $9^7/_8 \times 6^5/_8''$
Paris, Louvre (no. 2275)
(Page 62)

Study of Plants and a Man's Legs
(Plate 29)
Pen on paper, $9^7/_8 \times 6^7/_8''$
Paris, Louvre (no. 2264)
(Page 63)

Study of a Lion Mask and Architectural Motifs
(Plate 30)
Pen on paper, $11^1/_2 \times 7^7/_8''$
Paris, Louvre (no. 2290)
(Page 62)

Study of Masks, Feet, and Sandals
(Plate 30)
Silverpoint and pen on parchment, $7^1/_8 \times 5''$
Rotterdam, Boymans Museum (no. 521)
(Page 62)

Study of a Trumpeter
(Plate 31)
Pencil and pen on reddish paper, $11 \times 7^7/_8''$
Paris, Louvre (no. 2616 v.)
(Page 63)

Study of a Fife and Drum Player
(Plate 32)
Pen on reddish paper, $11^1/_4 \times 8''$
Paris, Louvre (no. 2614)
(Page 63)

Study of a Ceremonial Scene, a Trumpeter, and Male Heads
(Plate 33)
Pen on gray paper, $10^5/_8 \times 8^1/_8''$
Paris, Louvre (no. 2300)
(Page 63)

Study of a Male Profile
(Plate 34)
Pencil and pen on paper, $12^3/_8 \times 8^1/_8''$
Paris, Louvre (no. 2339)
(Page 64)

Study of a Male Head
(Plate 35, left)
Pencil on paper, $10^1/_4 \times 7^1/_2''$
Paris, Louvre (no. 2337)
(Page 64)

Study of a Male Head
(Plate 35, right)
Pencil on paper, $11^1/_4 \times 7^1/_2''$
Paris, Louvre (no. 2335)
(Page 64)

Study for a Flagellation
(Plate 37)
Pen on paper, $11^3/_4 \times 7^5/_8''$
Milan, Biblioteca Ambrosiana (F 214, no. 18)
(Page 64)

Study of Male Nudes, a Saint, and a Reclining Woman
(Plate 38)
Pen on paper, $11^3/_4 \times 7^5/_8''$

Milan, Biblioteca Ambrosiana (F 214, no. 18 v.)
(Page 64)

Study of Male Nudes and a Saint
(Plate 39)
Pen on parchment, $10^5/_8 \times 7^1/_2''$
Berlin Museum (no. 487)
(Pages 64, 65)

Study from the Antique
(Plate 40)
Pen on parchment, $7^5/_8 \times 10^7/_8''$
Milan, Biblioteca Ambrosiana (F 214, no. 13)
(Page 65)

Study of a Dancing Figure
(Plate 41)
Pen on parchment. Detail of a page measuring $7^3/_8 \times 9^1/_2''$
Oxford, Ashmolean Museum (no. 41 v.)
(Page 65)

Study of an Emperor's Head
(Plate 42)
Pen on reddish paper, $10^1/_4 \times 7^1/_8''$
Paris, Louvre (no. 2592)
(Page 66)

Study of a Winged Bull
(Plate 43)
Pen on paper $5^1/_8 \times 6^1/_8''$
Paris, Louvre (no. 2408)
(Page 66)

Study of a Reclining Bull
(Plate 44)
Silverpoint on parchment, $6^3/_4 \times 5^1/_8''$
Paris, Louvre (no. 2410)
(Page 66)

Study of a Horse
(Plate 45)
Pen on paper, $6^5/_8 \times 10^3/_4''$
Paris, Louvre (no. 2369)
(Page 66)

Study of a Man's Head
(Plate 46)
Pen on reddish paper, $10^3/_8 \times 7^5/_8''$
Paris, Louvre (no. 2608)
(Page 67)

Study of Male Profiles
(Plate 46)
Pen on reddish paper, $10^1/_2 \times 7^1/_2''$
Paris, Louvre (no. 2600)
(Plage 67)

Study of a Young Man Taking Off His Doublet
(Plate 47)
Pen on reddish paper, $10^1/_4 \times 14^1/_8''$
Paris, Louvre (no. 2597)
(Page 67)

Study of a Warrior
(Plate 48)
Pen on reddish paper, $11 \times 7^3/_4''$
Paris, Louvre (no. 2616)
(Page 67)

Study of Hanged Men, a Lady, and a Boy
(Plate 55)
Metalpoint and pen on paper, $11^1/_4 \times 7^3/_4''$
London, British Museum (1895-9-15-441)
(Page 69)

Study of Hanged Men
(Plate 56)
Pen on paper, $10^1/_4 \times 7^1/_8''$
New York, Frick Collection
(Page 69)

Study of Heads and an Archer
(Plate 57)
Silverpoint and pen, $6^7/_8 \times 9''$
Paris, Louvre (no. 2325)
(Pages 69, 70)

Study of a Man's Head
(Plate 58)
Pen on paper, $11 \times 7^7/_8''$
Paris, Louvre (no. 2621)
(Pages 67, 68)

Study of a Head
(Plate 61)
Pen and pencil on reddish paper, $8^5/_8 \times 7^5/_8''$
Paris, Louvre (no. 2315 v.)
(Page 70)

Study of a Young Man's Head
(Plate 62)
Pen on reddish paper, $5 \times 5^3/_4''$
Modena, Galleria Estense (no. 895)
(Page 71)

Study of a Horse
(Plate 63)
Pen on paper, $7^5/_8 \times 4^5/_8''$
Paris, Louvre (no. 2444)
(Page 69)

Study of a Woman's Head
(Plate 64)
Pen on reddish paper, $9^5/_8 \times 7^1/_8''$
Paris, Louvre (no. 2343)
(Page 70)

Study of a Woman's Head
(Plate 67)
Pen on paper, $9^7/_8 \times 6^3/_4''$
Paris, Louvre (no. 2342 v.)
(Page 70)

Study of a Woman's Head
(Plate 68)
Pen on paper, $9^7/_8 \times 6^3/_4''$
Paris, Louvre (no. 2342)
(Page 70)

Costume Study
(Plate 69)
Pen and watercolor on parchment, $10^3/_8 \times 7^1/_8''$
Bayonne, Musée Bonnat (no. 141)
(Pages 70, 71)

Costume Study
(Plate 70)
Pen and watercolor on parchment, $10^3/_4 \times 7^3/_4''$
Chantilly, Musée Condé
(Page 71)

Costume Study
(Plate 71)
Pen and watercolor on parchment, $7^3/_8 \times 9^1/_2''$
Oxford, Ashmolean Museum (no. 41)
(Page 71)

Study of a Dog
(Plate 72, top)
Pen on paper, $6^1/_4 \times 7^3/_4''$
Paris, Louvre (no. 2434)
(Page 68)

Study of a Dog
(Plate 72, bottom)
Pen and watercolor on paper, $7^1/_4 \times 9^5/_8''$
Paris, Louvre (no. 2433)
(Page 68)

Study of Cranes
(Plate 73)
Pen on paper, $9^3/_4 \times 6^3/_4''$
Paris, Louvre (no. 2469)
(Page 72)

Study of a Wounded Lizard
(Plate 86)
Silverpoint on parchment, $4^3/_4 \times 5^7/_8''$
Paris, Louvre (no. 2382)
(Pages 66, 67)

Study of a Man in a Turban
(Plate 87)
Pen on reddish paper, $10^1/_2 \times 7^1/_2''$
Paris, Louvre (no. 2609 v.)
(Page 68)

Study of a Young Man's Head
(Plate 88, left)
Pen on reddish paper, $8^1/_4 \times 7^1/_8''$
Paris, Louvre (no. 2594)
(Page 72)

Study of a Young Man's Head
(Plate 88, right)
Pen on reddish paper, $10 \times 6^7/_8''$
Paris, Louvre (no. 2595)
(Page 72)

Study of a Young Man's Head
(Plate 89)
Pencil on paper, $10 \times 6^7/_8''$
Paris, Louvre (no. 2333)
(Page 72)

Study for the Medal of John Palaeologus
(Plate 94)
Pencil on paper, $10^1/_4 \times 7^1/_2''$
Paris, Louvre (no. 2478)
(Page 73)

Study of Figures
(Plate 95)
Pen on paper, $7^7/_8 \times 11^1/_2''$
Paris, Louvre (no. M.I. 1062 v.)
(Page 73)

Study of Figures with a Cufic Inscription
(Plate 96)
Pen on paper, $7^7/_8 \times 11^1/_2''$
Paris, Louvre (no. M.I. 1062)
(Page 73)

Study of a Man in a Turban
(Plate 97)
Pencil on paper, $11^7/_8 \times 8^1/_8''$
Paris, Louvre (no. 2480)
(Page 73)

Study for the Medal of Filippo Maria Visconti
(Plate 98, left)
Pencil on paper, $11^3/_8 \times 7^3/_4''$
Paris, Louvre (no. 2483)
(Pages 73, 74)

Study for the Medal of Filippo Maria Visconti
(Plate 98, right)
Pen on paper, $11^3/_8 \times 7^1/_4''$
Paris, Louvre (no. 2484)
(Pages 73, 74)

Study of a Horse's Head
(Plate 99)
Pen on paper, $9^1/_4 \times 6^1/_4''$
Paris, Louvre (no. 2355)
(Page 75)

Study of a Horse's Head
(Plate 100)
Sepia on parchment, $4^1/_4 \times 3^7/_8''$
Paris, Louvre (no. 2405)
(Pages 75, 76)

Study of a Man's Head
(Plate 101)
Pen on parchment, $37^3/_8 \times 29^1/_2''$
Paris, Louvre (no. 2322)
(Pages 74, 75)

Study of a Procession and a Landscape
(Plate 105)
Pen on reddish paper, $10^1/_8 \times 7^1/_2''$
Paris, Louvre (no. 2595 v.)
(Page 74)

Study of "Luxury"
(Plate 106)
Pen and bistre on reddish paper, $5^1/_8 \times 6''$
Vienna, Albertina (no. 24018)
(Page 76)

Study of Male Nudes
(Plate 107)
Pen on parchment, $7^3/_4 \times 5^3/_4''$
Rotterdam, Boymans Museum (no. 519)
(Page 76)

Study of a Male Figure
(Plate 108)
Pencil on paper, $12^1/_8 \times 8^1/_8''$
Paris, Louvre (no. 2482)
(Page 75)

Study of a Young Man's Head
(Plate 118)
Silverpoint on parchment, $5^1/_2 \times 3^7/_8''$
Paris, Louvre (no. 2316)
(Page 76)

Study of a Boy Reading
(Plate 119)
Pen on paper, $6^1/_4 \times 7^7/_8''$
Paris, Louvre (no. 2299)
(Page 77)

Study of a Horse and Rider
(Plate 123)
Pen on paper, $7^3/_4 \times 10^1/_4''$
Paris, Louvre (no. 2368)
(Page 79)

Study of a Hare
(Plate 124)
Pen and watercolor on paper, $5^1/_2 \times 10^1/_4''$
Paris, Louvre (no. 2445)
(Pages 77, 78)

Study of a Stag
(Plate 125)
Pen and watercolor on paper, $10 \times 4^1/_8''$
Paris, Louvre (no. 2549)
(Page 77)

Study of a Duck
(Plate 126)
Pen and watercolor on paper, $6^5/_8 \times 8^5/_8''$
Paris, Louvre (no. 2462)
(Page 77)

Study of a Dog
(Plate 127)
Pencil on paper, $7^1/_4 \times 8^5/_8''$
Paris, Louvre (no. 2429 v.)
(Page 78)

Assorted Studies
(Plate 128)
Pen on paper, $7^5/_8 \times 10^1/_4''$
Paris, Louvre (no. 2368 v.)
(Pages 78, 79)

Study of Hoopoes
(Plate 129)
Pen and watercolor on paper, $6^3/_8 \times 8^1/_2''$
Paris, Louvre (no. 2467)
(Page 77)

Study of a Dog's Head
(Plate 130)
Pencil and watercolor on paper, $7^1/_4 \times 8^5/_8''$
Paris, Louvre (no. 2429)
(Page 78)

Study of a Hare
(Plate 131)
Pen and watercolor on paper, $5^1/_2 \times 8^7/_8''$
Paris, Louvre (no. 2445)
(Page 78)

Study of a Rabbit
(Plate 132)
Pen on paper, $5^7/_8 \times 7^7/_8''$
Paris, Louvre (no. 2439)
(Page 78)

Study of a Horse
(Plate 135)
Pen on paper, $7^7/_8 \times 6^1/_2''$
Paris, Louvre (no. 2378)
(Page 79)

Study of a Horse's Head
(Plate 136)
Pen on paper, $10^7/_8 \times 7^3/_4''$
Paris, Louvre (no. 2363)
(Page 79)

Study of a Woman's Head
(Plate 141)
Pen on reddish paper, $11 \times 7^7/_8''$
Paris, Louvre (no. 2589)
(Page 80)

Study of Two Bare Feet
(Plate 142)
Pen on reddish paper, $7^5/_8 \times 10^3/_8''$
Paris, Louvre (no. 2596 v.)
(Page 80)

Study of a Peewit
(Plate 143)
Pen and watercolor on paper, $6^1/_8 \times 11^1/_4''$
Paris, Louvre (no. 2465)
(Page 78)

Study of a Cockerel
(Plate 148, left)
Pen on reddish paper, $9^3/_4 \times 14^1/_2''$
Milan, Biblioteca Ambrosiana (F 214, no. 9)
(Page 78)

Study of a Seated Monk
(Plate 148, right)
Pen on paper, $10^5/_8 \times 7^5/_8''$
Paris, Louvre (no. 2332 v.)
(Page 81)

Study of Horses' Heads
(Plate 149)
Pen on paper, $11^3/_8 \times 7^1/_4''$
Paris, Louvre (no. 2354)
(Page 81)

Study of Shod Feet
(Plate 151)
Pencil on paper, $10^5/_8 \times 7^7/_8''$
Paris, Louvre (no. 2281)
(Page 80)

Study of Two Saints
(Plate 152, left)
Pen on paper, $10 \times 7^3/_4''$
Paris, Louvre (no. 2633)
(Page 80)

Study of the Madonna and Child
(Plate 152, right)
Pen on reddish paper, $7^3/_4 \times 10^1/_2''$
Paris, Louvre (no. 2623 v.)
(Page 80)

Study for a Medal of Alfonso of Aragon
(Plate 155)
Pen on paper, $6^1/_2 \times 5^1/_2''$
Paris, Louvre (no. 2486)
(Pages 81, 82)

Study for a Portrait of Alfonso of Aragon
(Plate 156)
Pen on paper, $11^1/_8 \times 8^1/_4''$
Paris, Louvre (no. 2481)
(Page 81)

Study of a Fantastic Landscape
(Plate 161)
Pen on paper, $7^5/_8 \times 10^3/_8''$
Paris, Louvre (no. 2280)
(Page 84)

Study of Figures in Costume
(Plate 162)
Pen and pencil on parchment, $9^7/_8 \times 13^3/_8''$
London, British Museum (1846-5-9-143)
(Page 82)

Study of a Wolf
(Plate 163)
Pen and watercolor on parchment, $6^1/_4 \times 8^7/_8''$
Paris, Louvre (no. 2424)
(Page 82)

Study of a Wildcat
(Plate 163)
Silverpoint on parchment, $5^7/_8 \times 9^1/_8''$
Paris, Louvre (no. 2422)
(Page 82)

Study of a Leg
(Plate 164, left)
Pen on paper, $9^1/_4 \times 7^1/_8''$
Paris, Louvre (no. 2263)
(Page 82)

Study of a Leg
(Plate 164, right)
Pen on gray paper, $9^5/_8 \times 6^7/_8''$
Paris, Louvre (no. 2275 v.)
(Page 82)

Study of Lynxes
(Plate 165)
Pen on paper, $9^7/_8 \times 7^1/_8''$
Paris, Louvre (no. 2418)
(Page 82)

Study of Horses and a Page
(Plate 166)
Pen on parchment, $5^1/_8 \times 4^1/_8''$
Paris, Louvre (no. 2372)
(Pages 82, 83)

Study of a Falcon
(Plate 167)
Pen and watercolor on paper, $8^3/_4 \times 5^3/_8''$
Paris, Louvre (no. 2453)
(Page 83)

Study of an Old Man
(Plate 168, left)
Pencil on paper, $10^1/_4 \times 7^1/_4''$
Paris, Louvre (no. 2338)
(Page 83)

Study of a Fat Man
(Plate 168, right)
Pencil on reddish paper, $10^5/_8 \times 7^1/_2''$
Paris, Louvre (no. 2606 v.)
(Page 83)

Study of Two Landscapes with Figures
(Plate 169)
Pen on reddish paper, $9^1/_2 \times 7^1/_8''$
Paris, Louvre (no. 2594 v.)
(Page 83)

Study of a Man's Head
(Plate 170)
Pen on paper, $10^1/_2 \times 7^3/_4''$
Paris, Louvre (no. 2281 v.)
(Page 83)

Study of Peacocks
(Plate 171)
Pen on paper, $10 \times 7^3/_8''$
Paris, Louvre (no. 2390 v.)
(Page 83)

Study of a Recumbent Deer
(Plate 172)
Pen on paper, $7^7/_8 \times 11''$
Paris, Louvre (no. 2489)
(Pages 83, 84)

Study of the Madonna Suckling the Child
(Plate 173)
Pencil on paper, $18^3/_4 \times 15^3/_8''$
Paris, Louvre (no. 2590)
(Page 84)

BIBLIOGRAPHY

A.E. "Riparazione all'affresco di Vittore Pisano in Sant'Anastasia a Verona," *Archivio Storico dell'arte*, 1890

ALBRECHT, I. R. "Zu Tito Vespasiano Strozza's und Basinio Basini's lateinischen Lobgedichten auf Vittore Pisano," *Romanische Forschungen*, 1888

ALEXANDRE, A. "Pisanello," *L'Art et les Artistes*, 1904

ANTAL, F. *La pittura fiorentina e il suo ambiente sociale nel Trecento e nel primo Quattrocento*, Turin, 1960

ARGAN, G. C., and LASSAIGNE, J. *De van Eyck à Botticelli*, Geneva-Paris, 1955

ARMAND, A. *Les médailleurs italiens du XVe et XVIe siècle*, Paris, 1883-87

ARSLAN, W. "Intorno a Giambono e a Francesco dei Franceschi," *Emporium*, 1948

AVENA, A. *Capolavori della pittura Veronese*, (Catalogo della Mostra), Verona, 1947

BABELON, J. *La médaille et les médailleurs*, Paris, 1927

———. *Pisanello*, Paris, 1931

———. "L'exposition Pisanello," *Beaux-Arts*, 1932

———. "Pisanello vers 1397-1455," *Les sculpteurs célèbres*, Paris, 1954

BALDASS, L. von. *Österreichische Tafelmalerei der Spätgotik*, Vienna, 1934

BAZZETTA, G. A. "Milano a Vittore Pisanello," *La Perseveranza*, 1908

BEAN J. *Les dessins italiens de la Collection Bonnat*, Paris, 1960

BELTRAMI, L. "Vecchi altari del Duomo di Milano," *Rassegna d'Arte*, 1902

BERENSON, B. *Italian Pictures of the Renaissance*, Oxford, 1932

———. *North Italian Painters of the Renaissance*, New York-London, 1907

———. *North Italian Painters of the Renaissance*, New York-Oxford, 1932

———. *Pitture italiane del Rinascimento*, Milan, 1936

———. *The Golden Urn*, Fiesole, 1897

———. "The Morelli Collection at Bergamo," *The Connoisseur*, 1902

BERNASCONI, C. *Il Pisano grand'artefice veronese della prima metà del secolo XV*, Verona, 1862

———. *Studio sopra la pittura del secolo XIV e XV e della scuola pittorica veronese dai medi tempi fino a tutto il secolo XVIII*, Verona, 1864

BERNICH, E. "Leon Battista Alberti e l'Arco Trionfale di Alfonso d'Aragona in Napoli," *Napoli nobilissima*, 1903

BERTOLOTTI, A. "Le arti minori alla corte di Mantova," *Archivio Storico Lombardo*, 1888

BIADEGO, G. *Il Pisanello* (discorso inaugurale della mostra di Belle Arti letto il 2 maggio 1892), Verona, 1892

139

————. "Pisanello," *Discorsi e profili*, Milan, 1903

————. "Pisanus Pictor," *Atti del R. Istituto Veneto di Scienze, Lettere ed Arti*, note I, 1908; notes II and III, 1909; note IV and V, 1910; notes VI, 1913

BIANCOLINI, G. B. G. *Notizie storiche delle Chiese di Verona*, Verona, 1749-71

BIERMANN, G. *Verona*, Leipzig, 1904

BIONDO, F. *Italia illustrata*, ed. Verona, 1482; written 1450

BISCARO, G. "Pisanus Pictor alla corte di Filippo Maria Visconti nel 1440," *Archivio Storico Lombardo*, 1911

BODE, U., and TSCHUDI, H. V. "Die Anbetung der Könige von Vittore Pisano und die Madonna mit Heiligen aus dem Besitz des Cav. dal Pozzo," *Jahrbuch der königlich preussischen Kunstsammlungen*, VI, Berlin, 1885

————. "Vittor Pisano," *Annuaire des Musées de Berlin*, 1885

BODE, W. von. "Zur neuesten Forschung auf dem Gebiete der italienischen Medaillenkunde," *Zeitschrift für bildende Kunst*, 1903

————; GRONAU, G.; and HADELN, D. F. von. *Archivalische Beiträge zur Geschichte der venezianischen Kunst aus dem Nachlass Gustav Ludwig*, Berlin, 1911

BOTH de TAUZIA, L. *Musée National du Louvre. Dessins, Cartons, Pastels et Miniatures des diverses Écoles* (Deuxième notice supplémentaire), Paris, 1888

————. *Notice des dessins de la collection His de la Salle exposés au Musée du Louvre*, Paris, 1881

————. "Vittore Pisano," *L'Art*, 1882

BOTTARI, M. G., and TICOZZI, S. *Raccolta di lettere sulla pittura, scultura e architettura*, V, Milan, 1822

BRENZONI, R. *Pisanello* Florence, 1952

————. *Rettifiche ai problemi pisanelliani in occasione della Mostra di Castelvecchio*, Verona, 1959

————. "La Resurrezione di Nanni de Bartolo e l'Annunciazione pisanelliana in S. Fermo Maggiore di Verona," *Per l'Arte Sacra*, 1932

————. "Per un attendibile catalogo pisanelliano," *Atti dell'Accademia di Agricoltura, Scienze e Lettere*, Verona, 1958-59

————. "Profilo pisanelliano," *Le Venezie francescane*, Verona, 1933

————. "Il ritratto dell'Imperatore Sigismondo," *Rivista di varia umanità*, 1958

BREVENTANO, S. *Istoria della antichità, nobilità et delle cose notabili della città di Pavia*, Pavia, 1570

CALABI, A., and CORNAGGIA, G. *Pisanello. L'opera medaglistica paragonata a quella pittorica, distinta dalla produzione di seguaci e falsificatori dei sec. XV e XVI*, Milan, 1928

CAMPORI, G. *Raccolta di cataloghi ed inventari inediti*, Modena, 1870

————. "I miniatori degli estensi," *Atti della R. Deputazione di Storia patria per le Provincie Modenesi e Parmensi*, 1872

CARLI, A. *Istoria della città di Verona*, Verona, 1796

CAVALCASELLE, G. B., and CROWE, J. A. *A New History of Painting in Italy from the Second to Sixteenth Century*, London, 1864

CAVATTONI, C. *Due opuscoli del Guarino Veronese che vengono a luce il dì delle nozze del Sig. Pietro Finato e Maria Antonietta Martinati*, Verona, 1860

————. *Tre carmi latini composti a mezzo il secolo XV in lode di Vittore Pisano*, Verona, 1861

CHARAVAY, E. *Inventaire des autographes et documents historiques réunis par M. B. Fillon*, Paris, 1878

CHENNEVIÈRES, H. de. *Les dessins du Louvre*, Paris, 1882-83

CHIARELLI, R. *Pisanello*, Milan, 1958

CIPOLLA, C. *Compendio della storia politica di Verona*, Verona, 1900

————. "Ricerche storiche intorno alla chiesa di S. Anastasia in Verona," *L'Arte*, 1914

COLASANTI, A. *Gentile da Fabriano*, Bergamo, 1909

COLETTI, L. *Pisanello*, Milan, 1953

————. *I Primitivi*, III, Novara, 1947

————. *Pittura Veneta del Quattrocento*, Novara, 1953

————. "Il Maestro degli Innocenti," *Arte veneta*, 1948

————. "Pittura veneta dal Tre al Quattrocento," *Arte veneta*, 1947

COURAJOD, L. "La part de la France du Nord dans l'œuvre de la Renaissance," *Gazette des Beaux-Arts*, 1890

CREIGHTON, G. "The development of Gentile Bellini's portraiture," *Arte veneta*, 1961

CROWE, J. A., and CAVALCASELLE, G. B. *A New History of Painting in Italy from the Second to Sixteenth Century*, London, 1864

CUPPINI, L. "Un ritratto di Michele Giambono a Palazzo Rosso," *Commentari*, 1962

DA LISCA, A. *S. Fermo Maggiore di Verona*, Verona, 1909

DAL POZZO, B. C. *Le Vite dei Pittori, degli Scultori ed Architetti veronesi*, Verona, 1718

D'ANCONA, P. *Umanesimo e Rinascimento*, Turin, 1953

DAVIES, M. *National Gallery Catalogues. The Earlier Italian Schools*, London, 1951

DE FOVILLE, J. *Pisanello et les médailleurs italiens*, Paris, 1908

————. "A quelle date Pisanello a-t-il exécuté la médaille de Jean François Ier Gonzague," *Revue numismatique*, 1909

————. "Pisanello d'après des découvertes récéntes," *Revue de l'art ancien et moderne*, 1908

————. "Pisanello et les médailleurs italiens," *Les grands artistes*, 1909

DEGENHART, B. *Pisanello*, Vienna, 1940

————. *Pisanello*, Turin, 1945

————. "Das Wiener Bildnis Kaiser Sigismund, ein Werk Pisanellos," *Jahrbuch der kunsthistorischen Sammlungen in Wien*, 1944

————. "Di una pubblicazione su Pisanello e di altri fatti," *Arte veneta*, 1953-54

————. "Le quattro tavole della Leggenda di San Benedetto, opere giovanili del Pisanello," *Arte veneta*, 1949

————. "Un'opera di Pisanello: il ritratto dell'imperatore Sigismondo a Vienna," *Arti figurative*, 1946

————. "Zu Pisanellos Wandbild in S. Anastasia in Verona," *Zeitschrift für Kunstwissenschaft*, 1951

————, and SCHMITT, A. "Gentile da Fabriano in Rom und die Anfänge des Antikenstudiums," *Münchener Jahrbuch der bildenden Kunst*, 1960

DELL'ACQUA, G. A. *Disegni di Pisanello*, Milan, 1952

————. *Pisanello*, Milan, 1952

DESTRÉE, J. *Notes sur les primitifs italiens. Sur quelques peintres de Toscane*, Brussels-Florence, 1899

DOGSON, C. "Ein Studienblatt des Vittore Pisanos zu dem Fresko in S. Anastasia zu Verona," *Jahrbuch der preussischen Kunstsammlungen*, 1894

DUPONT, J., and GNUDI, C. *La peinture gothique*, Geneva-Paris-New York, 1954

EPHRUSSI, C. "La date de la mort de Vittore Pisano," *Chronique des Arts*, 1883

———. "Les dessins de la Collection His de la Salle," *Gazette des Beaux-Arts*, 1882

———. "Les médailleurs de la Renaissance: Vittore Pisano par M. A. Heiss," *Gazette des Beaux-Arts*, 1881

FABRICZY, C. von. *Die Medaillen der italienischen Renaissance*, Leipzig, 1903

FACIO, B. *De viris illustribus*, ed. Florence, 1745 (written 1456)

FERRARI, O. "Un'opera di Niccolò de Pietro," *Commentari*, 1953

FILLON, B. "Les Médailleurs italiens du XVe et XVIe siècle," *Gazette des Beaux-Arts*, 1879

FIOCCO, G. *L'arte di Andrea Mantegna*, Bologna, 1927

———. "Niccolò di Pietro, Pisanello, Venceslao," *Bollettino d'Arte*, 1952

FISCHER, O., and PLANISCIG, L. "Zwei Beiträge zu Pisanello," *Jahrbuch der preussischen Kunstsammlungen*, 1933

FOGOLARI, G. "Il ciclo dei mesi nella torre Aquila di Trento," *Tridentum*, 1905

FOSSI-TODOROW, M. "The exhibition *Da Altichiero a Pisanello* in Verona," *The Burlington Magazine*, 1959

FRANCASTEL, P., and G. *Du Bizantin à la Renaissance*, Paris, 1959

FRIEDLÄNDER, J. *Die italienischen Schaumünzen des fünfzehnten Jahrhunderts*, Berlin, 1882

FRIZZONI, G. *La Galleria Morelli in Bergamo*, Bergamo, 1892

———. "Alcuni appunti critici intorno alla Galleria di Verona," *Rassegna d'Arte*, 1904

———. "I nostri grandi maestri in relazione al quinto fascicolo dei disegni di Oxford," *L'Arte*, 1907

———. "La data della morte di Vittore Pisano," *L'Arte*, 1883

FROHLICH-BUM, L., and STIX, A. *Beschreibender Katalog der Handzeichnungen in der Albertina*, I, Vienna, 1926

FRY, R. E. "Notes on a drawing and a painting of Pisanello," *The Burlington Magazine*, 1904

GAYE, G. *Carteggio inedito d'artisti dei secoli XIV, XV, XVI*, Florence, 1839

GESSNER, W. E. "Die Bedeutung des Veronesischen in der Malerei des Antonio Pisano," *Zeitschrift für bildende Kunst*, 1926-27

GNOLI, D. "Passaporto del Pisanello," *Archivio Storico dell'Arte*, 1890

GNUDI, C., and DUPONT, J. *La peinture gothique*, Geneva-Paris-New York, 1954

GOLLOB, H. *Gentile da Fabriano und Pisanello Fresken in Laterano zu Rom*, Strasbourg, 1927

GRASSI, L. *Storia del disegno*, Rome, 1947

———. *Tutta la pittura di Gentile da Fabriano*, Milan, 1953

GRONAU, G.; HADELN, D. F. von; and BODE, W. von. *Archivalische Beiträge zur Geschichte der venezianischen Kunst aus dem Nachlass Gustav Ludwig*, Berlin, 1911

GRUYER, G. *L'Art ferrarais à l'époque des Princes d'Este*, Paris, 1897

———. "Vittore Pisano appellé aussi le Pisanello," *Gazette des Beaux-Arts*, 1893-94

GUIFFREY, J. *Les dessins de Pisanello conservés au Musée du Louvre*, Paris, 1911-20

HABIC, G. *Die Medaillen der italienischen Renaissance*, Stuttgart, 1924

HADELN, D. F. von; BODE, W. von; and GRONAU, G. *Archivalische Beiträge zur Geschichte der venezianischen Kunst aus dem Nachlass Gustav Ludwig*, Berlin, 1911

HAUSER, A. *The Social History of Art*, I, London, 1951

HEISS, A. *Les médailleurs de la Renaissance: Vittore Pisano*, Paris, 1881

HENTZEN, A. "Die vision des Heiligen Eustachius von Antonio Pisanello," *Der Kunstbrief*, 1948

HERMANIN, F. "Una tavola di Stefano da Zevio a Palazzo Venezia," *Bollettino d'Arte*, 1923; 1924

HEVESY, A. "Zur Pariser Pisanello-Ausstellung," *Pantheon*, 1932

HILL, G. F. *A Corpus of Medals of the Renaissance*, 2 vols., London, 1930

————. *Dessins de Pisanello choisis et reproduits avec introduction et notices*, Paris-Brussels, 1929

————. *Portrait Medals of Italian Art*, London, 1912

————. *Pisanello*, London, 1905

————. *Selected Italian Medals of the Renaissance in the British Museum*, London, 1915

————. *The G. Dreyfus Collection, Renaissance Medals*, Oxford, 1931

————. "A last medal by Pisanello," *Pantheon*, 1931

————. "Forgery of Pisanello's signature," *The Burlington Magazine*, 1911

————. "Gallow-studies by Pisanello," *The Burlington Magazine*, 1920

————. "New Light on Pisanello," *The Burlington Magazine*, 1908

————. "Pisanello," in: *Allgemeines Lexikon der bildenden Künstler*, XXVII, by U. Thieme and F. Becker, Leipzig, 1935

————. "Pisanello's Portrait of a Princess," *The Burlington Magazine*, 1904

————. "Recent research on Pisanello," *The Burlington Magazine*, 1910

————. "Some drawings of the antique attributed to Pisanello," *Papers of the British School,* 1906

HUGELSHOFFER, W. "Circle of Pisanello," *Old Master Drawings*, 1927-28

JACOBSON, E. "Italienische Gemälde im Louvre," *Repertorium für Kunstwissenschaft*, 1902

KEARY, C. F. *Guide to the Exhibition of Italian Medals*, Department of Coins and Medals of the British Museum, London, 1893

KELLER, H. "Bildhauerzeichnungen Pisanellos," *Festschrift Kurt Bauch*, Berlin-Munich, 1957

KENNER, F. "Die Porträtsammlung des Erzherzogs Ferdinand von Tyrol," *Jahrbuch der kunsthistorischen Sammlungen des allerhöchsten Kaiserhauses*, 1896-97

KLINGSOR, T. "Les dessins de Pisanello," *Amour de l'Art*, 1923

KUNSTLER, C. "Dessins italiens des XIVe, XVe, et XVIe siècles," *Beaux Arts*, 1931

LANZI, L. *Storia della Pittura*, Bassano, 1795

LASSAIGNE, J., and ARGAN, G. C. *De van Eyck à Botticelli*, Geneva-Paris, 1955

LERMOLIEFF, I. *Die Galerie zu Berlin*, Leipzig, 1893

————. *Kunstkritische Studien über italienische Malerei, Die Galerie zu Berlin*, Leipzig, 1893

LIPPMANN, F. "Amtliche Berichte aus den königlichen Kunstsammlungen," *Jahrbuch der kunsthistorischen Sammlungen des allerhöchsten Kaiserhauses*, 1881

LOESER, C. "La Collection Beckerath au Cabinet des Estampes de Berlin," *Gazette des Beaux-Arts*, 1902

Longhi, R. *Officina ferrarese*, Rome, 1934

———. *Viatico per cinque secoli di pittura veneta*, Florence, 1946

———. "I resti del Polittico di Cristoforo Moretti," *Pinacotheca*, 1928

———. "Sul catalogo della Mostra di Verona," *Paragone*, 1958

———. "Una Mostra a Verona," *L'Approdo Letterario*, 1958

———. "Un frammento della Pala di Domenico Veneziano per Santa Lucia de' Magnoli," *L'Arte*, 1925

Lorenzi, G. *Monumenti per servire alla storia del palazzo ducale di Venezia*, Venice, 1868

Luzio, A., and Renier, R. "Fidelfo e l'Umanesimo alla corte dei Gonzaga," *Giornale Storico della Letteratura Italiana*, XVI, 1890

Maffei, S. *Verona Illustrata*, III, Milan, 1826

Magagnato, L. *Da Altichiero a Pisanello* (Catalogo della Mostra), Venice, 1958

———. *Arte e Civiltà del Medioevo Veronese*, 1962

Maineri, M. "Artisti veronesi in Roma nei secoli XV-XVI-XVII," *Vita Veronese*, 1960

Malaguzzi-Valeri, F. *Pittori lombardi del Quattrocento*, Milan, 1902

Manteuffel, K. Zoege von. *Die Bilder und Zeichnungen des Antonio Pisano aus Verona* (Inaugural Dissertation), Halle, 1909

———. "Uber zwei Handzeichnungen des A. Pisano," *Mitteilungen des kunsthistorischen Institut in Florenz*, 1912-17

Marcenaro, C. "Un ritratto di Pisanello ritrovato a Genova", *Studies in the History of Art* (dedicated to W. Suida), London, 1959

Marinelli, G. "Il Codice Vallardi e i disegni di Pisanello al Louvre (verso una nuova attribuzione)," *Emporium*, 1961

Marotte, L., and Nocq, H. *Les médailles d'Antonio Pisano*, Paris, 1914

Martinie, A. H. *Pisanello*, Paris, 1930

———. "Zeichnungen des Pisanello im Louvre," *Monatshefte für Bücherfreunde*, 1925

Matějček, A., and Pešina, J., *La peinture gothique tcèque,* Prague, 1950

Mazzini, F. "Pisanello," *Mostra dell'Arte lombarda dai Visconti agli Sforza*, Milan, 1958

Mellini, G. L. "La 'Sala Grande' di Altichiero e Jacopo d'Avanzo ed i Palazzi Scaligeri di Verona," *Critica d'Arte*, 1959

———. "Problemi di archeologia pisanelliana," *Critica d'arte*, 1961

Meyer, J. "Gentile da Fabriano und Vittore Pisanello in Venedig," *Livraison de la Königliche Gemäldegalerie zu Berlin*, 1896

Michiel, M. (Anonimo Morelliano). *Notizie di opere di disegno*, ed. Bassano, 1800; written c. 1520-40

Middeldorf, U. "B. Degenhart: Pisanello" (review), *The Art Bulletin*, 1947

Milani, L. A. "Vittore Pisano", *Protomoteca Veronese*, Verona, 1881

———. "Vittore Pisano, detto il Pisanello," *Protomoteca Veronese*, Verona, 1886

Molmenti, P. *La pittura veneziana*, Florence, 1903

Morassi, A. *Storia della pittura nella Venezia Tridentina*, Rome, 1934

————. "Lo Stefano da Zevio di Palazzo Venezia," *Emporium*, 1930

MORETTI, L. "Pisanello," *Catalogo delle pitture murali nel Veneto*, Venice, 1960

MÜNTZ, E. *L'arte italiana del Rinascimento*, Milan, 1894

————. *Les arts à la Cour des Papes pendant le XVe et le XVIe siècle*, I, Paris, 1878

————. *Les collections des Médicis au quinzième siècle*, Paris, 1888

————. "Archives et documents. Un dessin inédit de Pisanello au Musée de Cologne," *Revue de l'art ancien et moderne*, 1899

————. "Le Triomphe de la Mort à l'Hospice de Palerme," *Gazette des Beaux-Arts*, 1901

————. "Vittore Pisanello à propos de la nouvelle édition de Vasari publiée par A. Venturi," *Revue de l'art ancien et moderne*, 1897

NANIN, P. *Disegni di varie dipinture a fresco che sono in Verona*, Verona, 1864

NOCQ, H., and MAROTTE, L. *Les médailles d'Antonio Pisano*, Paris, 1914

PALLUCCHINI, R., *Catalogo, Mostra dei capolavori dei Musei Veneti*, Venice, 1946

————. *La pittura veneta del quattrocento*, Bologna, 1956

PARKER, K. T. *Catalogue of the Collection of Drawings in the Ashmolean Museum*, II, Oxford, 1956

PEŠINA, J., and MATĚJČEK, A. *La peinture gothique tcèque*, Prague, 1950

PLANISCIG, L. "Disegni per l'arco trionfale del Castel Nuovo di Napoli," *Jahrbuch der preussischen Kunstsammlungen*, 1933

————, and FISCHER, O. "Zwei Beiträge zu Pisanello," *Jahrbuch der preussischen Kunstsammlungen*, 1933

POPHAM, A. E. "Antonio Pisano, called Pisanello," *Old Master Drawings*, 1937

————, and POUNCEY, P. *Italian Drawings in the Department of Prints and Drawings in the British Museum*, London, 1950

POUNCEY, P., and POPHAM, A. E. *Italian Drawings in the Department of Prints and Drawings in the British Museum*, London, 1950

RAGGHIANTI, C. L. "Lo Studio dei disegni," *Commenti di Critica d'arte*, Bari, 1946

RANKIN, W. "Cassone Fronts in American Collections. A Birth-Plate of 1428 and the Triumph of Chivalry in the Bryan Collection," *The Burlington Magazine*, 1907

RASMO, N. "Contributi alla storia dell'arte veronese-tridentina (il ritratto dell'imperatore Sigismondo)," *Cultura Atesina*, 1956

————. "Il Pisanello e il ritratto dell'imperatore Sigismondo a Vienna," *Cultura Atesina*, 1955

————. "Note sui rapporti tra Verona e l'Alto Adige nella pittura del tardo Trecento," *Cultura Atesina*, 1952

RAVAISSON, F. "Une œuvre de Pisanello," *Revue archéologique*, 1893

————. "Une œuvre de Pisanello," *Mémoires de l'Académie des Inscriptions et Belles-Lettres*, 1895

REISET, F. "Une visite aux musées de Londres en 1876: Vittore Pisano," *Gazette des Beaux-Arts*, 1877

RENIER, R., and LUZIO, A. "Fidelfo e l'Umanesimo alla corte dei Gonzaga," *Giornale Storico della Letteratura Italiana*, XVI, 1890

RICCI, C. *L'Arte nell'Italia settentrionale*, Bergamo, 1911

RICCI, L. "Come debba chiamarsi il Pisanello," *L'Arte*, 1909

RICHA, G. *Notizie istoriche delle chiese fiorentine*, II, Florence, 1754-62

RICHTER, J. P. "Il Pisanello graziato," *Archivio Storico dell'Arte*, 1889

———. "The Pictures of the Veronese School," *Art Journal*, 1895

RICHTER, G. M. "Pisanello again," *The Burlington Magazine*, 1931

———. "Pisanello studies," *The Burlington Magazine*, 1929

RIDOLFI, C. *Le meraviglie dell'arte*, ed. Berlin, 1814

RING, G. *La Peinture française du XVe siècle*, Glasgow, 1949

ROSENBERG, J. *Great Draughtsmen from Pisanello to Picasso*, Cambridge, Mass., 1959

ROSSI, V. "Il Pisanello e i Gonzaga," *Archivio Storico dell'Arte*, 1888

———. "L'indole e gli studi di Giovanni di Cosimo de' Medici," *Rendiconti della R. Accademia dei Lincei*, 1893

RUSSOLI, F. *La Pinacoteca Poldi-Pezzoli*, Milan, 1955

SALMI, M. *Paolo Uccello, Andrea del Castagno, Domenico Veneziano*, Milan, 1938

———. "La *Divi Julii Caesaris Effigies* del Pisanello," *Commentari*, 1957

———. "Riflessioni sul Pisanello medaglista," *Annuali dell'Istituto italiano di numismatica*, 1957

SANDBERG-VAVALÀ, E. *La pittura veronese del Trecento e del primo Quattrocento*, Verona, 1926

———. "Niccolò di Pietro," *Art Quarterly*, 1939

SANTANGELO, A. *Catalogo del Museo di Palazzo Venezia*, Rome, 1948

SCHLOSSER, J. von. "Ein veronesisches Bilderbuch und die höfische Kunst des XIV. Jahrhunderts," *Jahrbuch der kunsthistorischen Sammlungen des allerhöchsten Kaiserhauses*, 1895

SCHMITT, A., and DEGENHART, B. "Gentile da Fabriano in Rom und die Anfänge des Antikenstudiums," *Münchener Jahrbuch der bildenden Kunst*, 1960

SCHUBRING, P. *Altichiero und seine Schule*, Leipzig, 1898

———. "Vittore Pisano," *Das Museum*, 1900

SCHULZ, H. W. *Denkmäler der Kunst des Mittelalters in Unteritalien*, IV, Dresden, 1860

SIMEONI, L. *Verona, Guida storico artistica della città e provincia*, Verona, 1909

SINDONA, E. *Paolo Uccello*, Milan, 1957

———. "Gotico e Rinascimento—Pisanello, Paolo Uccello e il Pittore dell'Adorazione," *Fede e Arte*, 1960

SIRÉN, O. *Dessins et Tableaux de la Renaissance italienne dans les Collections de Suède*, Stockholm, 1902

SPAVENTI, S. M. *Vittore Pisano, detto il Pisanello*, Verona, 1892

STERLING, C. "La peinture de portrait à la Cour de Bourgogne au début du XVe siècle," *Critica d'Arte*, 1959

STEVENSON, H. *Topografia e Monumenti di Roma nelle pitture a fresco di Sisto V della Biblioteca Vaticana*, 1887

STIX, A., and FRÖHLICH-BUM, L. *Beschreibender Katalog der Handzeichnungen in der Albertina*, I, Vienna, 1926

SUIDA, W. *Genua*, Leipzig, 1906

———. "Neue Studien zur Geschichte der lombardischen Malerei des XV. Jahrhunderts," *Repertorium für Kunstwissenschaft*, 1902

TAYLOR, F. H. *The Taste of Angels*, Boston, 1948

TESTI, L. *Storia della pittura veneziana*, I, Bergamo, 1915

———. "Quando nacque *Pisanus Pictor*," *Rassegna d'Arte*, 1911

146

————. "Vittore Pisanello o Pisanus Pictor," *Rassegna d'Arte*, 1910

THIIS, O. *Pisanello*, Oslo, 1941

THODE, H. "Pisanellos Todesjahr," *Zeitschrift für bildende Kunst*, 1884

TICOZZI, S., and BOTTARI, M. G. *Raccolta di lettere sulla pittura, scultura e architettura*, V, Milan, 1822

TOESCA, P. *Il Trecento*, Turin, 1951

————. *La pittura e la miniatura nella Lombardia dai piú antichi monumenti alla metà del Quattrocento*, Milan, 1912

————. "Di alcuni miniatori lombardi della fine del Trecento," *L'Arte*, 1907

————. "Domenico da Venezia," *Enciclopedia Italiana*, 1932

————. "Michelino da Besozzo e Giovannino de' Grassi," *L'Arte*, 1905

TSCHUDI, H. V., and BODE, U. "Die Anbetung der Könige von Vittore Pisano und die Madonna mit Heiligen aus dem Besitz des Cav. dal Pozzo," *Jahrbuch der königlich preussischen Kunstsammlungen*, VI, Berlin, 1885

————. "Vittor Pisano," *Annuaire des Musées de Berlin*, 1885

UZZEILLI, G. "Sui ritratti di Paolo dal Pozzo Toscanelli fatti da Alessio Baldovinetti e da Vittore Pisano," *Bollettino della Società geografica italiana*, Rome, 1890

VALENTINER, W. R. *Das unbekannte Meisterwerk in öffentlichen und privaten Sammlungen*, Berlin, 1930

VALLARDI, G. *Disegni di Leonardo da Vinci posseduti da Giuseppe Vallardi*, Milan, 1855

VAN de PUT, A. "Pisanelliana," *Old Master Drawings*, 1932

VAN MARLE, R. *The Development of the Italian Schools of Paintings*, VIII, The Hague, 1927

VASARI, G. *Le Vite*, ed. Milanesi, Florence, 1878-85; written 1568

VASOLI, C. *L'Estetica dell'Umanesimo e del Rinascimento*, Milan, 1959

VENTURI, A. *Grandi Artisti Italiani*, Bologna, 1925

————. "La data della morte di Vittore Pisano," *Per nozze Rovighi-Valcavi*, Modena, 1883

————. *Le Vite dei piú eccellenti pittori, scultori e architetti scritte da Giorgio Vasari, Gentile da Fabriano e il Pisanello*, Florence, 1896

————. *Pisanello*, Rome, 1939

————. *Storia dell'arte italiana*, VII, Milan, 1911

————. "Del quadro attribuito a Bono da Ferrara nella Galleria Nazionale di Londra," *L'Arte*, 1922

————. "Documento sul Pisanello," *Archivio Storico dell'Arte*, 1888

————. "Gentile da Fabriano und Vittore Pisano," *Jahrbuch der preussischen Kunstsammlungen*, 1895

————. "Giuseppe Biadego: Pisanus Pictor" (review), *L'Arte*, 1908

————. "Il Pisanello a Ferrara," *Archivio Veneto*, 1884; 1885

————. "Jacopo Bellini, Pisanello und Mantegna in den Sonetten des Dichters Ulisse," *Der Kunstfreund*, Berlin, 1885

————. "La scoperta di un ritratto estense del Pisanello," *Archivio Storico dell'Arte*, 1889

————. "Notizie sul soggiorno di Vittor Pisano alla Corte Estense e osservazioni sulla data fissata alla sua morte," *Archivio Storico veronese*, 1883

————. "Orme del Pisanello a Ferrara," *L'Arte*, 1933

———. "Per il Pisanello. Disegni inediti nella raccolta Bonnat a Parigi e nella biblioteca reale di Windsor," *L'Arte*, 1921

———. "Su alcune medaglie del Pisanello," *L'Arte*, 1935

———. "Un disegno inedito di Pisanello," *Miscellanea per le nozze Brenzoni-Giacometti*, Verona, 1924

———. "Un ritratto del Pisanello," *L'Arte*, 1918

———. "Vittore Pisano, detto Pisanello," *Protomoteca Veronese*, 1886

———. "Zu Pisanello und Jacopo Bellini," *Pantheon*, 1929

VENTURI, L. *Le origini della pittura veneziana*, Venice, 1907

———. *Pitture italiane in America*, Milan, 1931

———. "Due ritratti smarriti di Pisanello," *Arte veneta*, 1954

VOLPE, C. "Due frammenti di Gentile da Fabriano," *Paragone*, 1958

WEISE, G. *L'ideale eroico del Rinascimento e le sue premesse umanistiche*, Naples, 1961

WICKHOFF, F. "Die italienischen Handzeichnungen der Albertina," *Jahrbuch der kunsthistorischen Sammlungen des allerhöchsten Kaiserhauses*, 1892

WILDE, J. "Ein Zeitgenössisches Bildnis des Kaisers Sigismund," *Jahrbuch der kunsthistorischen Sammlungen*, 1930

WITTGENS, F. *Il Museo Poldi-Pezzoli a Milano*, Milan, 1937

ZANNANDREIS, D. *Le vite dei Pittori, Scultori e Architetti veronesi*, Verona, 1891

ZERI, F. "Un ritratto del Pisanello," *Paragone*, 1958

ZIPPEL, G. "Artisti alla corte degli Estensi nel Quattrocento," *L'Arte*, 1902

ACKNOWLEDGMENTS

The photographic material, nearly all of which was specially made for Istituto Editoriale Italiano, was supplied by:

ALBERTINA, Vienna: *Plate 15; Fig. 2.*
ALINARI, Florence: *Plates 57, 64, 72 (top), 98 (left), 135; Figs. 1, 8, 20, 22.*
BIBLIOTECA AMBROSIANA, Milan: *Plates 24, 25, 37, 38, 40, 148 (left).*
ARCHIVIO FOTOGRAFICO DELLA SOPRINTENDENZA ALLE GALLERIE, Naples: *Fig. 19.*
ASHMOLEAN MUSEUM, Oxford: *Plates 47, 71.*
BACRI COLLECTION, Paris: *Fig. 3.*
BIBLIOTHÈQUE NATIONALE, Paris: *Plates 92, 110, 111, 112, 113, 133 (bottom), 158 (bottom); Fig. 18.*
BÖHM, Venice: *Figs. 5, 6.*
MUSÉE BONNAT, Bayonne: *Plate 69.*
BOYMANS MUSEUM, Rotterdam: *Plates 13, 30 (right), 107; Figs. 4, 38.*
BRITISH MUSEUM, London: *Plates 16, 55, 109 (bottom), 114, 144 (bottom), 154, 162.*
CASTELLO SFORZESCO, Milan: *Plate 93; Fig. 35.*
CHIOLINI, Pavia: *Fig. 7.*
CRIMELLA, Milan: *Fig. 33.*
GALLERIA ESTENSE, Modena: *Plate 62.*
FINE ART ENGRAVERS, London: *Plates 122, 147, 150.*
FIORENTINI, Venice: *Plates 50, 53, 91.*
FOTOTECNICA, Bologna: *Fig. 34.*
FRICK COLLECTION, New York: *Plate 56.*
GABINETTO FOTOGRAFICO DELLA SOPRINTENDENZA ALLE GALLERIE, Florence: *Plates 133 (top), 144 (top), 153; Figs. 26, 27, 28, 30, 31.*
GASPARINI, Genoa: *Fig. 36.*
GIRAUDON, Paris: *Plates 2, 5, 20, 26, 29, 30 (left), 42, 43, 47, 58, 63, 87, 89, 94, 101, 105, 108, 118, 119, 131, 136, 141, 142, 152, 155, 156, 165, 171, 172.*
ISTITUTO DI STORIA DELL'ARTE FONDAZIONE G. CINI, Venice: *Fig. 24.*
KUNSTHISTORISCHES MUSEUM, Vienna: *Fig. 17.*
LANIEPCE, Paris: *Plates 17, 18, 27, 70, 104, 125, 126, 129, 130, 143, 167.*
MUSÉE DU LOUVRE, Paris: *Plates 19, 33, 34, 45, 61, 67, 68, 72 (bottom), 73, 86, 88 (left), 95, 98 (right), 99, 100, 124, 127, 132, 151, 163, 168, 169, 173.*
LUGT COLLECTION, Paris: *Plate 21.*
BIBLIOTECA MALATESTIANA, Cesena: *Fig. 15.*
MERCATALI, Milan: *Plates 1, 3, 4, 6, 28, 31, 36, 49, 54, 65, 66, 74, 75, 76, 77, 78, 80, 83, 84, 85, 90, 96, 102, 106, 109 (top), 115, 117, 123, 128, 134, 138, 139, 140, 145, 161, 166.*
METROPOLITAN MUSEUM OF ART, New York: *Plate 157.*
NATIONAL GALLERY, London: *Plates 120, 121, 146; Fig. 23.*
NATIONAL GALLERY OF ART, Washington, D.C.: *Plates 137, 158 (top).*
PAGLIARANI, Verona: *Plates 14, 22, 23, 35, 44, 46, 48, 79, 81, 88 (right), 148 (right), 170; Fig. 16.*
PEROTTI, Milan: *Plates 32, 97, 103, 116, 149, 164; Figs. 12, 13, 21, 29, 37.*
MUSEO POLDI PEZZOLI, Milan: *Figs. 9, 25.*
SANSOVINI, Rome: *Fig. 39.*
SOCIETÀ SCALA, Florence: *Plates 8, 9, 10, 11, 12.*
SOCIETÀ SCILLA, Florence: *Plates 51, 52, 59, 60, 82.*
SOPRINTENDENZA AI MONUMENTI E ALLE GALLERIE, Pisa: *Fig. 32.*
STAATLICHE MUSEEN, Berlin: *Plates 39, 159, 160; Figs. 40, 41, 42.*
VILLANI, Bologna: *Fig. 14.*
WELLS, Bergamo: *Figs. 10, 11.*

The plates for the color reproductions and medals were executed by ZINCOGRAFIA PASETTI, Milan; *the drawings by* DITTA ZUCCOTTI & CAPRARA, Milan; *and the rotogravure reproductions by* DITTA PEZZINI, Milan.

The drawings were printed by ARTI GRAFICHE TETTAMANTI, Milan; *the text and the plates of paintings and medals by* ISTITUTO EDITORIALE ITALIANO.